REPORTAGE DRAWING

DRAWING IN

Series editors:

Russell Marshall, Marsha Meskimmon and Phil Sawdon
Loughborough University, UK

'Thinking through drawing' has become a ubiquitous trope across the arts, sciences and humanities. The rich vein of thinking, making and visualizing through drawing that is being developed across these diverse fields affords an opportunity for sustained intellectual dialogues to emerge within, between or without traditional disciplinary boundaries. The Drawing In series provides a space for new perspectives and critical approaches in the field of drawing to be brought together and explored.

Published titles:

Drawing Difference, Marsha Meskimmon and Phil Sawdon
Drawing Investigations, Sarah Casey and Gerry Davies
Performance Drawing, Maryclare Foá, Jane Grisewood,
Birgitta Hosea and Carali McCall
Scenographic Design Drawing, Sue Field
Serial Drawing, Joe Graham
Reportage Drawing, Louis Netter

Forthcoming:

Drawing as Phenomenology, Deborah Harty
Looking at Life Drawing, Margaret Mayhew
Anatomical Drawing, Sue Field

REPORTAGE DRAWING

Vision and Experience

Louis Netter

BLOOMSBURY VISUAL ARTS

LONDON · NEW YORK · OXFORD · NEW DELHI · SYDNEY

BLOOMSBURY VISUAL ARTS
Bloomsbury Publishing Plc
50 Bedford Square, London, WC1B 3DP, UK
1385 Broadway, New York, NY 10018, USA
29 Earlsfort Terrace, Dublin 2, Ireland

BLOOMSBURY, BLOOMSBURY VISUAL ARTS and the Diana logo are trademarks of
Bloomsbury Publishing Plc

First published in Great Britain 2024

A catalogue record for this book is available from the British Library.

A catalog record for this book is available from the Library of Congress.

ISBN: HB: 978-1-3502-5309-4
PB: 978-1-3502-5308-7
ePDF: 978-1-3502-5311-7
eBook: 978-1-3502-5310-0

Series: Drawing In

Typeset by Newgen KnowledgeWorks Pvt. Ltd., Chennai, India
Printed and bound in India

To find out more about our authors and books visit www.bloomsbury.com
and sign up for our newsletters.

CONTENTS

INTRODUCTION

In Jaywick Essex, in the summer of 2021, I was drawing a woman I had just seen from memory on a windswept and untamed beach just outside the concrete fortifications protecting the below sea level town. I was lying down to give myself more control of the flapping paper, and the sand and grit of the saltwater were collaborating in my drawing, causing the graphite stick to stutter, leaving pock marks on the paper. The woman emerged from the drawing as a fragile wisp with hollowed-out eyes. In the end she was not just a person seen, she was a symbol, she was an experience captured. The drawing is an invitation to see what I have seen and to feel what I felt (Figure 1).

This book explores the history of reportage drawing and how it has shaped the contemporary act. It also looks at the way in which reportage drawing is understood as a record of direct observation and how the formal qualities reinforce this, bridging the experience of the artist with the viewer. This is done in the re-creative process of looking at drawing and re-performing its formal construction. There is also a connection to the artist's experience. I contend in this book that the subject of reportage, beyond drawing itself, is experience. The durational record of the drawing speaks to the layered experience of the artist, and this wider narrative of production is key to understanding the value of reportage drawing, its sustaining interest among artists and its potential as a unique piece of the media landscape.

In the early and mid-1990s, I studied illustration at Loughborough College of Art and Design under Mario Minichiello (see Chapter 9). We were encouraged to draw everything we could. Loughborough is a market town and this American found the hustle and bustle of traders and customers fascinating. I developed an obsession with probing the English character in my new home. Mario once said of my sketchbook, 'It's a gallery of faces. You need context.' He was right of course but I was slowly honing in. Something was happening in my drawing. I was aware that some essential fusion was taking place. A fusion of thought and form. The marks of the drawing were not merely in aid of representation; they etched out ideas, feelings and even judgements. Like Philip Rawson's (1969) concept of tenor and topic (see Chapter 2), I learned that stylistic choice can and should evolve out of the necessity and demands of the drawing. I was not

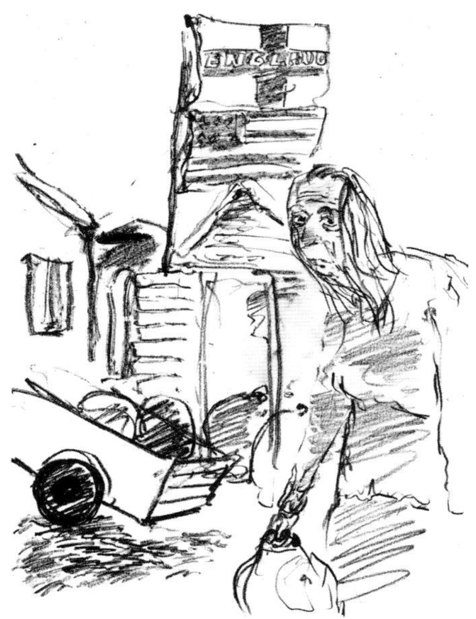

Figure 1 Jaywick, Essex, 2021.
Source: Louis Netter

attaching a 'style' as one would put on a new coat. My drawing was emerging out of a deep connection to my psychic world – the world of my thoughts, feelings and opinions. My drawing had become my refined world view. My 'talent' was less important than the ideas I brought to my work. Instead of diminishing the role of developing skills in drawing and painting and other media, the making of a work of art is about the concretization of ideas in visual form. With a developed command of the potentialities of one's own drawing, you can perform an expansive vocabulary of lines, marks and tones that emerge from a developed strategy to form, constituting a distinct language for understanding the world.

Reportage drawing becomes *the* way you see for many artists. It is a heightened kind of looking and documenting. Intensive looking and translating the observed into formal referents compel one, as Michael Taussig has noted, 'to *witness*, as opposed to *see*' and thereby 'be implicated in a process of judgement' (Taussig, 2011, p. 71). Drawing unfolds layers of thinking and seeing, which at its total fulfilment often surprises with both the connection to the subject and the wider symbolic power it projects. The drawing's meaning emerges from the palimpsest of thoughts, observations and conclusions on the paper. For all artists interviewed and written about in this book, the act of reportage drawing is layered with intentions, both artistic and conceptual, and is significantly shaped by the artists' orientation to their subject(s). Drawing forces you to look deeply, and when doing so, new insights emerge and the process of rendering vision into formal referents is a construction of meaning on the micro and macro level. The constellation of concerns that I have identified in this book around reportage drawings comes together to form, what I call (borrowed from Rawson (1969)), the graphic construct of the artist (see Chapter 2).

In Figure 2 we can see a dishevelled man smoking outside of a pub in Blackpool. I made this drawing from direct observation across the street on the inside wall of a closed shop. This man's proximity to the Old Bull sign makes a compelling and appropriate relay between text and image that completes a statement. That statement being that this man is like an old bull with a steely eye on anyone challenging him. It is also, with the simple contextual description that this was drawn in Blackpool, a statement about the economic and social deprivation of the place. On another level, the full reading and understanding of the image is singularly understood by the viewer based on what they bring to drawing itself: their own experience looking at drawing, their prejudices, perhaps their insecurities around art and expertise. These issues are explored in this book as the act of reportage drawing is seen in an expanded way, drawing out the complexities within its conception and construction. Famed educational theorist Elliot Eisner noted about the power of the arts to speak to other modes of human experience. He said:

> We appeal to poetry to say what cannot be expressed in literal language. We secure from images ideas and other forms of experience that elude discursive description. We experience through music qualities of lived experience that cannot be rendered in quantitative form. In short, our sensibilities and the forms of representation associated with them make distinctive contributions to what we notice, grasp, and understand. (Eisner, 2002, p. 204)

Drawing is both an abstraction and a referent to real things. It is both real and unreal, and therefore on the level of reportage drawing, it is a distraction to hold it up against the 'data' available in the photograph. A drawing is a human document of witness, and it is ultimately complicated by the subjectivities of the artists' experience. This book explores the concerns that make the act of reportage a highly valuable record of interaction between human and subject in a hyper-mediated world. This book explores the idea of drawing as a form of media and how it functions as such, allowing a new and challenging lens on the complexities of the world. Drawing is mediated vision through graphic means, but it is also created with a responsibility and fidelity to what is seen and understood. Experience and what constitutes experience play a large role in what is chosen, from the wide field of stimuli, to become a drawing. Reportage artists are not merely intrigued by what they see on location, they bring empathy and judgement to bear. Author Siri Hustvedt speaks of Goya's *Disasters of War* etching series and notes:

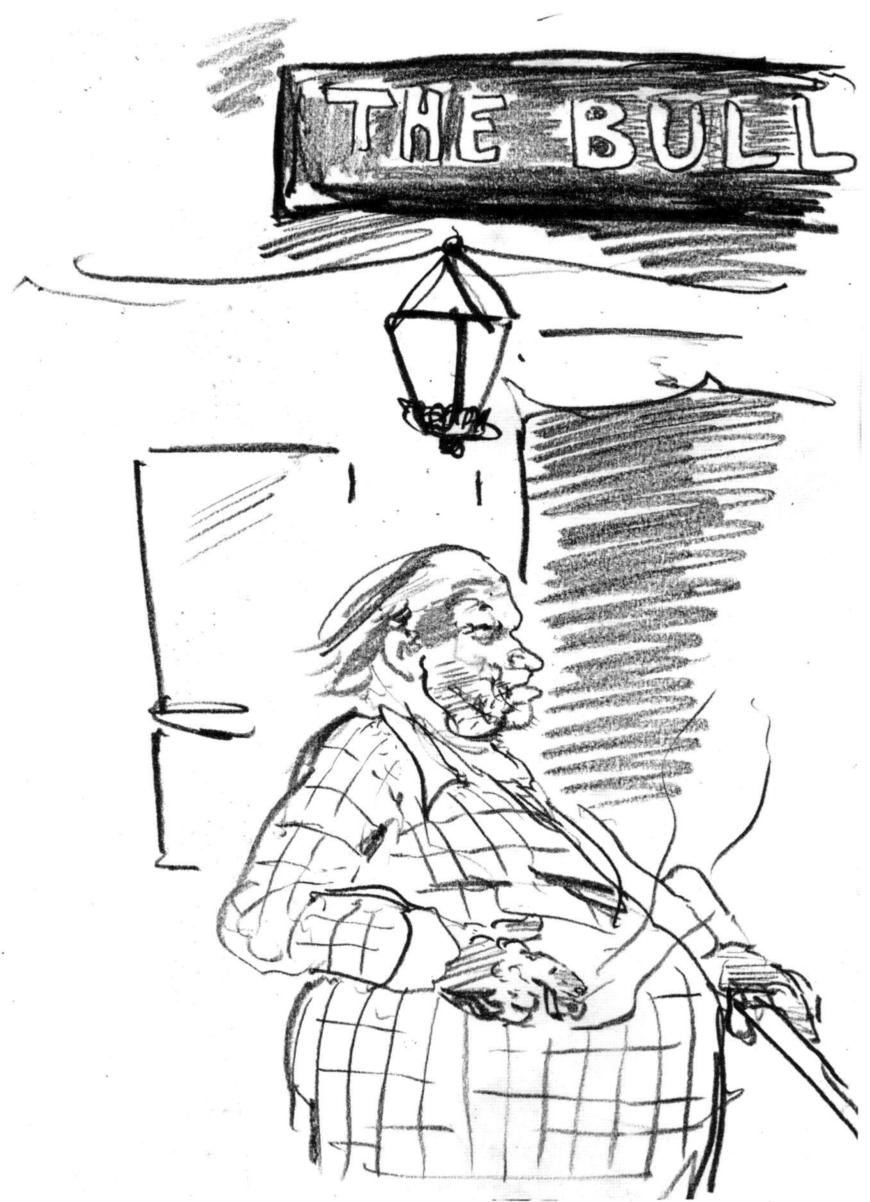

Figure 2 Blackpool, Lancashire, 2022.
Source: Louis Netter

> Although we can't know exactly what Goya saw during the Peninsular War, he obviously witnessed *enough*. It seems unlikely that the artist wandered about the countryside with a sketchbook as gruesome events were taking place in front of him. What he saw, heard about, and felt were realized afterward on paper and then in the plates … it is clear that emotion, especially strong emotion, keeps memories alive. (Hustvedt, 2013, pp. 326, 327)

Today, contemporary reportage finds its persuasive power in documenting protests, prisons, arms fairs, deprived cities and towns, migrant camps and all manner of human experience and struggle that marks on paper are so uniquely suited to capture. Drawings are an incitement to connect to the experience of the artist. As such, they are also a call to share a vision, a sentiment, a thought or thoughts. They can also be a call to action or deeper understanding.

The drawings done in the concentration camp Terezin outside Prague by Helga Weissová give us an intimate vision, from a child of only twelve years old, of the horrors of the Nazis. Felix Brummer notes in the book about Weissová's drawings:

> One can ask, what is so moving about these pictures? … they (the drawings) invite you to look at them with curiosity. Only then – aided by a comparison with your own inner images of a free childhood – come certain feelings and a special relationship to the artist as a child. Concerning this she herself has said 'the impressions that were to orient me from this point in time ended my childhood'. (Weissová-Hošková, 2017, p. 150)

More recently, Abu Zubaydah, a prisoner in Guantanamo Bay, produced a series of drawings that documented his torture and abuse in very spare and shocking images (see Figure 3). Zubaydah noted of his experience being waterboarded: 'They kept pouring water and concentrating on my nose and my mouth until I really felt I was drowning and my chest was just about to explode from the lack of oxygen' (Denbeaux et al., 2019). Guantanamo is also the subject of artist Molly Crabapple's reportage. She visited the site under tight restrictions and experienced the more banal aspects of the prison and problematic legal circumstances of the prisoners. Here, her drawings explore only what is allowed to be seen and this absence reveals a strange kind of invisible power to the images *not* drawn (Crabapple, 2013).

Ultimately, reportage drawing is, as Andrew Causey says, 'drawing-enhanced seeing' (Causey, 2017, p. 13). Drawing, through the invention of symbolic referents to the real, creates, quite literally, a re-creation of the act of seeing. Engaging in reportage drawing requires you to be fully present. Sights, sounds and even the weather contribute to how we enter the space of the subject. Whether human, animal or the built environment, the rendering of a subject is

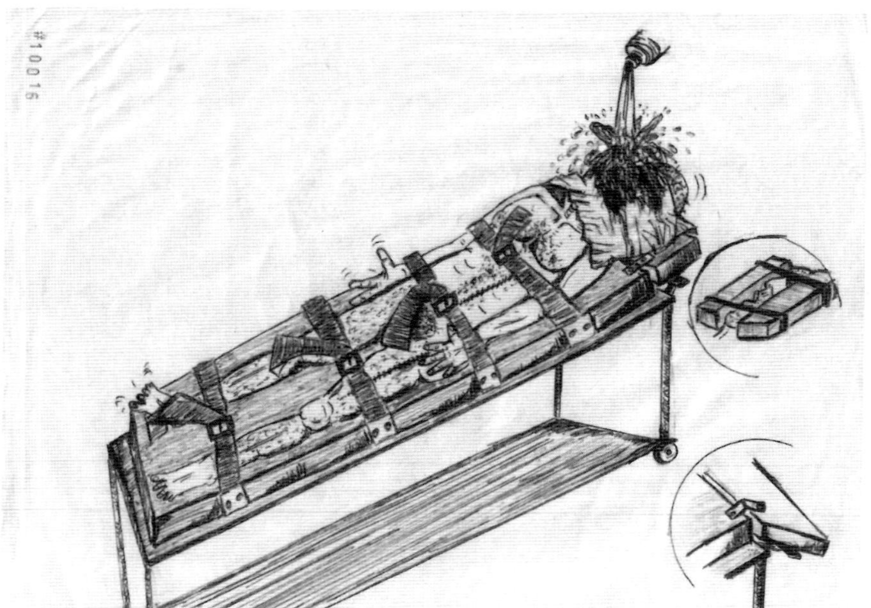

Figure 3 Guantanamo Bay torture, 2019.
Source: Abu Zubaydah

not just a pictorial record, it is a summative statement. This book explores how the history of reportage drawing has shaped the act today and how the form and function of the act reveal satellite concerns that fuse in the final drawing. The photographer's lens, with all of the sophisticated timing and skill that is required of a good photograph, ultimately reflects a human, creative intervention with a machine. The drawing, however, is a perceptual trace that is linked to the nervous system of the artist. Because of the durational aspects of drawing, it accumulates things seen, feelings felt and thoughts had. The final drawing is a revelation. It is an emphatic record. It is a smudgy, quickly executed mess of lines and marks, and it is an exquisite statement. It is primitive and sublime. This book demonstrates that practitioners of reportage drawing are engaging in it because the process of drawing is meaningful to them. It also represents meaning making and this is critical. Our drawings also challenge us. We see what we didn't expect. We care for those whom we despised. Drawing uncovers the nuances of the human experience and therefore it cultivates empathy. Jill Gibbons's work (see Chapter 6) depicts showgirls, attendees and traders at arms fairs in Europe plying their despicable trade. Her drawings, however, cultivate empathy or at least understanding, revealing exhaustion, boredom and pathos. Or, Loup Blaster (see Chapter 10), whose intimate drawings and animations reveal a deep connection to migrants in the Calais 'Jungle' and collectively help build creative networks of artists, musicians and activists who positively campaign for the human rights of migrants. Reportage drawings are intimate snapshots of experiences that come to be drawings because the subject calls to be drawn. The sustaining allure of reportage drawing is in the rich feedback the act provides. Our senses are united and even in the inevitable struggle for depiction, we see a mirror in every drawing, reflecting our humanity and a deep connectedness to our subject.

This book is structured to give a concrete understanding of form and formation of reportage drawing. The three chapters that look at the graphic construct of Jill Gibbon, myself and Gary Embury are an in-depth exploration of practice, orientation to the subject and theoretical aspects of wider drawing and reportage practice. These three examples give a vivid picture of the contemporary act and its guiding priorities as I see it. The subsequent 'artist spotlight' chapters are more of a survey of practice and explore different orientations to the act. They offer a more personal insight into the individual concerns and motivations of contemporary practitioners who come from different perspectives. The graphic construct chapters look at individual practice within the wider context of the contemporary field, while the artist spotlight chapters look at specific methodologies (Figure 4).

On recent trips to Prague with students, I did many drawings (Figures 5 to 7) which I felt captured the city. The city has a timelessness that Berger identified through a description of a drawing made by Roelandt Savery in Prague between 1603 and 1609. He noted:

> He (a beggar) is staring ahead, very straight; his dark sullen eyes are at the same level as a dog's would be. His hat, upturned for money, is on the ground beside his bandaged foot. No comment, no other figure, no placing. A tramp of nearly 400 years ago. We encounter him today. Before this scrap of paper, only six inches square, we come across him as we might come across him on the way to the airport, or on a grass bank of the highway above Latife's shanty town. (Berger & Savage, 2008, p. 48)

This is the other gift of drawing. It depicts a time but it is also timeless. It is idiosyncratically singular and yet it reflects the universal. It does this through symbolic means. A drawing is not only a representation but also a symbol. This book is not only a celebration of the drawing act but also a declaration of its value for documentation. Drawing is an antidote to the hyper-mediated world we live in. Drawing is a form of peace making and sense making. This is a complex and brutal world. Reportage drawing represents an old way to have new conversations and insights. Sharpen those pencils.

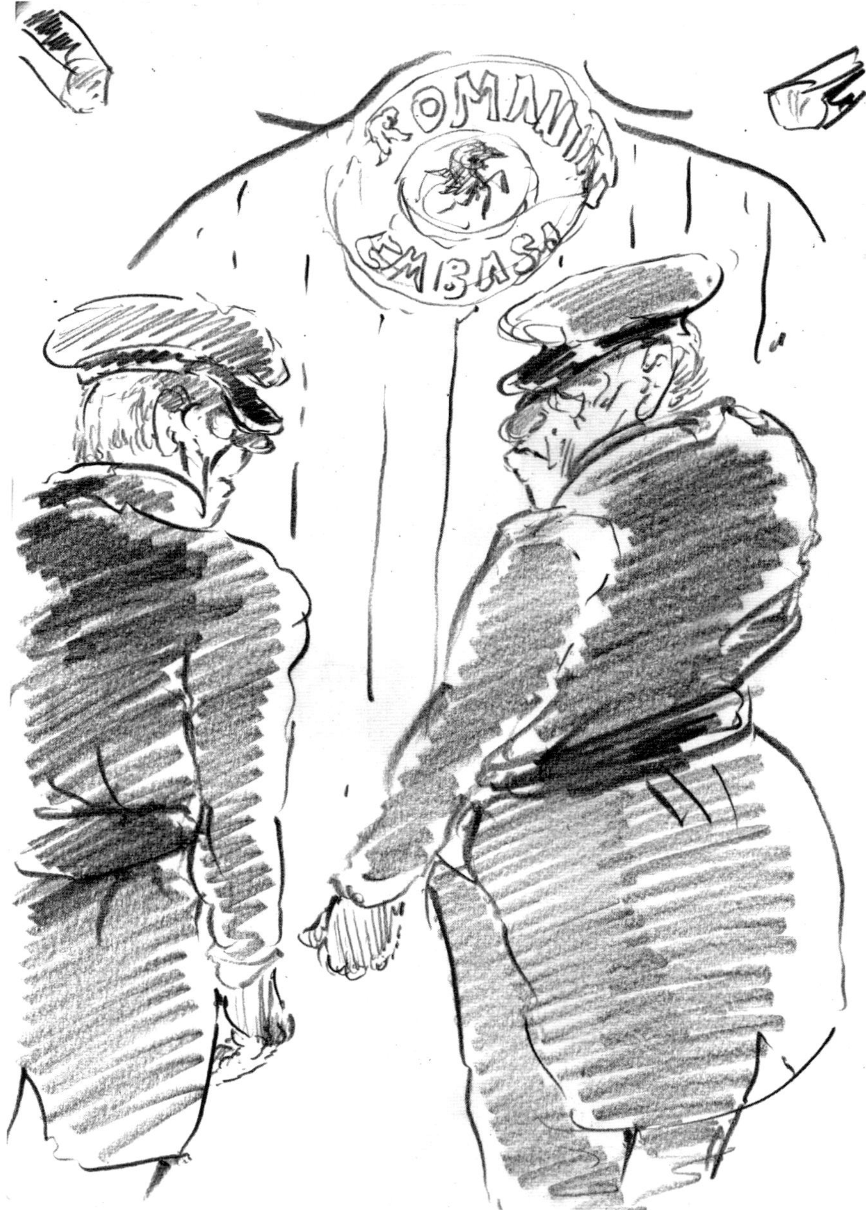

Figure 4 Old guards, Prague, 2023.
Source: Louis Netter

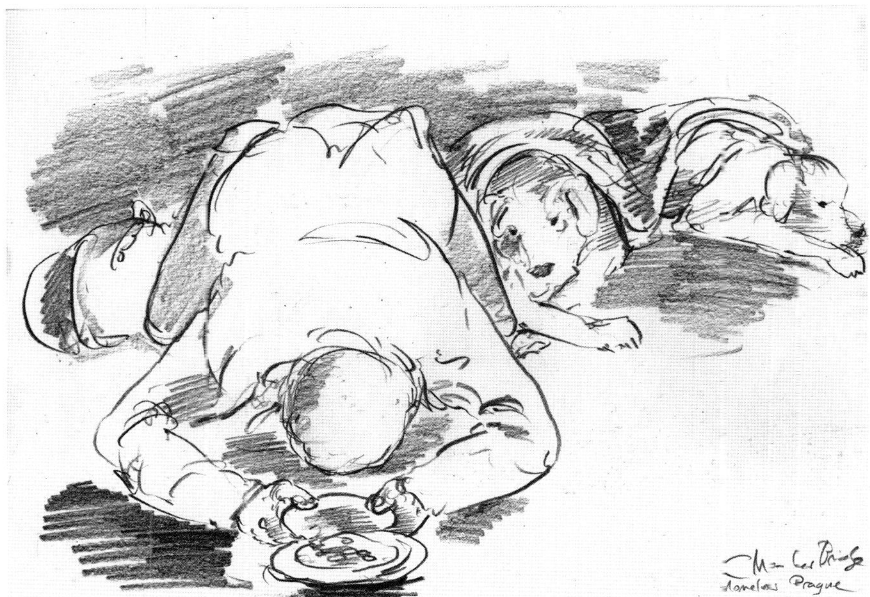

Figure 5 Beggar or Charles Bridge, Prague, 2022.
Source: Louis Netter

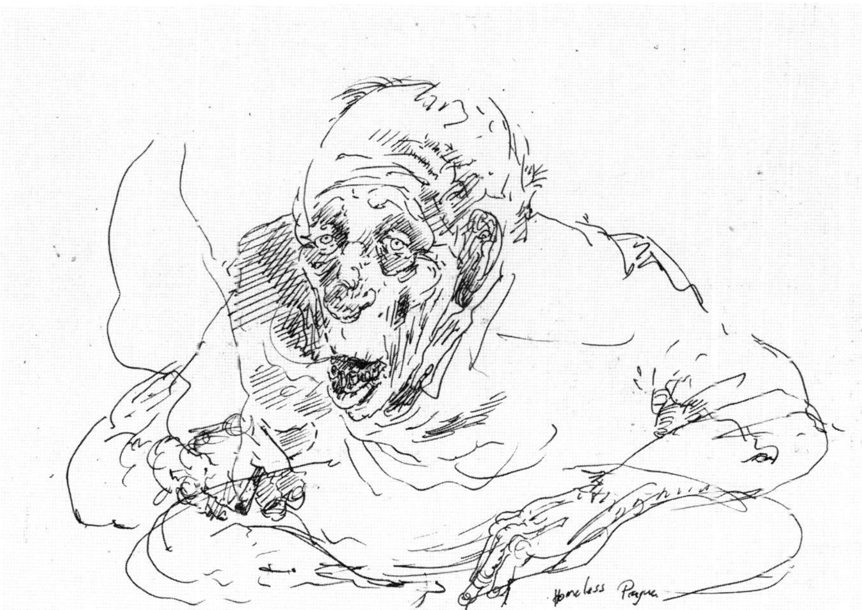

Figure 6 Beggar, Prague, 2022.
Source: Louis Netter

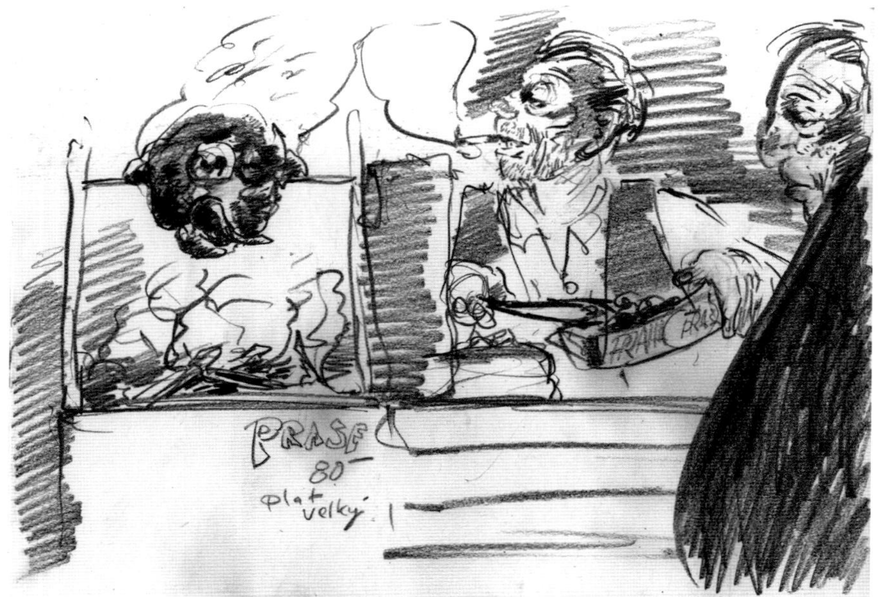

Figure 7 Pig head seller, Prague, 2022.
Source: Louis Netter

1

REPORTAGE DRAWING: HISTORY AND THE CONTEMPORARY ACT

The history of reportage drawing is long and truncated and is essential for formulating an understanding of its contemporary practice. Of central importance to this book is the shift in the perception of drawing from the nineteenth century to today. Issues of authenticity and origination were evolving in the nineteenth century with the constraints and new possibilities of print technology and, eventually, the photograph. Drawing in the form of wood block engravings delivered a generic news image to the public that removed the idiosyncratic and expressive hand of the artist. This presents a stark and valuable contrast with the practice today which centres around individualistic vision, experience and the drawing act.

On the level of drawing itself in the nineteenth century, individual artistic identities were subsumed by the newspaper production line and house styles. Commercial demands pushed artistic expression to the back of concerns and highlighted the purely informational function of the drawing. A distinction was clear, although not identified by the viewing public, between the original act of the reportage drawing and the reproduction. As noted anthropologist and author of *Lines* (2016) Tim Ingold notes, 'art creates; technology can only replicate. Thus was the artist distinguished from the artisan, and the work of art from the artefact' (Ingold, 2016, p. 130).

Photography played a crucial role in the nineteenth century as an evidentiary method of capturing what Susan Sontag called 'pieces of the world' in her book *On Photography*. Early photography was also connected to structures of power and control, and it soon became clear that the notion of 'reality' and the photograph's attestation of it was problematized by various factors (see below). Photography is also anchored to its subject in a way that drawing is not. John Berger noted the photograph 'belongs to its subject' and because they (photographs) preserve appearances, 'they do not in themselves preserve meaning'. Meaning, Berger noted, 'is the result of understanding functions' and the camera separates appearances 'from their function' (Berger, 1991, pp. 54, 55).

Drawing, in form and function, contrasts significantly with photography. While drawing may intend some capture or 'slice' of fluid reality, it is a necessary construction and its effects are the consequence of a 'species of lines' as noted by the late artist William Hogarth, which are descriptive and evocative (Hogarth, 1997, p. 50). Drawings are about depictive subjects and the drawing itself, its formation. Photography, however, is 'not a magical "emanation" but a material product of a material apparatus' and is 'not an alchemy but a history, outside of which the existential essence of photography is empty', as noted by John Tagg (1995, p. 3). The function of drawing compared to photography is of particular interest, with the nineteenth century providing a unique moment when drawing held the burden and responsibility of journalistic objectivity while simultaneously disappearing individual artistic language.

A brief history of reportage drawing

The demand for information about a newly connected world through trade, conflict and conquest tended to favour a more realistic, factual and unsentimental artistic reporting. This work was content driven and largely void of fanciful embellishment, relying instead on visual conventions of the time. Artists found work on expeditions to the new world and on Grand Tours with aristocratic clients, documenting their privileged excursions (Hogarth, 1986, p. 10). One such example of an artist exploring the new world was John White. White was asked to travel with Sir Walter Raleigh on his trip to North America in 1585 and White, along with his 'observer' Thomas Harriot, was commissioned to draw all varieties of plants, animals and people 'as you shall finde them differing' from the known English varieties (Hulton, 1984, pp. 7, 9). Unlike reportage artists of the nineteenth century, these early artists were rarely trained for their specific tasks and were often pulled from the commercial art trade. White himself was likely trained as a limner or miniature portraitist although it is difficult to know for certain (Hulton, 1984, p. 35).

The work is marked by a naivety in representation that was owed to the deficiencies in White's artistic training, most evident in clumsy anatomy and awareness of perspective. Still, in a break from earlier times, Elizabethans demanded a 'visual record' of new worlds instead of collected artefacts and this led to 'gentlemen', often socially connected, self-taught enthusiasts, joining expeditions (Sloan, Chaplin, Feest & Kuhlemann, 2007, p. 234).

Academies for artistic training in England (i.e. teaching drawing from nudes and learning perspective among other continental innovations) were not to be established until the eighteenth century (Hulton, 1984, p. 36). However, this work was commissioned solely to 'communicate information graphically' and any qualities seen in the work that signify artistic flourish or 'atmosphere' are 'unconscious by-products' (Hulton, 1984, p. 37). This is reportage drawing with a strict mission and tight brief to document and inform. Although notable artists of the time were producing individualistic artwork, this work is a direct outgrowth of the commercial art trade, with artists functioning more like craftsmen.

Overall, this tension between the limitations of the artist, their orientation towards the depiction of their subject and the commercial demands of the work carries throughout the history of reportage. Ironically, when reportage drawing has been most visible and consequential, artistic intent is marginalized.

The nineteenth century: Print and syntax

The nineteenth century saw dramatic moves in how drawing featured in everyday life. Through the proliferation of the illustrated press, the role of the reportage artist came to be central to visual media and communication. The reportage artist was an important figure but the primary aim of the work was clearly to serve, inform and entertain an image-hungry public. Drawing was prized for its ability to convey information and slotted into the machinery of popular print media. Drawing's prominence was in large part due to new and modified technologies for mass production in print. There were technical shifts in print techniques that had previously attempted to replicate the qualities of paintings for expensive reproduction in books and portfolios. This sought to satisfy the ever-increasing demand for accurate representation, which was adequately achieved through the mezzotint technique and, later, photomechanical reproduction, seen as potentially threatening to artists from sceptics such as John Ruskin (Jussim, 1974, p. 7). While print expanded the reach of drawing, it is questionable whether it elevated its status, flattening its qualities through necessary conventions and a production line print process.

The process of wood engraving for the illustrated presses is illuminating and highlights the division of labour and multiple hands that touched the work. In short, the wood block was painted with a thin layer of whitewash (to accentuate the lines to be engraved) and the sketch, which at this point had gone through a significant transformation from the field to accommodate scale, taste, house style and public expectation, was transferred and quickly went to specialists in drapery (called 'tailors') foliage (called 'pruners'), simple lines (called 'mechanics') and more skilled engravers for facial expressions (called, mockingly, 'butchers') (Brown, 2006, pp. 36, 37). While this description of the process came from a prominent North American publication called *Frank Leslie's Illustrated Newspaper*, this division of labour was commonplace and each newspaper, of which there were several competing, would have a definitive stylistic approach to their drawing and the depiction of events. A former employee of *Frank Leslie's Newspaper* noted 'each sort of line was the orthodox symbol for a certain form' and Leslie's paper quietly removed engravers' signatures signifying 'their subordination in the overall process' (Brown, 2006, p. 38). The invisibility of the artist and artistry in these prints linked them to their sixteenth-century counterparts in that despite centuries of individualistic, artistic achievement, commercial art was providing a purely informational, albeit occasionally sensational, record of events.

Central to the problem of removing the primary, eyewitness, artist from the print is in the syntactical differences as print scholar William M. Ivins (1969) puts it. Ivins also identified in artistic work that a 'graphic medium possesses its own graphic syntax' and that, like language, 'so too the structure and vocabulary of visual codes impose their own potentialities on visual communication' (Jussim, 1974, p. 14). Simply put, Ivins sees the artist's syntax as synonymous with visual language and the problem rests in 'making a visual statement about a visual statement', which is an inevitability in artist copy prints and production line reportage prints (Ivins, 1969, p. 61). Central to his concerns is the way in which the original syntax of the artist's work is lost, and copies were not just copies but 'translations' which often contained embellishments that ranged from the artistic, to trends in print techniques, not to mention the copyist's own limitations (Ivins, 1969, p. 67). The subsumed visual language of the artist also disconnects us from the durative process of drawing and the raw, denotative marks done in the field. The drawing was not anchored to singular artistic vision as it is today and, by virtue of its 'translations', eliminates the original act and the first-hand rendering of experience.

The special artist

The term 'special artist' was first used to credit coverage of the Crimean War (1853–6) and required an artist to be sent to the front lines where the story was unfolding. This required a set of skills far beyond the typical artist correspondent. The special artist had the skills of a journalist in identifying salient events combined with the artistic fortitude to get it down in drawing under dangerous conditions, often requiring a gun as well as a pencil (Hogarth, 1986, p. 30). War was big business for the illustrated press, and throughout the nineteenth century, wars provided large circulations for the *Illustrated London News* along with European counterparts in France (*L'Illustration*) and in Germany (*Illustrirte Zeiteung*) (Hogarth, 1986, p. 30). Virtuosity and artistic flair were present in the original drawings but disappeared in the process, retaining the original vision solely in detail, composition and some context-specific observations.

The special artist's role was born of necessity to meet the demand of weekly graphic newspapers that sprang up in the middle of the century, most notably in

London with the *Illustrated London News* and later with *The Graphic* (Hogarth, 1986, p. 10). In North America, *Frank Leslie's Illustrated Newspaper* and *Harper's Weekly* were main competitors and the Civil War provided rich subject matter for the special artist along with very vocal criticism of the images. Both papers contained a variety of information to the public, giving great prominence to the engravings, adorning sections ranging from 'penny encyclopaedias', to 'police gazette', 'travel journals' and 'satirical sheets', although focusing most on the reporting of news. Fires, weather oddities and humorous images from daily life dominated the press and more global news after the invention of the telegraph in 1844 (Hogarth, 1986, pp. 24, 30).

The eyewitness artist was responsible for a first sketch of the scene but 'there could be little motivation for comprehensive sketching'. Artists were acutely aware of their part in the larger chain of production and that contextual details were typically filled in by house artists, using a large, photographic resource (Brown, 2006, p. 34). This diminished role for the 'special artist' was not always so and the significance of their contribution to the final image was largely based on artistic capacity. However, because of the demands of the act and scarcity of correspondents (particularly in North America), publications like *Frank Leslie's Illustrated Weekly* solicited the general public, in particular soldiers, to submit sketches with promises that they would be paid 'liberally' (Brown, 2006, p. 47).

The public reception

Although the original field sketches rarely survived and the expressive act is lost in the final engraving, the dominance of drawing as *the* representation of the news is undoubtable and its public reception was critical (Brown, 2006, p. 34). A few 'special artists' did rise to prominence and engaged in a dialogue with readers. One such artist was Henri Lovie and he noted in a romantic description for *Frank Leslie*: 'A "Special Artist's" life is certainly not one of elegant leisure; but I like action, and have no objection to a spice of danger. I have several horses at various points, which have "come to me", and am prepared for whatever may turn up' (Brown, 2006, p. 52). The reality for the artist was likely less romantic but these exchanges show a desire by the public to connect to these artists, even when their 'hand' is many steps removed from the final imagery. This could also reveal a publications interest in validating the imagery and attesting to the accuracy of its reporting. Because a field artist is named and provides commentary on the event, the work is connected to an eyewitness. Just as the manner of production in contemporary reportage often belies the claim to direct recording, nineteenth-century publications enlisted the 'special artist' to validate, legitimize and personalize what was a constructed news image.

Social change

In 1869, *The Graphic* was founded in London by William Luson Thomas and prominence was restored to the individual artist and his (all men at this point) vision, aligning with the radical moral purpose of the weekly. With an openly Christian liberal slant, Thomas 'believed art should be enjoyed as much for its closeness to life and truth as for any aesthetic qualities it may possess' (Hogarth, 1986, p. 56). Aligned with Ruskin's interest in narrative in pictures, Thomas sought social change in his images and his 'sketches in London' series did have an impact on the 'public conscience' (Hogarth, 1986, pp. 56, 57). While this work does embrace a greater diversity of approaches and acknowledges individual artistic effort, the work is still rooted in the reportorial conventions of the illustrated press and it wasn't until the turn of the century that drawn language embraced a wider spectrum of qualities, atmospherics and potential for layered commentary.

The news image and witness

Noted art critic and theorist Jonathan Crary, in his attempt to rescript the narrative of the nineteenth century in terms of vision and art, notes about painting (although this could be replaced with drawing): 'paintings were produced and assumed meaning not in some impossible kind of aesthetic isolation, or in a continuous tradition of painterly codes, but as one of many consumable and fleeting elements within an expanding chaos of images, commodities, and stimulation' (Crary, 1990, p. 20). Crary also cites Walter Benjamin who 'saw the art museum … as simply one of many dream spaces, experienced … no differently from arcades, botanical gardens, wax museums, casinos, railway stations, and department stores' (Crary, 1990, p. 23). The nineteenth century can be seen as representing an early taste of what was to come, with an onslaught of images changing public perception of them as both enriching the public sphere and crassly cluttering it.

With a modernizing society towards the end of the nineteenth century, there is greater competition on the level of the image and thus the prominence and ubiquity of drawing result in its wider cultural disappearance. The artistic, cultural and technical achievements gained in art and drawing are largely flattened in commercial reportage, and drawings, at least popularly, are valued for their informative function, even when they provoke or titillate. Joshua Brown, quoting the poet Wordsworth, addresses the state of the Illustrated press after reading the *Illustrated London News* around 1846 noting (excerpted):

Now prose and verse sunk into disrepute
Must laquey a dumb Art that best can suit

The taste of this once-intellectual Land.
A backward movement surely have we here,
From manhood, – back to childhood; for the age-
Back towards caverned life's first rude career.
Avaunt this vile abuse of pictured page!
Must eyes be all in all, the tongue and ear
Nothing? Heaven keep us from a lower stage!

(Brown, 2006, p. 60)

A cultural hierarchy was evident and reportorial drawings in weekly newspapers were firmly in the mainstream appealing to the illiterate sectors of the public and indulging in pictorial accounts of salacious crime, punishment and scandal. This created a backlash against reportorial images and some publications sought to distance themselves from the rabble. This was evident in publications, particularly in the United States, that moved away from using images altogether and newer publications that did continue to use images, sought to identify with a more sophisticated reader, providing images 'suitable for framing' (Brown, 2006, p. 67). Other publications also emerged like the satirical publication *Puck* (1871), an American answer to England's *Punch* (Brown, 2006, p. 67). The second half of the nineteenth century was a time in which drawing was the shape and form of news and entertainment for the majority of the public. The rise of comic books in the 1940s and 1950s in America would see a similar phenomenon and a similar scepticism about the moral and cultural impact of drawing, representation and narrative.

The *Illustrated London News*, despite Wordsworth's criticisms above appeared to be less controversial, and balanced coverage, particularly of daily life, in an objective manner. Society was bifurcated between rich and poor, but it appears that both appreciated seeing their lives in pictures as evident in the enormous circulation of upwards of 300,000 by 1863 (Hibbert, 1975, p. 13).

The *Illustrated London News* also regularly featured dispatches from 'Special Artists' on the illustrations, including information about the events preceding the work and the after-difficult experience negotiating conflict zones. One such elaboration accompanied a dramatic engraving showing a large barricade in Paris near the Place de la Bastille during the revolution of 1848. It starts:

We append the substance of the notes taken by our Artist, of the appearance of the localities which he visited in sketching the accompanying Illustrations. That such was accomplished at great personal risk will be inferred by each reader; to whom also it will doubtless be satisfactory to learn that in his faithful and devotional discharge of duty, our Artist experienced no personal injury …

Although this scene appears too melodramatic to be true, still it is the very drama of reality. (Robertshaw & Vries, 1995, p. 63)

Several things are striking here. For one, the artist is capitalized as is illustrations in the text and the tone of the writing is clearly in reverent appreciation towards the artist and their service to the public in delivering this information. Also, this dramatic preface cleverly sets the stage to more specific detailing of the features of the image by establishing that the image is the product of an eyewitness. (One who managed to survive unscathed in what is a clearly violent and chaotic moment.) The acknowledgement of the image as almost unbelievable in its depiction and the claim that it captures the 'drama of reality' is again validated, tacitly, by the presence of the unnamed artist. Furthering this eyewitness, artist perspective, the article further notes:

> Our artist having taken a good view of the scene from inside the barricade on the Place de la Bastille, proceeded to the entrance of the Rue du Faubourg St. Antoine. 'Here,' he writes, 'I inspected the famous barricade: it was as high as the first floor, and more than ten feet deep; the top was covered with double rows of well-armed men. A small passage near the corners was left, through which I passed. When inside this barricade, I was compelled to work like everybody else at removing the pavement, only to show that I sympathised with the insurgents.' (Robertshaw & Vries, 1995, p. 63)

Beyond simply validating that the image was in fact the result of a first-hand observed event, the *Illustrated London News* is using the artist's narrative as a valuable adjunct to the news story. These details also enable us to 'enter' the image more effectively, imagining the artist navigating the terrain and engaging with the locals. This kind of rich narrative enables the reader to more readily accept the image as true, and to perhaps see all of the images in the *Illustrated London News* to be the product of a witness artist, more or less dramatized for effect. *Illustrated London News* is then self-validating and engaging in public relations on the level of truth, legitimacy and the delivery of the news. It is important to note that the *Illustrated London News* had only been in operation for 6 years and at this point circulation was below 100,000 (Hibbert, 1975, p. 13). Although the ubiquity of engravings in popular print culture and even the news was well established, it seems reasonable that these extended eyewitness accounts sought to reassure the public of the veracity of the images and that faithful reporting was taking place.

This kind of commentary happens in many instances throughout the *Illustrated London News* but one such instance is striking in which the 'Special Artist' and correspondent provide a joint dispatch. This particular report occurs during the American Civil War in 1863:

> (The Special Artist starts) 'The period chosen for my illustration is the moment when the last shell fired from the fleet burst over the battery; and the troops,

illuminated by the glare, are seen rushing to the parapet to repel the assault. Some of the enemy have already reached the crest of the work, but only to pay for their temerity by falling where they stand.' (Robertshaw & Vries, 1995, p. 146)

(Correspondent follows directly with) 'The horrible scene that met the eye the morning after the attack beggars description. All through the night we could hear the screams and groans of the wounded lying within a few yards of us; but as a continual fire was kept up by the advanced pickets it was impossible to do anything for them without running great risk of being shot.'

The image accompanied by this description of the moment that inspired it is a remarkable piece of evocative commentary and the orchestration of the image, which is highly elaborate, feels like a work of careful assemblage. The sights and sounds of the commentary draw us in to this violent scene. The drawing of the soldiers become effective referents to the real casualties of which six hundred are eventually dumped in a Confederate mass grave (Robertshaw & Vries, 1995, p. 146). As noted previously, it is not so much the effects of the drawing which engage us here (namely the visual language of the artist and the awareness of the 'hand') rather it is the construction of the image and the performance, clearly utilizing tropes of the drama of combat, but, through effective diversification of action, conveying the chaos of warfare. Here the image is evocative of this intense moment from the war but less through its formal means and more through staging and the relay between the artist and correspondent's testimony and what the image attests. It is reasonable to assume that these notes from the field helped to buttress the claim of the authentic witness but equally that without another credible media in competition (such as photography), an inherent truth was widely perceived by the public.

A contemporary 'reader' might want to look for artistic authorship here but what is striking about this and virtually all other illustrated news images is that the drawn effects are purely in service of the accurate depiction of events. The features of the image, from the environmental to the human and machine, are illusory of reality and not in direct response to it, as in contemporary reportage.

Photography

Susan Sontag called photographs 'pieces of the world' which she contrasts with writing and all other handmade arts. Other art forms she notes are 'interpretations' and photography's ability to 'furnish evidence' unsurprisingly found early use in 1871 by the Paris police to document inmates. Citing photography's implied veracity, Sontag notes, 'the picture may distort; but there is always a presumption that something exists, or did exist, which is like what's in the picture' (Sontag, 1979, pp. 4, 5).

This contrasts clearly with reportage drawing which, even at its most mimetic, cannot attest to a definitive moment other than the experience of the artist producing the work. The photograph however does not attest to moments of production and rather it freezes time and 'all photographs testify to time's relentless melt' (Sontag, 1979, p. 15). While the photograph is read as the result of a quick mechanical process, the drawing is seen as an unfolding of the process of its creation, and we connect to it as a 'made' thing and not a 'captured' thing. This is both a problem and an asset for the representational claims in the drawing.

The photograph, as Sontag notes, 'is both a pseudo-presence and a token of absence' (Sontag, 1979, p. 16). Unlike drawing, photographs do not point to the photographer and rather they capture an instant and are 'incitements to reverie' (Sontag, 1979, p. 16). While drawings are of and about things, they are also, as Rawson and others note, about drawing itself. Photographs are primarily concerned with how the 'camera makes reality atomic, manageable, and opaque' (Sontag, 1979, p. 23).

Where the roles overlap can be seen in the practice of the flaneur, roaming the streets at the end of the nineteenth century and seeing the 'picturesque' in the undiscovered street. Photographers like Paul Martin in London and Atget in Paris documented their respective cities' 'dark and seamy corners' (Sontag, 1979, p. 55). These images relate to reportorial drawings in that they share the same referent but differ greatly in form. While photographs 'don't seem deeply beholden to the intentions of an artist', drawings are the result of such implicit intentions (Sontag, 1979, p. 53). And while the photograph has become a way of experiencing something and recording participation, it is an 'act of non-intervention' (Sontag, 1979, pp. 10, 11). Although it could be argued that drawing too has an implicit physical distance from the subject, the act itself is an intervention, documenting but also mediating its subject matter(s). Also, the 'non-intervention' referred to is that of creating an 'image world' outside of the real, observed world (Sontag, 1979, p. 11). It is the distance necessary to capture the desired image and this requires the photographer to 'be in complicity with whatever makes a subject interesting' including a person's 'pain and misfortune' (Sontag, 1979, p. 12). This can be seen in war photography and presents the inherent conflict between fluid reality and 'slices' or 'miniatures of reality' the photograph provides (Sontag, 1979, p. 4).

This conflict is also conflated in the way photographs 'trade simultaneously on the prestige of art and the magic of the real' (Sontag, 1979, p. 69). The photographic conundrum is succinctly described by W. J. T. Mitchell who notes, 'it is praised for its incapacity for abstraction, or condemned for its fatal tendency to produce abstractions from human reality. It is declared to be independent of language, (as per Ivins) or riddled with language' (Mitchell, 1980, p. 274). In an age with sophisticated photo manipulation tools and hypersensitivity towards the manufacture of evidence, photographic imagery is seen with more suspicion, although with no alternative as comprehensively reflective of 'reality', it still holds tremendous power and persuasion.

Claims to representation, truth and vision

Umberto Eco saw the two forms (drawing and photography) as more related in that both reproduced perception. He notes, 'either a drawing or a photo, shows us that an image possesses none of the properties of the object represented; and the motivation of the iconic sign, which appeared to us as indisputable, opposed to the arbitrariness of the verbal sign, disappears' (Burgin, 1994, pp. 32–8). He then clarifies this saying the 'iconic sign' (drawing or photography) '*reproduces* the conditions of perception, but only some of them' (Burgin, 1994, pp. 32–8). The distinction being made by Eco is that full perception is more than the retinal image captured by the camera or represented in the drawing. He furthers this claim by stating that '*every image is born of a series of successive transcriptions*' which, according to his larger claim, makes all images, including photographs, correlative constructions comprised of 'codes of recognition' (Burgin, 1994, pp. 32–8). Truth for Eco appears to be less self-evident and requires a deeper analysis of the structural veracity of the image. Eco's claim is fundamentally simple, the drawing and the photograph are only part of the full experience of reality as they replicate a singular perception of that reality. As discussed in this book, it could be argued that drawing captures more layers of that perception by virtue of its form and formation.

The photograph has some specific problems with its claims to truthful representation which relate to its fragmentary nature. Allan Sekula notes, 'the photograph is an "incomplete" utterance, a message that depends on some external matrix of conditions and presuppositions for its readability' and 'is necessarily context-determined' (Burgin, 1994, pp. 84–109). This context relates to the specificity of the photograph in capturing a definitive moment. This burdens photography with the need for a 'discourse', which didn't bother the earliest practitioners like Fox Talbot and Morse who championed the 'unmediated agency of nature' (Burgin, 1994, pp. 84–109). The photograph can ther be seen to have a 'primitive core of meaning' from its early conception, thought to be analogous to nature and a fluid iconography, heavily dependent on how it is contextualized.

While John Tagg notes that the photograph 'as such has no identity' and that 'its history has no unity', this is in part because its identity and history are tied to its 'conditions of existence' and status as a technology (Tagg, 1995, p. 63). While drawings can evocatively convey the experience of a witness, they do not attest and frame an irrefutable 'reality'. Instead, they claim the experience of a thing seen, felt or remembered. This makes them durative records of experience and although historical in the sense that they reflect a specific encounter with a subject, the drawing itself is re-created by the viewer, reaching total fulfilment in the moments of its viewing. Therefore drawing is 'read' and understood differently by different viewers. The photograph however is always historical. As Tagg notes, 'photographs are never "evidence" of history; they are themselves historical', they 'encompass' or 'exclude' and therefore, as Berger noted, are separated from their 'functions' (Tagg, 1995, p. 65).

One debate that is essential to the discussion of representational truth and the photograph is about language. Berger and Ivins make the claim that the photograph 'has no language of its own' or, for Ivins, no 'syntax'. However, Eco claims above that the photograph is linked to perception and therefore is singular and has the specificity of the photographer's vision and is 'coded' (Tagg, 1995, p. 187). Tagg takes this further and draws upon a similar system of meaning making that is applied to drawing language. He notes, 'the meaning of the photographic image is built up by an interaction of such schemas or codes, which vary greatly in their degree of schematisation. The image is therefore to be seen as a composite of signs, more to be compared with a complex sentence than a single word' (Tagg, 1995, p. 187). If, as Eco and Tagg note, a language is in fact present within the photograph and, as Eco suggests, is part of the field of perception, then the photograph, like drawing, has a determinate truth only when its respective 'visual language' is understood. It could be argued that this is a barrier for the total reception of drawing as much as photography, particularly when so much about understanding drawing is by understanding and re-performing its construction. Something that will come easier to those who regularly 'perform' the drawing act.

The visual language of reportage drawing is not only on the level of codes, description and meaning. The language of drawing is, at the core, a language of invention and this is both a striking distinction from that of photography and a surprising asset in the claim to representational truth. While the artist's vision is inherently subjective, Gombrich notes, citing the reception of impressionist painters by the public, that

> Having learned this language, they went into the fields and woods, or looked out of their window onto the Paris boulevards, and found to their delight that the visible world *could* after all be seen in terms of these bright patches and dabs of paint. (Gombrich, 1972, p. 324)

The ability of the artist to utilize language to not just render reality but to fundamentally change the perception of that reality is key here. Because of the durative process of drawing and its inherent qualities, it does not compete with photography on the level of accuracy in depiction and rather presents artistic vision as a proposition. Gombrich, above, is identifying the flexibilty of artistic language and, to an extent, the willingness of the viewer to succumb to the illusory effects of artistic media. W. J. T. Mitchell notes, 'vision is as important as language in mediating social relations, and it is not reducible to language, to the "sign", or to discourse. Pictures want equal rights with language, not to be turned into language … to be seen as complex individuals occupying multiple subject positions and identities' (Mitchell, 1980, p. 47). The image, once separated from its maker and available to the viewer, is a propositional document, succeeding or failing on the terms of its own construction and coherence and asseting a range of ideas, both consciously woven into the image and subconsciously present.

The ubiquitous image – twentieth- and twenty-first-century reportage drawing as an alternative vision

Reportage drawing persisted through the twentieth century and now the twenty-first century as a distinct offering from the photographic image, and even when practised as journalism, it is valued for its highly individual and idiosyncratic lens through which to see our world. Mid-twentieth-century reportage saw a dramatic expanse of graphic constructs and closer links between the aims of caricature and reportage, asserting the voice of the artist and privileging the seductive and provocative over the purely informative. For this book, it is significant to chart the evolution of reportage drawing as it slowly detaches from commissioning structures of the second half of the twentieth century and evolves as a highly personal practice, engaged with the hyper-realities of modern life. Through individual graphic constructs, artists exploit the properties of drawing and understand inherent contrasts with competing media forms.

The twentieth century

At the turn of the twentieth century, as photography was rapidly becoming more mobile and a less burdensome technology, drawing in the form of reportage and social commentary was flourishing. Publications from around the world such as *The Daily Graphic/The Graphic* in the UK, *Simplicissimus* in Germany, *The Masses* in the United States, *L'Assiette au Beurre* in Paris and numerous radical publications in Russia decrying the violent suppression by the Tsarist regime tackled contemporary issues such as workers' rights, greed, poverty and episodic violence that predicted the deep fractures that were to reveal themselves at the onset of the First World War (Hogarth, 1986, pp. 84–109). During this period, graphic languages are wildly diverse in approach and traditions of caricature are incorporated into reportorial, observational drawing.

The range of approaches from direct reportage to more refined caricature mark a dramatic break from the conventional news images of the nineteenth century. This is largely due to both a liberalizing view of the image in a world that acknowledged (albeit slowly) the radical vision of the Impressionists and the ability to replicate practically any drawing media through photomechanical reproduction (Hogarth, 1986, p. 73). The idiosyncrasies of the artists' hand and their individual graphic constructs brought to the viewer a visceral account of the psychic world of the artist and an understanding of the turbulent dynamics of their modernizing societies. The publications noted above gave a temporary home to artist reporters, but after the invention of the Kodak Box Camera in 1889 and the innovation of faster film in 1905 and therefore greater practicality and utility, the artist reporter began to take on a hybrid role as reporter, commentator and satirist. Artists from across the disciplines of the fine arts also got involved (Hogarth, 1986, p. 74). Functionally, the artist was freed from the conventions of the news image and able to comment on a wider spectrum of issues and formally, individual graphic constructs were broadly applicable, imbuing the work with complex graphic vocabularies that reflected expanding visual appetites. Without the 're-codification' of the graphic construct of the artist as was commonplace in the print preparations of the nineteenth century, publications could now connect viewers to the artist's hand and mind, and reportage drawings could be 'read' as a work of singular vision with all of the layered intentions of the artist.

Throughout the First and Second World Wars, reportage artists found publication and significant exposure for their work (Hogarth, 1986, p. 152). Post-war, budgets were tight in Europe and most publications relied on photography. In America, there was more money and an explosion of liberal-minded special interest magazines that catered to a growing educated and affluent population (Hogarth, 1986, p. 152). Many of these reportage projects were attached to 'polemical essays' dealing with the fallout after the Second World War through niche stories tackling exploitation of workers, veterans' issues, infrastructure development and a variety of visual essays on an array of topics (Hogarth, 1986, p. 152). This move from the constructed, orchestrated and packaged news image to the freewheeling, emotive and expressive approaches to reportage post-war sees a total liberation from convention and a freedom, taken by artists, to move in their own stylistic direction, detached from any tradition or constraint. Paul Hogarth and Ben Shahn epitomize this move and can be seen respectively as significant in shaping modern reportage (Embury & Minichiello, 2018, p. 8).

Post-war in Britain, Ronald Searle comes back from Singapore where he was a prisoner of war and in 1946 exhibits his vivid drawings produced in captivity. This work caught the attention of Paul Hogarth and the two would go on drawing excursions in post-war Europe (Searle, 2010, p. 13). Searle's reportage work ran alongside his prolific humorous illustration career and found publication throughout the world in *Punch*, *The News Chronicle*, *Le Canarde Enchaine*, *Jours de France*, *Suddeutscher Rundfunk Fernsehen*, *Holiday* and *Life* (Searle, 2010, p. 6). Searle reflects the side of reportage that is laden with commentary and is unabashed about those intentions. Interviewed in 1977 about his reportage work he noted, 'One is not illustrating but pushing one's nose into life. On top of that one must have something to say – however crass. Reportage is not reporting, it is opinion and comment that takes it away from journalism into (minor) art' (Searle, 2010, p. 27).

Paul Hogarth's book *Graham Greene Country* shows the authorial potential of reportage which was visible in corners of the publishing industry in the second half of the twentieth century. This self-initiated journey takes the artist to the various locations of Graham Greene novels, and Hogarth's written accompanment offers an insight into his thinking and an engagement with his drawing which is as rooted in traditions of the cartoon as it is reportage. The correspondence between his written entries and his drawing is notable. Writing about residents on a beach in Clacton-on-Sea he notes, 'grotesque beetroot-faced retirees, who look as though they refused to be liberated when the camp closed stagger by, or absorb the warmth of the midday sun on battered deck chairs. (Hogarth & Greene, 1986, p. 54). Here it is clear that observation and comment are fused in the written description and so in the drawing which is both attentive to the structural accuracy of the architecture and solidity of setting, and more playful and stylized in the rendering of the beach dwellers.

Although stylistic tastes have shifted away from the approach of Hogarth, the work and its charm and commentary have a durability. As Martin Harison, former editor for *The Times*, notes in relation to the comparison between reportage drawing and other media:

Good art can feed the senses, teach without lecturing, and heighten the emotions or shock the soul. Photography can do all these things, but I feel with art those initial feelings will last and carry on being fresh, regardless of how far into the future the work is viewed. Film and photography seem to suffer more from association with a particular period and sharpness diminishes as the years go by. (Embury & Minichiello, 2018, p. 158)

While the commissioning structures for the reportage artist are stable but somewhat limited in the second half of the twentieth century, the commissioning of a war artist endures, and in the early 1980s, Linda Kitson is chosen for the Falklands War. Commissioned by the Imperial War Museum, her adventures and struggles to even participate and align with the logistics of the Royal Navy constitute a compelling meta narrative. Kitson's drawing follows on from a tradition of direct observation. Even though subjectivities and inevitable distortions exist, her work does attest to open, objective witnessing and raw unvarnished vision.

In the foreword to the book of her drawings produced during her time as a war artist, Frederick Gore notes of her work:

> Linda Kitson's particular gifts as a draughtsman are an ability to capture the essence of people, and even of things, so that they seem alive on the page, which she does by very rapid, simple means; and an extraordinary spatial awareness so that not only does she instinctively place her drawing beautifully on the paper but through the use of white areas and her immaculate sense of perspective she conveys the relationship of ship to sea to helicopter to land magically in two dimensions. (Kitson, 1982)

What is striking here is that drawing, as the loser in the battle with photography for prominence, is celebrated for the things it does in spite of its diminished status and, possibly, benefits as a unique piece of media, a compelling oddity. What Gore is identifying in the work of Kitson is the twofold experience of looking at drawing. As Michael Taussig notes, 'history is repeated in slow motion and the clumsiness of the artist actually adds to this *seeing seeing*, by which I mean to include as question the relationship between seeing and witnessing ... when an image surfaces at a moment of danger and just as quickly disappears if not seized' (Taussig, 2011, p. 89). Reportage drawing is valued for its evidence of the struggle to capture fluid reality; its currency is its fallibility and the distillation of what it does capture, not the comprehensiveness of its vision.

In the United States, a giant of twentieth-century reportage drawing is Robert Weaver. Weaver came to prominence as an illustrator in the 1950s but his work did not reflect the conservatism of his time. His work was loose, gestural yet structured, and had a bold openness that both grounded his depicted subjects as real people and as icons. The openness of his linework reflected his approach to reportage drawing which shared features with Gary Embury's work (see Chapter 8) in that the drawing feels like a perceptual trace of his vision. The honesty in this drawing was hugely appealing and his image construction demonstrated a sophisticated understanding of modern art, particularly expressionism, and developments towards rethinking the picture plane (Cath). He was regularly commissioned for *Fortune*, *Life* and *Sport Illustrated* magazines (among others) and his work was rarely altered from his field recording (Cath). Weaver had a huge influence on American Illustration for his refreshing use of raw drawing and bucking the trend towards highly realized, realistic, superficial and often twee illustration of his era. Ben Shahn, noted earlier for his enormous influence on the developing shape and conscious of reportage drawing, was a huge influence on Weaver but, from the perspective of raw, unvarnished drawn reportage, it is hard to see an equal to Weaver's highly visible contribution to the art. In many respects, even according to Weaver himself, it was Europe that moved his work towards greater sophistication and the visual essays in

L'Assiette au Beurre were hugely inspiring to the young artist and enabled him to imagine the expansive, responsive vocabulary that he eventually developed (*Saul Leiter and Robert Weaver, an artistic dialogue*). Weaver's later work such as the experimental *Vogelman Diary* demonstrated his strength in composition and the relay between evocative text and image. Although very happy with the label illustrator, his friends and admirers, such as his friend and photographer Saul Leiter, thought he could have been a highly successful fine artist for his abilities in painting and his intellectual temperament (*Saul Leiter and Robert Weaver, an artistic dialogue*).

Contemporary reportage drawing

The contemporary practice of reportage drawing is diverse in approach, subject and purpose. Because of shrinking budgets in print media across the board, reportage has less of a presence in print and has moved largely to the web. Reportage approaches still persist in print illustration as seen in the illustration collective *Ink* (now disbanded) whose members Rachel Gannon, Chloe Regan and Fumie Kamijo successfully incorporated reportage illustration and illustrative techniques into their commercial illustration. Rachel Gannon's work is particularly notable as she has produced her highly idiosyncratic reportage in a variety of locations and commissions including her residency at Luton Airport. These kinds of unique commissions persist and attest to the functional change in reportage. Reportage artists are providing a different perspective of space and place and capturing the poetics of those places through responsive artistic choices in situ.

Several experimental and experiential approaches to reportage have emerged over the past ten years and indicate the potential of the practice to grow and adapt in this fluid media environment. Jenny Soep's digital and traditional work at music festivals has enabled her to create drawings and then sell that work to musical acts. Linda Kitson is using an iPad to create the majority of her work, and collectives like First Hand bring together different reportage artists to create compelling collaborative work. The First Hand collective is well aware of the competition for eyeballs in the current media landscape and has a clear understanding of what it is trying to achieve with reportage drawing. The collective was formed after university by five core members and they engage with reportage through collaboration and seek to capture the unique textures of experience. They note in regard to their interest in drawing: 'drawing is a time-based activity, and the illustrator can edit information so that only the parts of the picture that tell the story need to be included. If we understand that drawing is not trying to do the same job as a camera, we understand that drawn visual journalism is an important method of conveying human stories (Embury & Minichiello, 2018, pp. 56, 57). This forward-looking group sees the immediacy of reportage and the speed of social media communications as presenting an opportunity for the active broadcast of their work. Online publication of their projects in *The Guardian*, *The Times*, *Eye Magazine* and *Varoom* validate their belief. They note about their media strategy that 'imagery is by far the quickest way to digest a situation and our lives are saturated with visual communication in the form of photographs and short video clips. Now is the perfect time to slice though this noise with an alternative method of communication that offers something more' (Embury & Minichiello, 2018, p. 59).

Much of the practice of contemporary reportage artists is self-initiated. Melanie Reim's coverage of election day in New York in 2016 shows the persistent desire of artists to engage with events that are significant and consequential (protests being particularly popular). Reim notes that 'the raw emotion of the reaction to this historical time is magnified when you take the time to draw it, as opposed to a clicking camera. I feel connected – and empowered, as much as we can be under the circumstances' (Brazell, 2017, p. 45). Reim's scratchy and colourful work captures the immediacy and atmospherics of place and her immersion is clear. As Reim notes above, reportage drawing in this way is personally fulfilling in that it enables a deeper understanding of the world, no matter how troubling those realities may be. Here the aesthetic of reportage is closely aligned with its purpose, namely capturing the energy of a live event and the frenetic chaos of the crowd. Reim's work represents a total break with the function of the camera and embraces the improvisation and responsiveness of hurried media in the thick of a fluid environment.

One figure in the world of contemporary reportage who deserves mention for his methods as much as his work is Olivier Kugler. Called the 'contemporary face of reportage illustration' by *Eye* magazine's John L. Walters, Kugler is one of the most visible practitioners working today finding publication in *Suddeutsche Zeitung*, *Reader's Digest*, *The New York Times*, *The New Yorker*, *New York Magazine*, *German GQ*, *Harpers* and commissions from organizations like *Oxfam, Medecins Sans Frontières* and *Black Sun Plc* to name a few (Walters, 2017, pp. 44, 45).

Kugler does not draw on location and rather takes photos with a simple camera and makes audio recordings. He later draws from his laptop using hard lead pencils and his work reflects this with its strong contour line and wealth of detail, no doubt aided by his use of photographic imagery (Walters, 2017, pp. 44, 45). Kugler's influences belie his current approach to reportage, citing the American illustrators Alan E. Cober and Robert Weaver as influences, both men who drew from life (Walters, 2017, p. 47). Kugler notes about the inclusion of overlapping action in his drawings and implied movement: 'I only draw what I see. That's why I want to start again when the subject moves!' (Walters, 2017, p. 48). This remark seems out of place with his working methods which do not involve direct engagement through drawing of subjects.

Kugler professes for his work a desire to tell stories first and foremost and it is perhaps this which dictates his methodology. Instructive for our understanding of Kugler in relationship to contemporary reportage practice is the way in which he uses available technology. What may seem like a cheat by some reportage artists who see drawing on location as fundamental to the act, Kugler offers something of a hybrid approach, acknowledging the value and quality of drawn lines but bringing in the photograph to provide more information. Does Kugler's method reflect a change in thinking about the role of photography in reportage drawing and, in the unspoken desire by commissioners to have their cake and eat it too, to have the qualities of drawing and the capacity for information afforded by the photograph, in one? This question remains contested but in the spirit of truly embracing the wide spectrum of reportorial methods, it is important to acknowledge and accept the role technology plays in aiding the artist. Drawing emerges as still valid because it connects to the maker through facture in ways that put both artist and viewer in the realm of the subject and the experience of the artist.

Contemporary reportage drawing: Authorial shifts and hybridity

There has also been a notable split between professional and enthusiast activity with the explosion of Urban Sketchers. This organization captures the important and previously unseen activity by professionals from a variety of fields within, and on the periphery of art and design along with amateur enthusiasts. For many within Urban Sketchers, this activity is about refining vision and the pure pleasure of engaging with their surroundings (and fellow artists). The important split between this activity and 'professional' reportage artists is in the terms of their engagement. In contemporary reportage drawing, practitioners are seeking subjects and circumstances that are both personally significant and provide some opportunity to exploit the political and social dimensions of their subject. The authorial shift in reportage drawing is not a refutation of its journalistic origins and rather takes those ideals and applies them inward. Contemporary practitioners are setting their own briefs and find sustenance in un-explored political and social terrain while miring the qualities of their own drawing. This contemporary moment for reportage drawing has come to be most vividly about drawing itself. In a crowded and quickly moving media landscape, drawing becomes a visible reminder of the power and limitations of the hand and all that tells us about vision, witness and the layers of understanding contained in marks and lines that are dashed out in confrontation with a world in flux.

Feliks Topolski was a Polish-born and British-based illustrator who became one of the most well-known and highly regarded illustrators during his most active period between the 1950s and 1970s. His work is highly relevant to the shape, form and concerns of contemporary reportage today. Although Topolski enjoyed many commissions and successes as an illustrator, his self-initiated *Topolski's Chronicles* and books, in particular *Holy China*, reveal an artist who is engrossed in the world and using drawing as a means of mediating his experiences and sharing them with the wider public. The fact that his drawing reflected a confrontation with reality in its brusque mark making and highly gestural language made his work both accessible as a conduit of experience and sophisticated in its disinterest in tidying up that vision. What we see and value in Topolski's drawing and what makes him relevant today is an awareness of what drawing can do and, in fact, what drawing is very good at, namely, insight into the workings of vision writ large. In Topolski's work and the work of many contemporary reportage artists, this connection to the perceptual qualities of line and the momentary (as Gary Embury notes 'time-based') qualities of the act are not purged but celebrated, even exploited. The legacy of Topolski's vision is that drawing is not about depiction alone, it is about vision and experience and reportage drawing can bring us to this convergence. It is a convergence of thought and action, of seeing and making sense of that seeing in drawing. Topolski notes in *Holy China* what he is seeing:

> China: tinny high-voiced song-and-music (knob it down but cannot off) and train clangour turn the sand-coloured panorama into a pantomime of communal rhythm; little horsecarts trot to it, clusters of burdened carriers sway to it, smoke puffs with it over dusty villages, strings of peasants in the fields dig and fork in unison with the train-steward hoeing his vacuum cleaner. (Topolski, 1968)

Topolski's commentary condenses observations which can be seen in his drawings, and the identification of rhythm and linear references like strings suggest that the commentary and drawing can be seen as counterparts, riffing of each other and not, in this case, establishing either a hierarchy or a preferred order of viewing/reading. Although clearly *Holy China* is a book that highlights Topolski's drawing, his writing does more than provide contextualization, it speaks to the same procedural thinking inherent in the drawing and touches upon challenges that are reflected in the artwork. One such notable case is below in which Topolski expresses the revelation of just how different the functions of art and life are in Mao's China and how the constructed and the real confound Western perceptions.
He notes:

> Young men cluster attentively around some gadgets, obligingly they are queried, and the translated answer is: 'Discussing the quality of titanium foil.'

And again, as often the scene takes the shape of a staged socialist-realist painting-poster-sculpture – their truth to life, of life's to the picturings of it, is of such a perfect fit that the doubting Thomas from the West is tempted to see reality as a make-believe for his benefit. This utopia-aiming intensity discomforts the Westerner, accustomed to a vitality fed on opposition and indignation: here, Art and Life, for better or worse, idealize one another. (Topolski, 1968)

The above quote exhibits the kind of thinking that goes on behind the drawing. Thoughts that reside in the drawing in some way. Equally, this reflects the thinking of the artist about the image. Thinking which reveals that every image represents a debate of some sort and that his own images of China are polluted with his perceptions as a Westerner but equally, valid concerns that the 'reality' presented to him may not be true. The later concern is one that is central to reportage drawing and shapes individual orientations to the act. While the journalist has some responsibility to truth, the reportage artist has this same responsibility to vision and that can be equally as difficult. Although the textual elaborations are not a requirement of reportage drawing, the interplay is often lively and, like the drawings, reflects a construction of vision and experience. As Gombrich notes, 'we must try to relearn the difference between stimulation through self-projection, which, when applied to art, so often passes for "appreciation", and that enrichment that comes from an understanding, however dim and imperfect, of what a great art is *intended* to convey' (Gombrich, 1963, p. 85). In reportage drawing, this enrichment manifests itself in the intersection between the artists' record of experience and the viewers re-creation of that experience. The success of the drawing is in how well the artist traverses the space between witness, recording and mastery to convince us of his or her vision. The thinking on the page which is typically at a more advanced stage in a 'finished' drawing is at an early, tentative and searching stage in reportage drawing. Art theorist Rudolph Arnheim notes, 'In the course of the creative process the work goes through elaborations that require that the artist distinguish, with severe discipline, between what suits the nature of his subject and what is accidental impulse' (Arnheim, 1969, p. 439). In reportage drawing, this process is left as a record of thinking. The moves of the artist from attention to attention is evident in the marks and lines on the page and because of this we feel close to the artists' thinking and the 'enrichment' that Gombrich speaks of can be seen as the intimacy felt with the artists' hand. The fact that reportage practice persists in this media world may be due to this important connection to raw intention and strategies to form that are seen in reportage drawing and its close relative, the sketch.

For Topolski, the relationship between text and image is more fluid. The text does occasionally provide what could be discerned as journalistic inquiry but more often, like the drawing, is episodic, textural and anecdotal. The writing provides some context for the drawing but it is not a requirement for access. Topolski's drawings are rich and elaborate evocations of vision and they involve us in the drama of his thinking in ways that cannot be textualized.

Victoria Lomasko's *Other Russias* (2017) is a collection of writing and drawing in which both play a more definitive role. Lomasko's drawing is bold and less open in its construction than the sketchy indications of typical reportage. The book is broken into two sections which are 'invisible' and 'angry' and it looks at forgotten parts of Russian society through interviews and drawings done on the spot. Lomasko's drawing is built with thick black lines and a cartoonist's flair for exaggeration, both subtle and amplified. She often includes her subjects' own words in the drawing and her commentary is stripped down, setting the scene with just enough to understand the context. The voice of the people she has interviewed is integral and these utterances are open, honest and often, devastatingly, emotional and raw. Although the text here has a more important role in completing the drawing, it also creates, as Barthes notes, a 'relay-text' in which 'the unity of the text is realised at a higher level, that of the story' (Barthes, 1977, p. 41). This is a critical point. Functionally, Lomasko's *Other Russias* is telling us a wide-ranging narrative first and foremost and the text is important for understanding the complexities of the lived experience of its subjects. In one such section of the book called 'Feminine', Lomasko looks at women and their unique plight navigating boredom and desire in the hinterlands. Lomasko notes in this section that she 'tried to move away from reportage and toward symbolism in this series' and 'the portraits here are not so much images of specific people as they are archetypes: the faded, lonely woman, the slutty boozer, the rigid old Soviet woman, and so on' (Lomasko, 2017, p. 35). This quote reflects the flexibility within the field of contemporary reportage to embrace other kinds of seeing, documenting, commentary and construction.

Jill Gibbon (see Chapter 6), a reportage illustrator known for drawing in arms fairs across Europe, notes, 'drawing is capricious, forever wandering away from what is seen or intended' (Gibbon, 2018). While this may seem like a departure from the seen, what we saw in Topolski's textual divergences equally occur in the drawing and sometimes these archetypes necessitate creation because, as Lomasko notes, the symbolic is sometimes more important and urgent than mere recording. It also does not mean that these archetypes are a wholesale invention. They are often a condensation of the observed, an amalgamation of features to create a symbolic whole. George Grosz took this one step further. For him the drawings of people he observed were also part of him. He noted:

Arrogantly, I considered myself a natural scientist rather than a painter or even a satirist. Actually, however, I was everybody I depicted: the rich, gorging, champagne-guzzling man favoured by fate, as well as the one out there

> holding out his hand in the pouring rain. There were two equal parts of me. In
> other words, I participated in life. (Grosz, 1998, pp. 125–6)

Reportage drawing demands this kind of empathetic leap of imagination and drawing, no matter how caustic, trades on the humanity of its forms, both in its facture and the idiosyncrasies of depiction. Lomasko's drawings, like all drawings, render something anew and our engagement with the text in *Other Russias* creates a compelling correspondent connection to the world of/in the drawing.

Kate Evans's book *Threads* explores the daily life of immigrants stuck in the no man's land of the 'jungle' in Calais in a comic that trades heavily on a reportage-style eyewitness drawing (2017). The drawing is stripped bare of ornament, stylistic indulgence or contrivances. What results is a drawing language and comic storytelling approach which feels urgent and honest. The occasional clumsiness of the drawing reinforces what we imagine is the speed of execution but also the circumstances of its creation in an under-resourced migrant camp. There is an inherent flatness to the compositions and the overall colour is applied somewhat crudely, giving the images the impression that they are conduits of experience and not articulated drawings to be admired for their mastery. However, in this media environment of high polish, these drawings and the overall humble aesthetic of *Threads* is highly effective. Evans notes in the book when talking about her supplies, 'thick cartridge paper. I want the pictures to feel weighty and professional, even if they don't look it' (Evans, 2017, p. 75). I think she is aware of the aesthetic she is creating but equally, it emerges out of the limitations of her own hand and as much as this may be an artistic limitation, it does the opposite of limit the text; it amplifies the rough, chaotic and tragic elements of the narrative. Equally, like Lomasko's bold but economic line art, the aesthetic of *Threads* disappears hierarchies of author/artist and subject and grounds the narrative in a dialogue of equals. As noted previously, reportage drawing is effective in eliciting compassion through the knowledge that the artist has borne witness to something and, through the active means of representation in drawing, constructed that vision with intention.

My own drawing reflects similar concerns and orientations to the act as above but unlike some contemporary reportage, my work functions more as visual essay. My work is aligned with many of the tenets of journalism, but it seeks something more textural, experiential, personal and less comprehensive. In 2009 I started my drawing blog *Life's Too Short for Nuance* and it was intended to capture the reportage drawing that I had been doing all around New York where I was living at the time. The practice evolved as my confidence grew and I realized what I was trying to achieve. In short, this was a more comprehensive image of my experience. This did not mean that my drawings intended to tell a comprehensive story. However, it did and does mean that my drawings are intended to be a reification of the ecstatic moment(s) of experience and the textures of that experience. I often produce my drawing after the fact but my visual memory has been tuned by years of practice and I can both conjure and construct memory on the page with surprising accuracy. I have often been surprised that the drawings contain so much of the seen, especially when I see the same people after they have been drawn.

Contemporary reportage drawing is a fluid practice with practitioners utilizing the comic format (Evans), a hybrid text and image reportage (Lomasko) and more stand-alone statements like Jill Gibbon and myself. All practitioners engage in the act of drawing to mine meaning. Drawing connects to our psyche in surprising ways and is a document that feedbacks to the artist and the viewer, unfolding new understandings. It is also a human document made for humans. Reportage is attracted to spectacle but it almost always uncovers something else, something more nuanced.

Drawing is always a balance between the seen, the felt and the intended. Because of this, reportage drawing elicits a connection to the inner space of the artist but equally, the world of the subject. A world created new in marks and lines which, like our world, shifts and moves, acquiring new meanings and perspectives with every viewing.

Conclusion

The nineteenth century saw reportage drawing as a prominent part of visual culture and the primary vehicle for the delivery of the news of the day. However, field drawings were subsumed into a production line approach to constructing the news image which eliminated the qualities of their graphic construct. Artistic intent through the responsive line of the artist and the construction of the image was lost to conventions and amplifications which occurred when field drawings were re-worked into wood engravings and idiosyncrasies were flattened. This presents a stark contrast to contemporary reportage drawing as artistic intent through individual graphic constructs is key to the act and distinguishes it from analogical forms like the photograph. In the nineteenth century, reportage drawing was attempting to fulfil the public desire for the accurate representation of events and, consequently, homogenized and disappeared distinctive graphic constructs. Today, the act is almost wholly engaged with the tension between the challenges of the act and the respective strengths and limitations of the artist working in situ. In near total contrast with the nineteenth century, today reportage artists are seeking to reveal, through the construction of their images, the durative process of reportage and the inherent subjectivities of drawn notation, seeking images which are expressive of a time, place and experience rather than mimetic representation. Developments in print and photography changed public perception of the image in the nineteenth century and enabled a more expansive approach to representation, ushering in modernism. These developments largely centred around an awareness of the limitations of representation in the photograph and a desire to capture the complexities of modern culture through expressive rather than mimetic or mechanical means.

Developments in art from realism towards Impressionism and then total breaks from representation into abstraction led to a re-examination of what representation is and what can be represented. Speaking of a Manet painting called *In the Conservatory*, Crary identifies two competing strains in late-nineteenth-century art which shape how we see art and perception today. He notes:

> *In the Conservatory* is a figuration of an essential conflict within the perceptual logic of modernity, n which two powerful tendencies are at work. One is a binding together of vision, an obsessive holding together of perception to maintain the viability of a functional real world. The other, barely contained or sealed over, is a dynamic of psychic and economic exchange, of equivalence and substitution, of flux and dispersal that threatens to unmoor the apparently stable positions and terms that Manet seems to have effortlessly arranged. (Crary, 2001, p. 92)

In contemporary reportage the diversity of approaches, and complex intentions in individual graphic constructs, push our understanding of the observed and observable world towards new realizations, unbound by convention or objectivity and invested in the plasticity and potential of drawing itself. As Crary notes above, like modernism's inherent tensions, contemporary reportage was shaped by an art world moving towards abstraction while a complex and conflicted world needed rendering in the figurative language of reportage drawing. Many of the psychic features of modernism's shifting movements were incorporated in the evolving graphic languages of the reportage artist.

At the core of reportage drawing's stubborn persistence as a media and practice is our innate connection to the act of drawing and how it reflects something fundamental about human vision and understanding. Ingold reflects on how the sketch and its tremulous searching and non-straight lines reflect how we understand surfaces. He notes, 'whereas the abstract geometrical line, in the depiction of an edge, represents the junction of two *planes*, an actual edge in the built environment is formed by the junction of two *surfaces*'. He furthers, 'we perceive the environment not from a stationary point, nor from a succession of such points, but in the course of our movement along what Gibson calls "a path of observation"' (Ingold, 2016, pp. 169, 171). Seen in the context of reportage drawing the unique properties of drawing as a record of perception relate to how we not only see the world but also understand its construction. As a depictive media, drawing does not merely mirror the world that we live in, it creates a new perception of the world and as noted previously, aggregates our own perceptions of the subject. The survival of reportage drawing is then less about a defiant posture towards other media and more a recognition that it offers something functionally different. Berger makes the following observation about a figure he is drawing noting, 'every line I draw reforms the figure on the paper, and at the same time it redraws the image in my mind. And what is more, the drawn line redraws the model, because it changes my capacity to perceive' (Berger & Savage, 2008, p. 112). While this is from the perspective of the drawer, this same phenomenon is occurring with the viewer. Contemporary reportage with its myriad of graphic constructs reflects the multiple ways in which we can enter the experience of the artist engaging with the subject and share the range of perceptions that are imbedded in the drawing. The continued practice and proliferation of reportage drawing is contingent on the awareness of its unique properties and its connection to multi-layered experience. American philosopher John Dewey notes, 'the doings and sufferings that form experience are, in the degree in which experience is intelligent or changed with meanings, a union of the precarious, novel, irregular with the settled, assured and uniform – a union which also defines the artistic and the esthetic' (Dewey, 1929, pp. 290, 291). Drawing is fundamentally an abstraction and yet, in terms of reportage drawing, it is depictive. The layers of experience contained in the drawing can be seen as an abstract, conceptual overlay on top of and within the depictive elements of the drawing. This is the essence of the contemporary act and distinguishes it from the nineteenth-century conventional image.

2

THE GRAPHIC CONSTRUCT OF REPORTAGE DRAWING AND THE RE-CREATIVE EXPERIENCES

The currency of contemporary reportage drawing is in its proximity to its subject and how this is conveyed in the graphic construct of the artist. This construction is then a vehicle for a re-creative experience and a communion with both the durative process of drawing and the layered experience of the artist's engagement with the subject. Through the properties of drawing that form the construct, we engage with the total experience of drawing including the negotiations in situ, and we understand the experience through the filter of the artist's intentions. These are implicit or explicit in the methods and stylistic choices of the artist.

Although reportage drawing is typically identified by a complex range of analogical marks, it is also the summation of aesthetic, conceptual and procedural concerns at the point of drawing. Being a composite of multiple concerns including a desire for commentary and provocation, the correspondent, analogical record is further complicated, and the association with conventional documentary aims is weakened. What arises is a new understanding of experience in and of the image, one that embraces the personal imprint of the artist but still maintains an essential anchorage to the observation of people and places.

The immediately identifiable aesthetic of the graphic construct of reportage drawing shares the features of the sketch, especially the raw, unclosed forms that convey the urgent, improvisation that connects us to the making of the drawing and, by extension, the engagement with the subject. The raw forms of a 'first thought' sketch mirror the reportage drawing in approach and the dual concerns of articulating observed forms and departing into imaginative applications. The sketch is more than a way of framing the act of reportage, it is a way of seeing how the larger aesthetic reads as a direct engagement with its subject.

Noted drawing theorist Philip Rawson's terms 'tenor', 'topic' and 'realia', or the visual reality of the artist, are significant to this book and enable a closer understanding of the make-up and function of the reportage artist's graphic construct. Although there are myriad stylistic approaches and orientation towards subject matter among reportage artists, the 'tenor', or the purposeful rendering of the drawing, reinforces the engagement with a live subject and aims to draw the viewer into a confrontation with artistic perception, not away from it in stylistic indulgence. The reportage drawing is a record of negotiation between the artist and subject and thus reflects the propositional terms of the artist's graphic construct. This reflects a merger of concerns, inclinations and limitations on the part of the artist and renders, at its fulfilment, a 'half-created' record of collaboration between artist and subject.

Schema and the way in which drawing becomes a schematic language is critical to see how reportage drawing, in contrast to most conceptions, is schematic and therefore relies on conventional visual language. This language, however, comprised of refined perception and invented forms, is beyond 'schematic restatement' and reflects developed forms and strategies for the rendering of forms. This schematic language is an identifiable part of the artist's graphic construct and contributes to the artist's aesthetic.

In reportage drawing, the constituent forms and the subject unify in a graphic construct that is layered with descriptive, symbolic and metaphoric intent. Analysing these intentions and the effects of the work provides a more complete understanding of the structural relationships between drawn forms, their relation to the individual's experience drawing in situ and how the graphic construct enables a re-creative experience of the drawing itself.

First thoughts – the impromptu record of thought and action

The sketch and the freedom of its forms have been useful to artists for clarifying thinking, relying on action over deliberation that is reflected in the manner of its making and the aesthetic impression of unforced honesty. The sketch is also, to an extent beyond the challenges of reportage, an exploited aesthetic property of reportage drawing. Philosopher and theorist on drawing, perception and photography Patrick Maynard, citing Rawson's ideas about the procedural nature of drawing and its effects, notes 'productive process and history is not only an important aspect of the appearance of drawings, it is a factor that may be actively exploited by the drafter for drawing purposes, including depictive and representational ones. In these terms, we learn more about the efficiency of drawing as an imagining-seeing technology' (Maynard, 2005, pp. 191, 192). Maynard is referring to the way in which the artist controls the perception and re-perception in drawing and how the effects, including stylistic choices, can be manipulated for desired reading. For reportage drawing, the loose gestural quality that pervades the act attests to its production but could equally belie it. The impromptu marks and gestures that are associated with reportage drawing have been conventionalized and the contemporary practitioners included in this research have distanced themselves from those flattening qualities, seeking, as much as possible, a singular, idiosyncratic language.

From the fifteenth to the eighteenth centuries, drawing was developmental practice and a preparatory activity for the realization of ideas intended in other media (Rosard, 2002, p. 22). Disconnected from the intentions of the act these historical sketches enable a 're-enactment of the drawing gesture' and 'our mimic re-creation of the creative acts' (Rosand, 2002, p. 23). This closeness to the durative process of drawing and the artist's own articulations make the sketch (and by extension the reportage drawing) a valuable originary act' (Rosand, 2002, p. 23). Taylor breaks down the historical forms of drawing as the sketch, the study and the cartoon, each confirming the place of drawing as almost purely developmental (Taylor, 1957, p. 97).

However, extracted from its historic role as largely preparatory, the sketch and its isolation of the 'drawing gesture' is highly valuable to the reportage artist. In contrast to a 'finished' drawing, the sketch and reportage drawing derive their potency from an awareness of their construction, not an elimination of it. Equally, the inventive forms that emerge from the quickly executed drawing imbue it with the energy of raw vision and provide the building blocks for schematic language, mostly through refinement and a building of the 'storehouse' of memorized forms.

The sketch has historically provided the artist with everything from the pre-visualization of a composition, to the specific qualities of a pictorial component (like drapery for example) and, an end in itself, retaining the vitality of rendered thought, unaltered for public consumption (Rawson, 1969. Reportage drawings share the impromptu gestures of the sketch and closeness to the operations of thought. As drawing theorist David Rosand notes, 'the drawn mark is the record of a gesture, an action in time past now fixed permanently in the present; recalling its origins in the movement of the draftsman's hand, the mark invites us to participate in the recollection of its creation' (Rosand, 2002, p. 2).

Additionally, and perhaps most importantly, the reportage drawing benefits from its perception as a piece of intimate artistic creation. The uncovering of private sketches of the past has given viewers a privileged look at how the artist constructed forms and conceived their work in the most fundamental ways. Reportage drawing exploits this, not only revealing its construction but relinquishing control, leaving indicative marks, half-finished forms and awkward lines. These diosyncrasies enable the viewer to engage with the drawing as a wrestle between the experience of the subject and the strengths and limitations of the artist. John Berger identifies this struggle as a dialogue and notes 'it is a ferocious and inarticulated dialogue. To sustain it requires faith. It is like a burrowing in the dark, a burrowing under the apparent. The great images occur when the two tunnels meet and join perfectly. Sometimes when the dialogue is swift, almost instantaneous, it is like something thrown and caught' (Berger, 2008, p. 77).

Studies after nature – observation and refinement of vision

The history of the sketch is often confused by assumptions made about the nature of the work. Because of the spontaneity of the sketch, they were often mistaken for 'studies after nature' but more often than not these studies preceded or predetermined compositions that followed and emerged purely from the imagination (Rawson, 1969, p. 295). This is an important distinction for reportage drawing. While it is marked by the brevity of its construction and intimates direct recording, the practice of the act is broad and combines a variety of methods, including working from memory or imagination. However, the rigorous observation from nature develops a confidence in the rendering of forms that, after much practice, can be fluidly manipulated and recalled on demand. This was part of the practice of notable artists such as Leonardo, Michelangelo, Rembrandt, Hogarth and Daumier to name a few. For reportage artists, this practice is less a false construct of the observed than a prodigious use of visual memory.

Victorian polymath John Ruskin focused his drawing tuition on studying nature and noted that drawing strategies emerge to depict natural subjects and when you do 'you must now therefore have recourse to some confused mode of execution, capable of expressing the confusion of Nature' (Ruskin, 1971, p. 70). The confidence of an artist's graphic construct is evident in the sketch and the ability to create reductive, economical forms, developed from rigorous observation. Ruskin, speaking of the sketches of 'great men', emphasizes the value of 'economy' in the sketch and notes to judge the sketch 'you must know the beauty and nature of the thing he was drawing. All judgement of art thus finally founds itself on knowledge of Nature' (Ruskin, 1971, p. 82).

Ruskin's orthodoxy was not without some understanding of the limits of human vision and skill. Ruskin's three laws of sketching from nature, 'subordination', 'individuality' and 'incomprehensibility', acknowledge the difficulty of the task but says of great masters (like Turner) that they are able to create 'a perfect expression of grace and complexity' (Ruskin, 1971, p. 121). Ruskin is aware that the expression of nature is more important than mere depiction, made clear by his contention that 'nothing is ever seen perfectly, but only by fragments' (Ruskin, 1971, p. 120).

Ruskin's observational loophole is well exploited in reportage drawing. The observation present in reportage is almost always fragmentary but the conveyance of the observed subject to the viewer is in the selective detail, the 'individuality' of the seen. As Ruskin implies, it is not the total capture of nature that is essential but rather an acknowledgement of its complexity and an effort towards some resolution. Ruskin makes this distinction clear, noting how one should approach natural subjects. He said:

> You must invent, according to the character of tree, various modes of execution adapted to express its texture … it is the intention of Nature that the tenderness and transparent infinitude of her foliage should be felt, even at the far distance, in the most distinct opposition to the solid masses and flat surfaces of rocks or buildings. (Ruskin, 1971, p. 123)

Berger provided a glimpse into his own procedural thinking during a life drawing class and this account confirms the value of study from nature. What is evident here is how the drawing unfolds from an engagement with the subject and how the resolution of the image is tied up with the artist's own matrix for success, often anchored to a perceived rightness or truth to what was observed. For Ruskin and Berger, some form of submission to the circumstances and realities of your subject is necessary and instead of shortcutting towards a resolution, one must grapple with the complexities of the 'real'. He notes, 'I had to resist the temptation to make every line over-emphatic' and 'yielded to the oncoming forms'. He then notes, 'I saw and recognized quite ordinary anatomical facts; but I also felt them physically.' Also, echoing Ruskin's warning about 'habits' he wonders 'which spontaneous gestures had evaded the problem, and which had been instinctively right'. And finally, he reflects on the final image noting 'I saw my drawing and the actual man coincide – so that, for a moment, he was no longer a man posing but an inhabitant of my half-created world, a unique expression of my experience' (Berger, 2008, pp. 7–9). This is aligned with Berger's broader definition of drawing as 'an autobiographical record of one's discovery of an event – seen, remembered or imagined' (Berger, 2008, p. 3). Rawson echoes this noting, 'in creating the image of his world man creates his image of himself' (Rawson, 1969, p. 9). Drawing reflects a complex strategy to rendering reality and, hence, is a total picture of individualistic vision, personhood.

This notion of a 'half-created' world is significant here. Because reportage drawing is a formulation of a graphic construct, rendered subjects are imbued with layered referents of individual vision. Additionally, as Berger notes, the engagement with the subject is like a collaboration. The success of this collaboration rests on how the artist perceives the capture of the subject and also on how the multiple aims of their graphic construct are satisfied, including personal commentary. The success of the drawing is in the ability of the artist to negotiate the creation of a 'half-created' world with the subject and, importantly, convey that negotiation to the viewer in a way that invites the re-creation and re-experience of the act.

Speed, mastery and performance – the record of quick perception and the capture of fluid reality

French poet and essayist Charles Baudelaire famously quoted Delacroix saying, 'If you have not sufficient skill to make a sketch of a man throwing himself out of a window, in the time that it takes him to fall from the fourth floor to the ground, you will never be capable of producing great machines' (Baudelaire, 2006, p. 62). Baudelaire goes on to support the comment and his thoughts on Delacroix's aims which he notes are 'to achieve an execution quick and sure enough to prevent the smallest particle of the intensity of action or idea from evaporating' (Baudelaire, 2006, p. 62). The speed evident in the sketch and reportage drawing is seen here as a demonstration of mastery and 'genius', and although this is connected to the legacy and history of the sketch, improvisation and invention characterize the persistent interest in the sketch in scholarship and practice (Petherbridge, 2010, pp. 26, 27).

Speed is noted as not only a critical component in the practice of reportage drawing (whether circumstantially required or self-imposed), it is also a readily observed aesthetic quality. It indicates the rush to capture fluid reality and it is the mark of urgent creation, pushing the artist's capabilities. In line with the historical perception of speed as mastery, reportage trades in the perception that it is an urgent act, that the drawing somehow emerges from the environment, which it often does. The viewer becomes another participant and enables the re-creation of the act and re-experience of the circumstances of its production.

Anthropologist and avid drawer Michael Taussig reflects on his own drawing of a fleeting moment witnessed from a taxi in a tunnel in Columbia. He notes, 'far from splattering perception into a diffuse morass of sensation, the high-velocity speed-up and disappearance of the world into an endless tunnel of night accentuates with a cruel clarity the glimpse of things but for an instant seen ... a glimpse can be enough' (Taussig, 2011, p. 125). Taussig's own drawings are disconnected from an aesthetic expectation and his own interest in the drawing as an artefact is as a crystallization of some smuggled truth in hurried lines, some connection to his own emphatic memory.

Tenor, topic and visual reality – understanding how the graphic construct projects meaning and connects us to artistic intent

The attributes of individual graphic constructs vary widely among reportage artists, especially those who avoid some of the more conventional approaches. A surprising diversity of approaches to the act denotes widely varied concerns and differing notions about what constitutes success in the image and how one perceives the conveyance of experience. Philip Rawson's delineated terms 'tenor' and 'topic' are useful for fleshing out the graphic construct and the relationship between the subject and treatment of the subject. Rawson defines the tenor as promoting 'the extension of forms into space; second is the special meaning enclosed in the topic, which may or not be an obvious direct product of the tenor though it may be "hung on" it' (Rawson, 1969, p. 5). The tenor can be seen as the construction of the drawing and the formal relationship between the graphic symbols. As Rawson notes, 'the meaning lies not in the tenor, but in how it is treated' (Rawson, 1969, p. 5). He furthers this later noting, 'no tenor is ever the final resting point of the meaning, its terminus … the artistic tenor is never a single actual thing, nor even a recognizable class of things. It is a fact of the world which is referred to for the sake of the sense of "external reality" or "positive truth" it can give to the image' (Rawson, 1969, p. 250). This directly relates to the reportage drawing and the way in which the graphic construct attempts the capture of fluid reality and attests to experience.

These two terms are useful for reportage drawing in that the subject and the treatment of the subject are dialogic. The graphic construct is often a consequence of the demands of the act and relate, in varying degrees depending on the individual practice, to the orientation to the subject. The practice is less shaped by differing contentions about objectivity and more about the way tenor and topic summate experience and what the artist deems salient in that experience. What is striking, however, is that this dialogue between language and subject is fundamental to understanding artistic motivations, especially as the outward aesthetic of reportage drawing can belie more subtle intentions about individual perception, commentary, and stylistic concerns.

Rawson sees the graphic construct as inseparable from artistic vision and the summation of an artist's construct resides not solely in 'notional realities' depicted but in the 'system of relationship' between graphic forms. This creates a stylistic, graphic structure which relates to itself and marks, at its total fulfilment, the visual reality of the artist or 'realia' (Rawson, 1969, pp. 32, 33, 35). Rawson also notes, importantly, that graphic constructs or 'drawing styles' create very distinct visual realities and have different 'structural functions' (Rawson, 1969,

p. 33). These structural functions are multiple and complex and require from the spectator a 'well-stocked mind' to know how the drawing, and drawing itself, shapes meaning (Rawson, 1969, p. 32).

What the artist is creating in a drawing is then, according to Rawson, the proposition of a construct which depends on knowledge of both the terms of the artist's perception and the correspondent language to describe it. Rawson relates the success of this negotiation between artist and spectator as crucial to the success of the drawing. As Rawson notes, the artist 'makes up his drawings out of elements no one can see in any object' (Rawson, 1969, p. 21). Rawson furthers this, saying, 'drawing is not seeing … On the contrary, works of art are in fact made; they are artistic constructs, based on ingrained scanning procedures … A language of form or structure creates its own kind of reality' (Rawson, 1969, pp. 22, 23).

Schema

Schema can be seen as invention, a developed strategy for the depiction of subjects through one's available means. Influential professor of Art Education Viktor Lowenfeld says of schema as it relates to children's drawings as 'drawing is essentially an abstraction or schema from a large array of complex stimuli and demonstrates the beginning of an ordered thought process' (Lowenfeld & Brittain, 1987, p. 223). Gombrich saw schema as relating to artistic development and refinement. Schema for Gombrich was a part of artistic training and was both an element of rote memorization through practice and the development of an artist's own vocabulary of form. Gombrich notes 'for in a way our very concept of "structure," the idea of some basic scaffolding or armature that determines the "essence" of things, reflects our need for a schema with which to grasp the infinite variety of this world of change' (Gombrich, 1972, p. 155). For the reportage artist, schema relates to the strategies and approach to forms which in the act must be called upon quickly with little deliberation. Schema in reportage drawing is refined perception and relates to a consistency in an artist's graphic construct (what outwardly can be called 'style' but in the act of reportage, for some, is less consciously cultivated). An awareness of schema and its formation enables a greater understanding of an artist's graphic construct and how, particularly in the act of reportage drawing, purist claims to objectivity and direct recording are put in question by the condensation of prior perception that resides in schematic forms. Schema does not, however, preclude the artist's own on-the-spot invention, and schema development is very much a continuous and inventive process. What resides as conventional in terms of the approach to form is still, itself, an invention, the result of refined perception and the merger of a constellation of aims.

The balance between capturing the specificity of the observed and applying a schematic, stylistic approach is in the intentions of the artist. Gombrich notes that children 'do not draw what they "see" but what they "know"' (Gombrich, 1994, p. 8). Schema can be seen as a merger of the two: a developed strategy for the rendering of form based on observation (the seen) and internalized forms (the known), which may be layered with creative intentions. For most contemporary reportage practitioners, stylistic indulgence is undesirable, and the effect of direct observation and recording is the conduit through which we achieve a communion with the experience of the artist. Schema, however, is not always rooted in simplistic convention and can comprise condensed perceptions and strategies for the depiction of all manner of things in the observable world and, importantly, amplifications applied to them. As Gombrich notes, schema 'stands for' something and that form in drawing can have a wide range of sophisticated referents (Gombrich, 1994, p. 19).

Notes on visual language

Philip Rawson's 'tenor' and 'topic' are central to this book because both terms confirm the larger contention of this research: primarily that visual choices are dialogically bound to conceptual orientations towards the subject. The terms relate to the practice of reportage drawing and the way in which completed drawings reflect a condensation of intentions and that visual language is only part of the larger graphic construct of the artist. Other significant theorists on semiotics, language and its components will be explored below including prominent linguists M. A. K. Halliday, Michael O'Toole and Theo Van Leeuwen.

M. A. K. Halliday's notion of 'tenor' is not unlike Rawson in that both see the word as affective but also interdependent with other factors to enable as Halliday notes an act of meaning' (Halliday & Webster, 2009, p. 16). For Halliday, meaning is the product of several aspects of the system of language such as mode, field and tenor and how the relations between those factors shape meaning. Halliday notes, 'The meanings so created are not, of course, isolates; they are integrated systems of meaning potential. It is in this sense that we can say that the meanings are the social system: the social system is itself interpretable as a semiotic system' (Halliday & Webster, 2009, p. 55). To clarify Halliday's notion of what the social system constitutes as it relates to an 'instance' of meaning he notes, 'for this purpose we interpret the situation as a semiotic structure; it is an instance, or instantiation, of the meanings that make up the social system'. He further notes, 'the social action: that which is 'going on", and has recognizable meaning in the social system; typically a complex of acts in some ordered configuration, and in which the text is playing some part; and including "subject-matter" as one special aspect' (Halliday & Webster, 2009,

p. 57). Like Rawson, Halliday sees tenor as 'interpersonal' and relating directly to the 'field' ('significant social action') and 'mode' ('symbolic organisation') (Halliday & Webster, 2009, p. 58). However, Rawson's 'tenor' and 'topic' relate directly to how we understand drawing and how meaning is constructed in the choices of the artist. Rawson notes:

> And it (drawing) conveys that meaning not by a general similarity of surface but by a structure of symbolic elements which are formulated as method. At certain points the structure rests on a foundation of visual analogies between human perceptual experience both of graphic forms and of realities. Therefore the first thing to query in the study of any drawing is: To what features of experience do its basic visual elements ultimately correspond and how do they do so? (Rawson, 1969, p. 24)

While Halliday is laying out a structure for understanding written language through a matrix which enables greater understanding of its formal make-up and relational logic, Rawson's tenor and topic acknowledge that visual language is idiosyncratic and meaning is highly dependent on, among other things, the capacity of the viewer to analogize with the forms of the artist. Rawson notes, 'certain groups of marks will constitute references to everyday objects of use, i.e. will be representational. Others will serve structural functions according to the artist's usual principles.' He continues, 'but the main bulk of the marks will not just refer directly to everyday objects but will "qualify" them by investing them with analogous forms from quite other fields of experience' (Rawson, 1969, p. 26). For Rawson, the framework for analysing drawings is limited by the essential collaboration between the artist and viewer for fully 'reading' the image through understanding the critical dialogue between tenor and topic. Halliday does acknowledge this essential dialogue although 'topic' for Halliday can best be described as some merger between his terms 'mode' and 'field'. He notes:

> In the first place the distinction between style (or 'form', or 'manner') and content is largely illusory; we cannot really separate what is said from how it is said, and this is just as true of everyday language as it is of myth and poetry. In the second place, the factors of field, mode and tenor operate as a whole, not in isolation from each other; the linguistic reflection of any one of them depends on its combination with the other two. (Halliday & Webster, 2009, p. 77)

While there are clear overlaps between Rawson and Halliday, Rawson acknowledges the specific qualities of drawing as a communicative language and that unlike written language broadly, there is not a common vocabulary of forms in drawing that enable such analysis nor a sufficient model for analysis that could incorporate all the intentions of the artist. This is precisely the reasoning behind the development of the graphic construct and mapping the practice of the reportage artist. Without a broader understanding of the orientation to the subject and the experience of the artist, we cannot comprehend the summation of intentions in the drawing which, as Rawson notes, 'summarize and condense the psychological meaning of the graphic forms of which they are composed' (Rawson, 1969, p. 247). Halliday notes similar complexity in linguistics in a variety of examples and most notably in relation to Rawson and drawing as a communicative language, in the 'voice' of the text. Halliday notes:

> The interpersonal voice provides the interaction: mood, modality, person, polarity, attitude, comment, key. The textual voice provided the organization: thematic and informational prominence; grammatical and lexical cohesion among the parts. The 'character' of the text is its pattern of selections in these various voices, and the way they are combined into a single whole. (Halliday & Webster, 2009, p. 373)

The above is perhaps the closest alignment with Rawson in that the drawing, like the 'voice' of the text, is playing multiple communicative functions and cohering the structure and meaning. For Rawson, 'voice' could be replaced with 'type' (here type can be seen as 'style' or a formalized (conventional) approach to form). He notes:

> The types of all kinds must continually appeal to many tenors in actual experience. The subject itself may even be a symbol for the 'ultimately real' (as in strictly religious icons). A wide range of types representing all the accepted existential ground needs to be evoked and clad in a large repertory of forms symbolic of the accepted extent of Being. This adds to the central numinous image a whole current apparatus of visual reality. (Rawson, 1969, p. 258)

For Rawson, and importantly for this book, drawing and 'tenor' and 'topic', broadly, are not seen as applicable to an established and stable language as in linguistics and, rather, refer to the multiplicity of artistic approaches to form and both individual artistic inclinations towards form and meaning, and cultural traditions and understandings which have implications for methods of representation. Halliday's analysis of linguistics function and structures could be useful in framing the act of drawing and his comprehensive approach is reflected in the approach to the design of the graphic construct in this book. However, Rawson's 'tenor' and 'topic' relate more specifically to the graphic forms of drawing and his view of the 'visual reality' of the artist is a more fitting way to see the way that 'tenor' and 'topic' constitute the world view of the artist and become an individual symbolic language, dependent on the 'linked chains of emotive affect they arouse; that is, upon their *content*' (Rawson, 1969, p. 29).

Michael O'Toole's approach to the analysis of art builds from Halliday's semiotic approach and explicitly seeks a dispassionate, accessible and comparable structure to find a common 'grammar' in the discussion of works of art (O'Toole, 2011, p. 16). For O'Toole, artworks can be broken down using a structural framework which reveal the meaning of the work through an analysis of the structural intent of its components. O'Toole notes, 'I would want to argue that what is often referred to as the "aesthetic" quality of a work of art is primarily the impact on us of purely formal relations – including colour, line, and volume' (O'Toole, 2011, p. 27). By seeing the image as a 'text', it is liberated from 'external' factors which, for O'Toole, have shrouded art history in a realm only accessible to specialists who are overly concerned with context and lineage (O'Toole, 2011, pp. 120, 121). O'Toole notes 'engaging first with the modal function at least involves viewers directly and personally with what they see on the canvas' and 'at least the judgment is based on what everyone can see for themselves in the painting before them' (O'Toole, 2011, pp. 126, 129). While this method does provide a clear structure for analysis which allows for close analysis without (or at least before) contextual information, for this book, the position and inclinations of the artist were of greater import and the meaning and intentions of the image were framed through the narrative of production. My interest in the image was to frame the contemporary act of reportage from the perspective of its practitioners and, through the image, highlight distinct orientations (both aesthetic and conceptual). Although O'Toole's method on the surface appears to extract aesthetic choice from conceptual intent, he notes, 'I am not thereby claiming total "objectivity", and a kind of spurious "scientific" status for the analysis; on the contrary, I want to show how a consistency in the method of approach both generates new subjective insights about a work and shows us the boundary between the subjectively perceived and the objectively describable' (O'Toole, 2011, p. 131).

Both O'Toole and Halliday use a matrix-like system for organizing their analysis and this most closely relates to the graphic construct model designed in this book to map the aesthetic and conceptual concerns of the artist. O'Toole notes 'one starts by grouping meaningful elements into compatible sets and then arranging them in a hierarchy of sets and cover-sets. The rank-scale of Halliday's linguistic model and my semiotic model do this anyway. One can then construct matrix arrays that match potential meanings against a well-defined set of features' (O'Toole, 2011, p. 164).

Linguist David Machin notes that this framework for analysis laid out by O'Toole has problems in that 'the code is conflated with the interpretation based on extensive book knowledge'. Machin points to O'Toole's analysis of Boticelli's *Primavera* in which he invokes art historical critique. Machin notes the difficulties presented to modal analysis, noting 'contextual and production knowledge are vital parts of our analyses. But we must be careful to distinguish where we rely on historical and contextual information and where our own system of analysis begins' (Jewitt, 2017, p. 187). For this book, the aim is a holistic view of the practice of reportage drawing and the image and its effects are valuable primarily for the way in which they cohere the intentions of the artist and how they reflect the contemporary practice. While the modal and multimodal approach to analysis of the image is useful in understanding the image itself, the path of analysis in this book sees the image as a record of experience and a sum of a narrative of production. Aesthetic properties and effects are significant in terms of their relation to artistic choice. In almost direct opposition to the dispassionate aims of O'Toole, this book privileges personal choice, inclinations and orientation over formal elements (although important and seen through the lens of choice, intention and the aesthetic and impression of the sketch).

Theo Van Leeuwen's expanded application of semiotics seeks to explore methods of analysis for a variety of established and emerging forms of media, utilizing 'rules' but equally acknowledging that 'rules can never control every detail of what we do. In a sense every instance of sign production and interpretation is new' (Leeuwen, 2005, p. 50). Leeuwen's approach to social semiotics borrows from the tools of analysis developed by Halliday in linguistics and expands it to all aspects of communication. Leeuwen sees communication as always within a social context and both physiological and technical. He notes 'we can communicate not only with our voice but also with musical instruments; not only with facial expressions and gestures but also through the clothes we wear and the way we groom our bodies'. He continues: 'the use of these resources is also socially regulated, for instance through the question of who is given access to them and in what roles – as producer, consumer, or, with today's more interactive media, something in between ... this means that social semiotics is by and large about the *how* of communication. How do we use material resources to produce meaning?' (Leeuwen, 2005, p. 93). Leeuwen sets out four main areas of investigation for multimodal texts, being rhythm, composition, information linking and dialogue but stresses that, like Halliday and O'Toole, they work in conjunction to formulate meaning (Leeuwen, 2005, p. 179).

Conclusion

The graphic construct of the reportage artist is primarily concerned with rendering observed subjects within one's artistic and circumstantial limitations. The features of the sketch as both an aesthetic and artistic limitation are key to understanding how subjects are captured and conveyed in fluid environments and how the immediacy of the sketch, in form and practice, rids the drawing of undesirable affectations. Although the forward aesthetic of reportage drawing is related to the sketch, this often belies layered intentions and differing methodologies, such as memory drawing, which are not directly responsive or from direct observation. What emerges is an understanding of the artist's graphic construct which is propositional and invites participation in the artist's own experience of the subject through drawing. This mediated experience through drawing is complex and reflects layered referents to a range of observed and felt perceptions in situ. The graphic construct is then a composite or summation of a range of concerns and is informed by observational practice and an engagement with the potentialities of one's own drawing.

3

THE PERCEPTION AND RECEPTION OF DRAWING

Reportage drawing is an act of rendering one's environment through the graphic construct of the artist. The complex make-up of the graphic construct and its layered intentions and fulfilment in drawing reflect the merger of conscious and intuitive thought and action. The viewer engages with the drawing on the propositional terms of the graphic construct and comes to integrate his or her own understanding of the subject with the new terms established in the drawing.

At its most basic level, a first pass at an image is a judgment. As art theorist and perceptual psychologist Rudolph Arnheim notes, 'judgments are sometimes thought to be a monopoly of the intellect. But visual judgments are not contributions of the intellect, added after the seeing is done. They are immediate and indispensable ingredients of the act of seeing itself' (Arnheim, 1954, p. 2). Arnheim is proposing here that perception is an intelligence unto tself and he makes this claim repeatedly. Psychoanalyst Ernst Kris furthers this saying that seeing is also experiencing and that the artists message 'is an invitation to common experience in the mind, to an experience of a specific nature' (Kris, 1964, p. 39). As Rawson has noted, the success of drawing for the viewer is in how he or she can match and 'analogize with' the tenor and topic. This quick judgment can then lead the viewer away from the image or into it, engaging with the re-creative process of looking and re-experiencing the totality of the drawing. Gombrich identifies a necessary willingness and readiness to collaborate with the artist and 'call up our conceptual image under his guidance'. A constructed experience is made of 'hints' intended to evoke the 'external form (Gombrich, 1994, p. 10).

What enables the viewer to engage with a drawing is the 'aesthetic illusion' created through the graphic construct of the artist. This illusion exists in the 'thinly separated' world of artistic creation from the 'real' world (Kris, 1964, p. 42). As Kris notes, 'the "reality of play" can coexist with a certainty that it is play only' (Kris, 1964, p. 42). This illusion is more than superficial and extends through experiential modes of understanding form. Arnheim notes:

> In looking at an object, we reach out for it. With an invisible finger we move through the space around us, go out to the distant places where things are found, touch them, catch them, scan their surfaces, trace their borders, explore their texture. It is an eminently active occupation. (Arnheim, 1954, p. 33)

The above confirms the re-experience of the image and notes the participation of the viewer in mimicking the process of its creation, like Berger's 'half-created' collaboration with his subject. Arnheim is seeing vision as active rather than passive as the viewer seeks, through 'generalization', an understanding of the image through his or her own field of knowledge (Arnheim, 1954, pp. 33, 35). As Arnheim notes, 'eyesight is insight' (Arnheim, 1954, p. 37). The recording of these insights constitutes the formation of the reportage drawing, and the sensory tracing of surfaces, linked to a corporeal understanding of form, encourages the viewer to re-enter into the act of rendering fluid reality.

The propositional terms of the artist's graphic construct invite the viewer to participate in the world created by the artist. When this world departs too far from the comprehensible world of the viewer, there is 'overdistance', and the spectator is unable to 'find a point of identification' (Kris, 1964, p. 47). What the artist ultimately hopes for is some form of integration. Some merger between the world presented to the viewer and the viewer's own reality. Kris, aligned with Arnheim's contention that 'eyesight is insight', sees this process of integration as separate from meaning making and notes, 'pictures do not convey a thought or meaning only, they catch reality for the man who is to see them. Seeing contains both elements: that of recognizing what is known, the element of thought, and that of actually holding reality' (Kris, 1964, p. 50). When the viewer sees a representation of a human figure in an artwork (common to the largely figurative nature of reportage drawing), they have a 'bodily' experience and work from recognition to self-identification, one supporting the other. Kris then concludes, 'we started out as part of the world which the artist created; we end as co-creators: We identify ourselves with the artist' (Kris, 1964, pp. 55, 56). The viewer is then the co-creator of the already 'half-created' world of the artist.

It is notable that this integration also occurs at the point of drawing. Arnheim notes that art functions within the polarities between the 'multiplicity of reality' and the 'simplicity of form' (Arnheim, 1954, p. 140). Echoing Ruskin, Arnheim notes that 'order in nature can be discovered only when the capacity for grasping order is developed in the mind' (Arnheim, 1954, p. 140). This relates to the processes within reportage drawing as fluid reality is reduced quickly into a range of marks that stand in for their real-world referents. The condensed forms of schematic language are shaped by repeated observation and enable their quick application in situ. The sum total of this immediate and stored observation is an ownership of the subject, a re-imagining and re-creation in drawing. While the drawing reflects a 'reduction of reality', there is no 'simile of nature' and 'independent of the level of resemblance, nature has been re-created' (Kris, 1964, p. 52). But this integration of the subject is not merely a process of perceptual functions, it is also a process of the imagination, and artistic works, like their literary counterparts, extend from the real towards the imagined. As Kris notes, 'the familiar figure of the painter in search of a model, a scene, a tree with specifically shaped branches, can well be compared to that of writers engaged in a similar quest, they scan the world around them for observations or themes which would stimulate their imagination' (Kris, 1964, pp. 53, 54). Additionally, the process of drawing is one of a multitude of choices and while these may have anchorage in observed people and places as in reportage, they are formed by artistic intent. Arnheim recognizes this as inherent in the expressive content of an artwork and notes, 'in the course of the creative process the work goes through elaborations that require that the artist distinguish, with severe discipline, between what suits the nature of his subject and what is accidental impulse' (Arnheim, 1954, p. 439). Often seen as the marker of a mature artist, the adept command of both the technical facility of drawing and its conceptual underpinning results in work that not only achieves greater solidity but also confidently coheres the choices of the artist.

On the level of drawing, beyond integration, which is necessary for an understanding of the image, the manner of depiction, the graphic construct of the artist, requires a new appraisal of the subject itself. Patrick Maynard neatly summarizes this saying:

> It is not only of great significance for depiction that our interpretation of depicted scenes is (obviously) strongly influenced by our perception of the properties of the lines generating them, but that our visual experience of these lines – what we notice about them, how we group and orient them – is reciprocally influenced by our imaginative perception of the scene we take them to depict. That this experience feeds back into the interpretation of the scene is an elementary fact of perception with great significance for depiction. (Maynard, 2005 p. 200)

Maynard describes an essential loop between the denotive marks of the artist and our own understanding of their form and function. The enjoyment and ultimate rendering of meaning within the image is dependent on our connection to the intended total effect of the images and how the constituent parts reflect not just things but sensations, atmospherics, feelings and other textures of experience. As noted previously, a certain conversant knowledge of drawing is required to potentially unlock more challenging evocations within a drawing, but that corporeal, re-performative aspect of drawing, aided by its transparent construction, enables most viewers some entry into its inherent logic and effects.

The summation of the graphic construct and schematic forms of the artist renders not only meaning in the drawing but also emotion. How the emotive intent of the artist connects with the viewer is reliant upon a complex extension of the image towards an internalized, mutual experience. Gombrich quotes Dewey saying, 'the meaning of an expressive object, on the contrary, is individualised'. He goes on to say, 'the esthetic portrayal of grief manifests the grief of a particular individual in connection with a particular event. It is *that* state of sorrow which is depicted, not depression unattached. It has *local* habitation' (Gombrich, 1994, p. 53). The localization here is specific to the way the drawing is constructed and choices have been made about portrayal. Dewey is also making the point that the content of a work of art is our entry into the experience depicted (and our re-experience viewing it). A drawing fixes a certain reading of its subject and the sum of its construction produces effects, some intentional and some not. An artist is hyper-conscious of these effects and, as above, can create highly localized and specific sensations within a work that ultimately speaks to the sophistication of the artist's repertoire, both technical and conceptual.

As noted earlier, the new 'co-created' world of the viewer and the re-creative experience enable multiple insights into the procedural moves of the artist, the effects of the graphic construct and a new lens on the depicted subject. As Kris notes, referring principally to representational art but using the following as an example,

> The person who hums verse or melody, who repeats to himself passages and can thus re-experience the original experience, is in a similar position. Do we then refer to a reproductive rather than to a productive activity? Are we entitled to speak of identification with the artist when his work has become part of the inventory of our memory or when we can 'recall' or 'perform' it? (Kris, 1964, p. 58)

The moves of the artist in the drawing enable us to imagine its production and 'perform' and, by extension, 'reproduce' the original act of creation. This participation is essential to reportage drawing which constructs an experience that is anchored in direct observation but is the sum of a vocabulary of forms which are an assemblage of percepts. Familiarity with an artist's visual language can greatly aid its reception and perception. To produce the desired intent of the image in one's mind, it is essential to synchronize with the language present and metaphorically speak it as your own. The drawing then slots into all of the other visual artefacts in your storehouse and its meaning is made in relation to those other objects and your intimate amalgamation of them into your whole thinking and feeling self.

Conclusion

Our understanding of a work of art and drawing in particular requires an effective bridge between the experience of artist within the work and the viewers' ability to align with it, re-perform it and integrate that experience as their own. Our perception of reportage drawing is aided by our understanding that it is a made thing by an individual. We understand its construction as a formal struggle to capture and depict and as such, we re-construct as much as we seek a conclusion. Although reportage drawing has a laid-bare construction, its effect is immediate. We engage with the marks and lines and quickly see their referents in people, things, architecture and so forth. The visual language of drawing is evocative but is ultimately anchored in individual vision and, as such, t engenders empathy, understanding and a granular amalgamation of the experience(s) of the artist.

4
THE REDUCTIVE LINE: CARICATURE AND COMMENT

Caricature features in reportage drawing as both a conscious amplification of an observed subject in order to direct attention to a concern or render that subject as emblematic, and a result of the demands of the act, exaggerating through a reductive, economical line. Although traditionally a practice of refinement and simplification in order to elicit an emotional response or judgment upon a subject, the caricature and its expressive potential can be seen as a means of drawing us closer to the observed through accentuating salient features. The way in which the caricature can make the particular universal is relevant to reportage drawing as observed figures become symbolic of larger societal issues. Both the contemporary practice of reportage drawing and caricature (as seen in the work of cartoonists) are equally concerned with the potential of drawing to further our understanding of the world we live in and challenge formal conventions of what drawing can and should be and do.

The way in which caricature features in reportage drawing differs with artists' own intentions for their work and how they perceive a fidelity to the observed subject. Although perceived by some to be a departure from strict observation, for others it represents an amplification of the observed, a capture of not just observable features but of essences and personhood. As noted below, caricature, like some contemporary reportage drawing, aims to achieve two things simultaneously: the capture of an observed subject and the potential of that subject for wider symbolic meaning, both eliciting a greater understanding of the subject.

Reportage and caricature

The struggle to capture subjects in fluid environments results in reductive, economic lines that compress salient features and can share the attributes of the caricature. For some this is part of a graphic construct that seeks commentary through pushing and pulling features of observed subjects, articulating themes and held beliefs. For others, the move to caricature represents a stylistic indulgence, pulling the drawing away from observation towards crude comment. What is important to acknowledge, however, is that the tradition of caricature and the reductive, symbolic and synthesized line that defines it is significant to many approaches, even to guiding figures in the field such as Ronald Searle, Paul Hogarth and Ralph Steadman.

Aligned with the aim of much contemporary reportage and drawing itself, Gombrich and Kris note of caricature: 'It is not its proximity to reality that proves its value but its nearness to the artist's psychic life' (Gombrich & Kris, 1938). In the caricatured line we are drawn to the attentions of the artist in a way that complements observation. Looking at the impact of caricature on the development of art, one can see clear links with the thinking of Ruskin, Berger and Rawson, who privileged not only observation but also invention. Gombrich and Kris note about the impact on work after the seventeenth century and the discovery of caricatures by Bernini and others: 'The artist was no longer bound by fixed patterns, as in the Middle Ages; he was not even bound to the imitation of reality ... Imagination rather than technical ability, vision and invention, inspiration and genius made the artist, not merely the mastering of the intricacies of handicraft. From an imitator he became a creator' (Gombrich & Kris, 1938). Although schematic languages and conventions marked much work after the seventeenth century, the potentialities of drawing and the imaginative capabilities of the artist were liberated.

Bernini is a significant and early figure in the development of caricature. Lavin notes in reference to Bernini's contribution to caricature and satire, 'as a work of art the drawing is slight enough – a few tremulous, if devastating pen lines sketched in a moment of diversion on a wisp of paper ... the work represents a monumental watershed in the history of art: it is the first caricature that has come down to us of so exalted a personage as a pope' (Lavin, 1981). Bernini's significance was not exclusively the invention of caricature as that had been seen in the work of Carracci and others, but in the implicit ridicule of a known and powerful person. This is a very early instance of an artist wilfully distorting the features of a figure through the means of reductive drawing, using the tools of the artist usually reserved for the faithful rendering of likeness. As Lambourne notes, 'after the renaissance, with the awakening of a new interest in man as an individual, caricature – the comic distortion of an *individual* man – could begin' (Lambourne, 1983, p. 5).

The term 'caricature' comes from the root to 'charge' or 'to load' (Petherbridge, 2010, p. 346). Sharing qualities of the sketch, the caricature finds its ultimate completion in the mind of the viewer, piecing together the available clues in the economical drawing (Petherbridge, 2010, p. 349). Gombrich notes that this reduction is the synthesis of essential, communicative forms. He notes in reference to the work of Daumier, 'and condensation, the telescoping of a whole chain of ideas into one pregnant image, is indeed the essence of wit' (Gombrich, 1994, p. 130). In relation to the work of the reportage artist, these condensed marks reflect quick, summative vision and, like the cartoonist, seek a kind of quick reading, an immediate recognition of form. What is happening in the cartoon as in much reportage drawing is the establishment of a graphic language, part of a larger graphic construct that marks out an artistic conception of reality. Rawson notes, 'implicit in every drawing style is a visual ontology, i.e. a definition of the real in visual terms' (Rawson, 1969, p. 19). In this constructed reality, the cartoonist and reportage artist are directing attention towards areas of interest, summative judgments that are manifest in marks and lines.

The language of the cartoonist and the reportage artist is built from a synthesis of vision, and the vocabulary of that language marks refined perception and thought. Shahn noted of artists like George Bellows and Paul Klee that 'these artists found in such casual aspects of reality a form of life, a means to create an *oeuvre*, to build a language of himself, his peculiar wit and skill and taste and comprehension of things' (Shahn, 1957, p. 8). This language for the caricaturist is one with an 'absence of contradictory clues', its concise language pointing us clearly at its intentions (Gombrich, 1972, p. 336). Gombrich neatly sums up the relationship between reality and artistic reality as 'all artistic discoveries are discoveries not of likeness but of equivalences which enable us to see reality in terms of an image and an image in terms of reality' (Gombrich, 1972, p. 345). This reflects the core way in which the graphic construct of the cartoonist and the reportage artist functions through the correlation between what is seen and understood and what is created, which is the new 'reality' of the drawing. The main difference between the application of the visual language for the cartoonist compared to the reportage artist is that the cartoonist's reality is not dependent on a directly observed reality. The cartoonist establishes a visual vernacular to manufacture a new reality, likely inspired by the real but ultimately an imaginative fabrication.

The caricaturist, and some inclined reportage artist's tableau, tends towards the traditions of caricature in ridicule and biting satire and shares the darker vision of the world presented to us in the grotesque. Barthes notes that it is not only the artist's tableau which indicates meaning but the treatment of the tableau in 'gestures' or 'the coordination of gestures' (Barthes & Heath, 1977, p. 76). For the cartoonist and the reportage artist, these gestures tend towards extremes with the intention of some kind of visual provocation. Central to the grotesque and to caricature is exaggeration. Eduards and Graulund note, 'caricature also relies on a metonymic relationship to its subject, for it takes parts of the whole in order to stand in for the totality' (Eduards & Graulund, 2013, p. 67). This synthesis is noted above as a necessary element of both caricature and reportage illustration, but this synthesis, as it relates to the grotesque and commentary more broadly, is the rendering of symbolic forms which carry ideas. This symbolic form is a fundamental part of the grotesque as the grotesque 'reflects a specific culture and society. Its symbolic nature enables us to see things we cannot fully grasp, but points to a "noble" truth that is beyond the limits of normative human thought' (Eduards & Graulund, 2013, p. 21). A sublime truth sought by many caricaturists and reportage artists is achieved in a symbolic rendering of a reality in which specific concerns are highlighted. The element of the grotesque in revulsion or shock attempts to push the viewer out of a comfortable notion of reality towards the extreme, rendering a space that is magnified, drawing us back, with new understandings, to our own reality. Connelly notes:

> Monstrosity and abjection elicit an overwhelming desire to draw a boundary between ourselves and their fearful otherness. This response reveals a fundamental element common to both: each in its way defies our attempts to objectify it, to re-present or grasp it in our own minds, and in so doing calls our position as independent subject into question. (Connelly, 2014, p. 116)

The above quote calls to mind Dewey's 'mutual adaptation of the self and the object' that occurs between artist and subject and viewer and a work of art (Dewey, 2005, p. 45). While the above quote refers to a more extreme visual form or depiction, it is important to understand how grotesqueries play upon and question the nature of the subject and, therefore, the viewer's relation to the subject. The function of the grotesque in reportage balances delicately between the real and exaggerated, careful not to stretch into low ridicule or fantasy. The grotesque figure is then a symbol of not just hideous perversion but of essential contrast. As Eduards and Graulund note in reference to the grotesque in American fiction, 'in this, grotesque figures and images lie in sharp contrast to the economic and social mythologies of an "American Dream" or the religious utopic vision of the "city on the hill"'. They further note, 'it has proved an enduring genre for examining social and cultural concerns, as well as issues of race, gender, and class' (Eduards & Graulund, 2013, pp. 12, 13). The caricature captures the 'passing illusion and the lasting characterization' and, as such, it marks not just figures, events and places that reflect a time, but their extended and symbolic meaning (Gombrich, 1994, p. 138). It could be argued that iconic forms of caricature, satire and the grotesque are effective magnifications of the real and not, as they are often seen, departures into indulgent folly.

The way in which the cartoonist and reportage artist employ their graphic construct to render meaning in an image is through metaphor. These metaphors are not necessarily in far-fetched imaginative invention (as is more common in the cartoon) and are, rather, particularly in relation to the work of reportage artists, in the amplification of physical attributes and the development of types who reflect larger themes. As Lubbock notes, 'a caricature makes it clear that it is a deliberate, artistic reshaping, not a depiction of a face that is itself strangely shaped … its strange shapings aim to mockingly emphasise a character that is already there. Its insults aren't stuck on. In caricature the face is made to give itself away' (Lubbock & Coutts, 2012, p. 93). The above quote makes it clear that the crux of a caricature, going back to its origins, is how it extends from the actual (a real person) towards the metaphorical. In the hands of the cartoonist or the reportage artist, people have a kind of plasticity, they can be shaped to specific ends and can compress multiple overt and subtle ideas through playing upon our innate understanding of the 'type' being depicted. For Gombrich, the challenge for the caricaturist is to render the light and dark textures of the world through 'physiognomic' expression, attending to the critical contrasts that exist between the polarities (Gombrich, 1994, pp. 138, 139).

From the local to the universal, the cartoonist and reportage artist are confronted with the same problem, the problem of language. The rendering of metaphor in drawing is a challenge of communication and that rests on the clear intent of the visual language. Noted cartoonist Steve Bell suggests:

> Since by definition such a language is beyond words, our only means of understanding it is subjective. We can only judge whether such a language works for us by reacting spontaneously to its effect on our eyeballs. This is why cartoonists (and some reportage artists) keep referring back to existing imagery, to imagery which is so well known that it can provide a framework on which to hang other meanings, comments, cheap laughs or political obsessions. It is not just a desire to save effort (which it obviously does); instead it is a genuine attempt to establish some visual common ground. (A Sense of Permanence?, 1997, pp. 33, 34)

Art theorist W. J. T. Mitchell notes that 'caricature is, in this sense, a form of disfigurement and iconoclasm' (Mitchell, 1980, p. 132). The caricature dismantles its subject through 'character assassination' and builds a new image, a reflection of it for public consideration (Lubbock & Coutts, 2012 p. 91). The moral dimension of caricature is clear in its refined language and the clarity of the graphic construct, overt in its intentions through the choices in its depiction. This is also true of the reportage artist; however, anchorage to the directly observed is critical and this distinguishes the work from the cartoon in its closer attention to direct recording (although this varies according to individual artist methodologies). The reportage drawing which seeks to elicit some comment does so in the forming of the drawing. Commentary is mixed up with observation, and the inclinations of the reductive, economical marks and lines are extended towards commentary. Because of this, reportage drawing that imbeds commentary is a kind of performative process that synthesizes observation and commentary and presents a unique record of our society and a new lens to see the modern 'carnivalesque body' which has taken new forms in the street, in boardrooms and in arms fairs (Connelly, 2014). What distinguishes reportage drawing from the modern face of caricature is that the subjects are typically not known and recognizable and therefore, caricature elements point to broader themes around social issues and politics. In this sense, there is a connection to the broader tableau scenes of eighteenth- and nineteenth-century caricaturists such as Hogarth, Gillray, Cruickshank and Rowlandson. In these scenes, like in many reportage drawings, particularly those of protest, both the individual and the collective reflect broader ideas about society and human drama.

Contemporary caricature further departs from reportage drawing in the push towards the extremes. English caricature prior to the mid-nineteenth century and after Hogarth was characterized by prurient humour and in some cases (as with Gillray especially) prone to extreme and even crude characterization and metaphor. This wild departure in caricature from the real towards the fantastic was pulled back again in the caricature of Daumier who, as noted by Hofmann, 'upon their shoulders (English caricaturists) stands Daumier, who gave monumental artistic expression to this English directness and who knew to control its wildly flowing frenzy' (Hofmann, 1957, p. 36). The move in caricature from the fantastical or at least highly charged and frenzied tableau of English cartoonists to the drama of the street occurred in France when

> both branches of development, therefore, needed the assistance of a third element before caricature could fully evolve. The closeness to reality of the popular cartoon had to be refined, the concern with physiognomy of 'high' art had to be directed towards the inexhaustible scenes of everyday life. In this process the traditional partiality of French art for the day-to-day events of the human scene played an important part. (Hofmann, 1957, p. 39)

The caricature was then to be associated with scenes of everyday life and, like the artwork of Daumier, closely resembles the look and feel of some reportage drawing, particularly in the loose gestural approach and the synthesis of observation and comment. The appeal of Daumier's cartoons is not only in his play with familiar types but also his individualization of such types, imbuing personhood and the idiosyncrasies of actual people, a feat of his prodigious observation and memory.

Today, cartoonists like Ralph Steadman, Steve Bell, Gerald Scarfe, Jules Feiffer and others have developed visual languages that are consciously untethered from realism and indulge in expressive departure for expressive means. Besides the inevitable proportional solidity that defines all successful drawing, never mind cartooning, artists like Feiffer noted a shift in his method towards direct drawing without any preparation: 'I started doing drawings that way, and my god they were working. And they had an immediacy that – to me – was much more important than their obvious crudeness' (Groth, 2004, p. 17). This relates to new thinking about drawing and an isolation of the expressive gesture through, in this case, the exploration of immediate drawing (see Embury, Chapter 8). For Steadman, the nature of 'style' is important and he notes, referring to the work of Grosz, 'you don't simply say, "I'll do this for a style" – bang! – and that's your style. It came out of a stringent approach, an acid-tight way of how to draw these poor bastards of the Weimar Republic' (Groth, 2004, p. 100). For Steadman, the cartoon is an emotional response but, equally, its form relates as much to freedom from restraint (the governing rules of art and decorum) and deeply personal convictions. Expanding the conception of the cartoon Steadman notes, 'if the playwright is using expressive word-forms to make a point, he's really exaggerating the situation in order to make his point. Well, that's a cartoon form as far as I'm concerned! It's a very important area to consider. In fact, I think all basic expressive impulses are *cartoon* impulses' (Groth, 2004, p. 135). Here the cartoon is seen as a broader practice of exaggeration and expression and this, along with visual metaphor as seen in all cartoonists, especially Gillray and today, Bell, is the core component of the cartoonists' repertoire. The reportage artist, although amplifying the observed through cartoonist/caricaturist means, does not intend to depart from the subject and rather develops their commentary through eliciting a closer examination of the real. The overlaps are clear and it is perhaps extreme metaphor and fantasy alone that truly distinguish the acts of cartooning and reportage drawing as separate entities.

As noted previously, many reportage artists see the indulgence in caricature as an undesirable distraction from the real and observed. Because the reportage artist self-regulates their anchorage and fidelity to the observed, they also manage the balance between the real and the exaggerated. I have yet to see a full exploration of the ethics of reportage illustration; however, Irish illustrator Eva Kelly has attempted to develop a framework which is heavily based on ethics established in the field of photo journalism. Noting an NPPA (National Press Photographers Association) code of ethics which states 'our primary goal is the faithful comprehensive depiction of the subject at hand' and 'we believe it is wrong to alter a photograph in any way that deceives the public' (2016) Kelly notes that this notion of distortion is a part of other ethical codes and frameworks and yet acknowledges that no such code governs reportage drawing (2016). Kelly, in an interview with reportage illustrator Veronica Lawlor puts the question of whether reportage drawing needs an ethical code (2016). She thought there should be but also made salient points about the editorial decisions of the artist and how, ultimately, reportage drawing is self-regulated in that it is fundamentally created by the artist. Still, she notes, 'bending the truth' is unethical in any medium (2016). While the talk of a formalized ethical code for reportage drawing may highlight important considerations in the act (a sentiment echoed by Kelly and Lawlor) it is impossible to gauge within any artist's work. The nature of reportage drawing is that we faithfully submit to the artists' recording. There can be no reason to question the veracity of the vision based on what we can see unless aspects of the work are either so distorted or the solidity of the drawing is weak and inconclusive. Again, the ethical dimensions of the work are essentially regulated and controlled by the artist. That said, because of the demands of the act, the unique skill set required to partake in it is unlikely that those who practice reportage are eager to deceive. Equally, reportage drawing does not portend to be verifiable evidence and functionally provides a meditation on the real rather than a durable record of it. This is not to say that reportage drawing does not effectively capture people and places. It is, however, made up of the symbolic language of drawing and as a made thing by humans, it can't have a blanket code which could encompass the various orientations, practices and aesthetic variety. However, a series of overarching principles could be established and perhaps should as a way of, if nothing else, validating the contribution reportage drawing makes to visual journalism, and as such, it should be seen as a serious endeavour.

In relation to caricature and the ethics of reportage, it can be seen in two ways. Caricature in response to what is seen and approached with a desire to reductively capture people and places would, in my opinion, reflect reasonable judgment and would not distort a viewer's sense of the locale or its people. However, caricature that is not responsive to the locale and reinforces held stereotypes or judgments would not be acceptable. The question remains whether these two can be detected and observed as distinct orientations by the viewer. I believe they can. The consumer of reportage drawing has an expectation that there is a fidelity to the observed, an anchor in reality. These can be seen in the idiosyncrasies of the drawing and the perceptual trace evident in the drawing. The aforementioned smuggled truth within reportage drawing is a tacit understanding and belief that what has been depicted was seen and experienced by the artist. A currency of authenticity is an essential feature of reportage drawing. Can a highly skilled artist fudge these lines? Probably, but if they can connect us to their experience, they must have done something right.

Conclusion

Reportage drawing and caricature share several aims and from the historical practice to the contemporary, observation is key to both traditions as is an awareness of the expressive potential of drawing. While the journalistic-orientated reportage artists may see expressive caricature as an unwelcome deviation from aims, both seek a deeper understanding of society and our place in it through the practice of drawing. However, as the modern caricaturist aims to dismantle or comment upon known subjects, the reportage artist is seeking to elicit a closer examination of the everyday. While both practices of reportage drawing and caricature share the same modes of exaggeration, the reportage artist, through an amplification of the observed, is seeking a closer examination of the unknown or, at the very least, the unexamined. Visual metaphor, which is a key element of caricature, is found in the reportage drawing in its final form, as the drawing is both a record of the observed and a statement about the individual or collective as a symbolic form.

This book contends that contemporary reportage drawing has evolved from a more narrowly focused news image to a place in which the modalities of drawing and a range of personal intentions merge. Within those intentions and the dialogue with one's own drawing, caricature plays a role in imbuing subjects with intent and pushing the form of reportage to new places. While the caricaturist is seeking explicit comment through the graphic immediacy of line, the reportage artist is more likely engaged with caricatural elements as a result of the demands of the act and/or as a means of accentuating an aspect of the observed. The primary distinction is then that the conceit of the reportage artist is always that the observed subject is real and the indulgent, surrealistic fantasy and metaphor of contemporary caricature is an undesirable departure from this. For the reportage artist, the most valuable aspect of caricature is in its immediacy and synthesis of forms and how this reflects, in form and function, the impression of a first thought and observed subject. The range of approaches and engagement with drawing practices, including caricature, indicate a move in the contemporary practice from purely journalistic intentions, towards a range of commentary, reflecting as much contemporary attitudes towards professional and citizen journalism and developments in drawing as a media and mediation.

5
EXPERIENCE, PLACE AND MEANING MAKING

While the act of reportage is diverse in its approaches, the individualistic witness is at its core and whether pre-meditated or more spontaneous, the nature of experience is key to the artist's engagement with its subject. Experience as it relates to reportage drawing is referring to the experience of the subject in situ and the re-creation of that experience in drawing. This then provides for the viewer a re-experience of the artist's encounters in the field through their rendering of it in drawing. Arnheim sees experience through the lens of expression as 'artistic expression seems to be something more specific. It requires that the communication of the data produce an "experience," the active presence of the forces that make up the perceived pattern' (Arnheim, 1954, p. 425). Here, Arnheim is referring to the generation of experience through an association with understood and internalized physiognomic traits like gesture, facial expression and so forth. For the purposes of this book, experience of place is about the salient aspects of that place that reside in the drawing. Dewey notes 'events turn into objects, things with meaning. They may be referred to when they do not exist, and thus be operative among things distant in space and time, through vicarious presence in a new medium' (Dewey, 1929, p. 138). For reportage drawing, the experience in situ is about navigating meaning and making choices which inform a highly synthesized and personal rendering of that experience. Dewey's conception of experience is in how we define it and for Dewey, it is a heightened connection to an event, both within the realms of artistic production and beyond. This is critical as we can see a wider spectrum of experience as relevant to reportage drawing and, as noted, residing within its facture.

Dewey's larger contention about art as experience is crucial here. His theories about art centre around the notion that the circumstances of its production are the true nature of its aesthetic. As Leddy notes, 'art products exist externally and physically, whereas, on his (Dewey's) view, the work of art is really what the physical object does *within* experience' (Leddy, 2006). Dewey is concerned with a conception of art that is less defined by the resulting object and is a negotiation with one's environment and medium through attentive action. While the resulting drawing is key to this book, Dewey's examples of aesthetic experience mirror those of the reportage artist in situ and speak to the motivations of the act. This is further explored below but this democratic notion of experience and its centrality aligns with the aims of this book and how reportage emerges from and reflects experience.

Lastly, how experience relates to space and place will be explored through the work of geographer Yi-Fu Tuan, geographer Doreen Massey and social scientist Michel De Certeau. Primarily concerned with architectural spaces, Tuan's thoughts about meaning and response to spaces relate to how experiences are translated into drawings. Massey is concerned with expanding the notion of place to incorporate other fields of experience. De Certeau is briefly cited to provide a contrast with Tuan's notion of mythic space and De Certeau's call to explore the unexplored.

Experience

Experience is one layer to reportage drawing but an experience is only understood as such because we have applied sufficient thought and action to render it meaningful. The experience of drawing is equally an experience of thinking and an exploration of the experiential formation of a reportage drawing must also take into consideration the role of thinking, and specifically observational thinking, as it relates to the act. The conversion from experience and thought to its concrete form in drawing, just as space is transformed into place, is an act of meaning making, and this summation is also key to understanding the ways in which artistic intent fuses with other concerns, for example, the desire to imbue the work with commentary and negotiate artistic limitations of skill and circumstance.

Dewey's complexly layered ideas about art as experience and experience as art can be neatly summed up by him as 'constituted by interaction between "subject" and "object," between a self and its world, it is not itself merely physical, nor merely mental, no matter how much one factor or the other predominates' (Dewey, 2005, p. 256). This neatly sets up Dewey's contention that experience, as it relates to art making, is the impetus and the sum of an interaction with the environment. He sees the artist as a 'live creature' and notes a heightened awareness, like that of an animal, with an 'attentive eye', seeking the things that arouse the interest of the artist (Dewey, 2005, p. 3). On the goal of exalting experience in art theory he notes:

> This task is to restore continuity between the refined and intensified forms of experience that are works of art and the everyday events, doings and sufferings that are universally recognised to constitute experience …
>
> We must arrive at the theory of art by means of a detour. (Dewey, 2005, p. 2)

In the above quote Dewey conflates art as experience and experience as art (which he clarifies). This is his sole contention, which he un-picks, in a variety of cogent examples. Dewey observed a distance present between how we engage with the art object through museums and an intellectualistic approach to art. It is not only a problem of the institutionalization of art but of an un-tethering from the material of art. A separation between experiences shared by all and those within artworks is seen by Dewey as making art an exclusive domain and one that is perceived to require specialist knowledge, something he refutes. Dewey notes 'for many persons an aura of mingled awe and unreality encompasses the "spiritual" and the "ideal" while "matter" has become by contrast a term of depreciation, something to be explained away or apologised for' (Dewey, 2005, p. 5). Dewey calls for a return of art to its core, to its making but also to its materiality. In doing so he brings it back to the public in relating art to other 'modes of experiencing' (Dewey, 2005, p. 9). In contrast, current theoretical orientations are flawed as he notes 'no amount of ecstatic eulogy of finished works can of itself assist the understanding or the generation of such works' (Dewey, 2005, p. 11) Exploring the circumstances surrounding production and orientations towards the subject within reportage drawing seek to reveal within the act that it emerges from a live engagement with a subject and that these myriad factors and approaches enable entry into the diverse practices in contemporary reportage. If the photograph is valued for its ability to furnish evidence, then reportage drawing must consider what it does, functionally, to capture salient experience.

Inherent in this, which is of particular relevance to reportage drawing, is the twofold nature of artistic experience. Broadly, Dewey sees life as a series of interactions between the 'live creature' and his/her environment. The twofold experience is that of the artist in their environment and the experience of creating the work. Dewey sees these two experiences in very similar ways. An experience, including an artistic experience, is necessarily formed of some negotiation, struggle and overcoming within one's environment. The direct experience that we are concerned with in reportage drawing summed up by Dewey 'comes from nature and man interacting with each other. In this interaction, human energy gathers, is released, dammed up, frustrated and victorious. There are rhythmic beats of want and fulfilment, pulses of doing and being withheld from doing' (Dewey, 2005, p. 15). Dewey sees the artistic experience (or, as he calls, the aesthetic experience) as containing a necessary struggle. Without it there isn't sufficient energy to formulate the work and that the work is a kind of harmonious balance of energies (Dewey, 2005, p. 15). In the act of reportage, the experience that Dewey speaks of relates to both the experience of seeking subjects (the hunt) and the act of drawing as containing the same elements. Relating experience to those most acute animalistic qualities of the savage Dewey notes:

As he watches what stirs about him, he, too, is stirred. His observation is both action in preparation and foresight of the future. He is active through his whole being when he looks and listens as when he stalks his quarry or stealthily retreats from a foe. His senses are sentinels of immediate thought and outposts of action, and not, as they so often are with us, mere pathways along which material is gathered to be stored away for a delayed and remote possibility. (Dewey, 2005, p. 18)

The phrase 'action in preparation' is a fitting way to think of the anticipatory gaze in reportage drawing, which surveys the field for subjects. Whether stationary or moving, this surveillance mentally prefigures subjects for suitability in drawing and this act shares qualities of a hunt. Although this quote does not relate to reportage drawing or an artistic act, it does reflect the heightened sensory awareness and mental preparation and action that exists. As mentioned above, this quote could equally describe the making of a drawing in situ as it does the preliminary stalking of its subject. The nature of reportage drawing merges thought, action and experience in a unified whole although neither is subsumed in the act and instead permeate the drawings and can be recalled, vividly, by the artist post facto. In a complex prefiguration that occurs in the mind, subjects are remembered in varying levels of detail in a kind of temporal storehouse, to be drawn out later. These are often surprisingly convincing and attest to the power of Dewey's 'sentinels of immediate thought'. Dewey sees artistic experience as a heightened communion with our senses like those in the animal kingdom but with the advantage of imbuing them with 'conscious meanings' and 'deliberate expression' (Dewey, 2005, p. 23). In reportage, many artists see deliberation as an enemy of spontaneity although the two are not mutually exclusive as noted below.

Dewey lays out several features of having an experience that have informed this book. For one, Dewey notes that an experience is a 'consummation not a cessation'. He goes on to clarify this by noting that life is a 'thing of histories, each with its own plot, its own inception and movement toward its close, each having its own particular rhythmic movement; each with its own unrepeated quality pervading it throughout' (Dewey, 2005, p. 37). This fulfilment for Dewey is more layered and has an 'individualising quality' (Dewey, 2005, p. 37). What emerges here is the singular notion of experience. Dewey takes this further and sees the unity achieved in an experience as being due to a 'single quality that pervades the entire experience' (Dewey, 2005, p. 38). He notes that in spite of constitutive parts, 'one property' above all shapes our conception of the experience (Dewey, 2005, p. 38). Teasing out this notion of a singular feature that marks experience, Dewey relates it to a conclusion and notes 'in fact, in an experience of thinking, premises emerge only as a conclusion becomes manifest. The experience, like that of watching a storm reach its height and gradually subside, is one of continuous movement of subject-matters' (Dewey, 2005, p. 39).

The assessment of subject matters is central to reportage drawing as practitioners often state a desire for the unexpected in their drawings in situ and survey the field extensively prior to committing to drawing. More importantly, however, is this notion of a 'single quality' that marks the observed and identifies it for suitability in drawing. For reportage drawing, one can look at the totality of experience in situ and the drawings themselves to find this quality. It may reside singularly and distinctively in individual drawings, or it may pervade a collection, identifying a thematic or visible connection between them.

The emotional content of a work of reportage is folded into other more obvious concerns at the point of drawing such as the circumstantial challenges on the ground. However, emotions and the rendering of emotions in drawing show the attentions of the artist and, in terms of the experience of place, assign value to place in the fulfilment of the subject with intent. When we speak of the emotional content of drawing we are speaking of the total impression of the subject and this can be overt or subtle depending on the rendering. The fundamental importance of the emotional content of the image is that it reflects the overriding aim and desire for the drawing and that an emotional affect is a concluding statement on the subject and therefore the experience of the subject.

Emotional and expressive aims for the image have been a controversial aspect of modern art with many artists denying such explicit intent. Speaking of Stravinsky's contention about music and expression Read notes, 'if music seems to express something, it is an illusion, and not a reality. Expressiveness is simply an additional element which by habit we (the spectators) impose on a work of art – a descriptive label which we then confuse with the essence of the work of art.' Quoting Stravinsky directly Read notes, 'when we suddenly recognize our emotions, they are already cold, like lava' (Read, 1967, p. 64). While this reflects a somewhat extreme denial of explicitness in terms of a work of art, it is important to acknowledge the subjectivity around emotion and the emotional effect of images. For the purposes of this research, we are looking at the emotional content of reportage drawing as representing a determination about the subject and therefore the place and experience of place, and that the rendering of emotion is an extrapolation or amplification of observed subjects.

Emotion is a constituent of experience although Dewey does not see it as distinct but rather 'the moving and cementing force' (Dewey, 2005, p. 44). This unifying force is embedded in experience and is to some extent or another essential. But Dewey also sees emotion in thinking and draws communities of intellectuals (non-artists) and artists together as having a 'dependence on emotionalised ideas' that are essential for new insights in all fields and rely on an imaginative and emotional conceit (Dewey, 2005, pp. 76, 77).

Dewey does not dwell on the content of experience and rather speaks more broadly about the theoretical underpinnings of what an experience is. He does however note that every experience moves towards 'a mutual adaptation of the self and the object' and results in an 'institution of a felt harmony' (Dewey, 2005, p. 45). This interpenetration of self and object, or artist and subject, is both evident in reportage drawing and the reportage drawing experience. The drawing experience speaks to this as the artist is occupying the same space as their subjects and negotiating, in often dynamic settings, a perch from which to capture them. This hunter and prey dynamic quickly becomes more intimate in drawing as the summative judgment of the artist on the subject becomes realized. As Michael Taussig notes, drawing upon Walter Benjamin, drawing is 'to become and behave like something else' (Taussig, 2011, p. 23). And, as Taussig notes, 'drawings acquire their own reality' (Taussig, 2011, p. 30), a reality in which the subject is sealed in the graphic construct of the artist and a bond is recorded between artist, subject and experience.

For Dewey, the evaluation of a work of art is not in the calibration of its authenticity and rather that these conclusions are largely intuitive. Furthering his notion of the singular pervasive thing that defines an experience, Dewey notes 'the penetrating quality that runs through all the parts of a work of art and binds them into an individualised whole can only be emotionally "intuited"' (Dewey, 2005, p. 200). Dewey sees this quality as individualistic and 'it is the idiom in which the particular work is composed and expressed, that which stamps it with individuality' (Dewey, 2005, p. 200). He is also citing the artist's graphic construct here, binding the artist with the expressive qualities of the work. The acknowledgement of the intuitive, subjective and individual qualities of a work of art aligns with his contentions about experience itself. This wider view of art as experience is neatly summed up by Dewey as 'this sense of the including whole implicit in ordinary experiences is rendered intense within the frame of a painting or poem' (Dewey, 2005, p. 201).

Space and place

In reportage drawing, spaces and places are the backdrop or central subject of the artists' tableau. Yi-Fu Tuan sees place as 'a pause in movement' and that pause 'makes it possible for a locality to become a centre of felt value' (Tuan, 1977, p. 138). He cites the human necessity of stopping to care for the injured or eat and the built-up associations we make with those places we assign value to. Tuan also speaks of how humans are capable of metaphoric notions of place and home, even thinking of home as a person (Tuan, 1977, p. 139).

The assigning of value that is self-evident in reportage drawing is reliant on the rest and the pause. In order to draw one must choose a place to stop or 'perch', and this vantage point allows one to survey the territory of their subjects. That choice of perch may or may not be imbedded in the area of their subjects (e.g. the top of a hill looking down) but it does involve a compelling choice. Often, reportage drawing necessitates a perch that is hidden or at least sufficiently distanced from the subject. Still, the pause is key and this moment of reflection enables the artist to survey and assign value and interest to his/her surroundings, thereby preparing for the selection of a subject.

There are also times when the location is significant to the nature of the subjects found there and this context is crucial to the understanding of the work. Jill Gibbon's work is a good example. To 'read' her drawings without the important knowledge that they were drawn in an arms fair in Paris is to diminish their meaning and power, just as the knowledge of her surreptitious sketching gives us further entry into her hurried scrawls.

Our engagement with place connects to our collective experiences, thoughts and emotions we bring to them. Doreen Massey sees space as not just external or localized but rather a psychic orientation to the world. She notes:

> For if experience is not an internalised succession of sensations (pure temporality) but a multiplicity of things and relations, then its *spatiality* is as significant as its temporal dimension. This is to argue for a way of being and thinking otherwise – for the imagination of a more open attitude of being; for the (potential) outward lookingness of practised subjectivity. (Massey, 2005, p. 58)

Significant to reportage practice, the above quote highlights the way that reportage drawings condense not just physical and observable features of an object but its psychic make-up, a 'spatiality' that condenses thought and intention in the concrete form of a drawing, a new space. Massey also calls for a more singular, individual and therefore subjective outlook which aligns with her contention that space is a 'multiplicity' and that 'practised space' is a 'relational construction' through 'material engagement'. She notes 'if time unfolds as change then space unfolds as interaction' (Massey, 2005, p. 61). Massey's argument is for greater complexity when speaking of place and a move away from the overly vague categories of the global and local to advance more granular, heterogeneous approaches (Massey, 2005, p. 61). Massey's conception of time, temporality and space is relevant to the practice of reportage drawing as the drawing, like Massey's notion of space as 'material' and time as a 'product of human experience', is a fusion of the two. Massey notes that 'time is either past or to come or so minutely instantaneously *now* that it is impossible to grasp. Space, on the other hand, is *there*' (Massey, 2005, p. 117). Reportage drawing as rendered experience is central to this book but seeing the two concepts of time and space (broadly), it is equally important to see it occupying a middle ground, a negotiated compromise between the 'now' and the 'there'. A reportage drawing fixes the temporalities of experience in the concrete form of a drawing, thereby making a new space, of the moment and beyond it. Massey paraphrases a remembered passage from the writer Raymond Williams who observed a woman from the window of a train. She notes 'he catches a picture, a women in her pinny bending over to clear the back drain with a stick. For the passenger on the train she will forever be doing this. She is held in that instant, almost immobilised … From the train she is going nowhere; she is trapped in the timeless instant' (Massey, 2005, p. 119).

Tuan sees place as an object that is a 'concretization of value'. Noting the concept of the pause, it is a place that one dwells as opposed to a space which Tuan implies is associated with movement (Tuan, 1977, p. 12). This value however, needs to be fixed and Tuan notes that as we move through spaces we move 'from inchoate feelings for space and fleeting discernments of it in nature to their public and material reification' (Tuan, 1977, p. 17). Tuan notes that space becomes place when we are 'thoroughly familiar' with it and that we have 'kinaesthetic and perceptual experience' of it along with formed concepts of the space (Tuan, 1977, p. 73). Because Tuan sees experience as holistic and multi-sensory, this transformation of spaces to places involves a complex 'reification' which, in drawing, gives solidity to the layers of experience. It can also be noted that the process of becoming 'thoroughly familiar' and therefore moving from space to place can occur in the act of drawing itself, in the process of understanding through hyper-attention.

Mythical space is a concept Tuan advances as the space that we create with the available knowledge that we have at a given time. Born of necessity or some accumulation of personal understandings, mythical space cannot be 'readily verified, or proven false, by the evidence of the senses' (Tuan, 1977, p. 85). Tuan distinguishes two types of mythical space: one is at the edges of known, pragmatic space and the other is a 'spatial component of a world view' and is a 'conception of localised values' that people live within (Tuan, 1977, p. 86). The second is particularly relevant to reportage drawing. It would be limiting to view the graphic construct of the reportage artist as serving a purely representational purpose as the symbolic language of drawing as a whole necessitates a kind of approximate knowledge, a mythic language. A language of forms that, like those in mythic space, are based on an accumulated understanding of the world which, inevitably, does not have an exact analogue in reality.

As Tuan notes, 'mythical space is an intellectual construct. It can be elaborate. Mythical space is also a response of feeling and imagination to fundamental human needs' (Tuan, 1977, p. 99). De Certeau, exploring New York city through walking, makes the claim that the city itself is mythic because it is caught between place as a location and a 'dreamed place'. He notes:

> The moving about that the city multiplies and concentrates makes the city itself an immense social experience of lacking a place … The identity furnished by this place is all the more symbolic (named) because, in spite of

> the inequality of its citizens' positions and profits, there is only a pullulation of passer-by, a network of residences temporarily appropriated by pedestrian traffic, a shuffling among pretenses of the proper, a universe of rented spaces haunted by a nowhere or by dreamed-of places. (De Certeau, 2011, p. 103)

Here, mythic space is less a mental construct based on fragments of experience and needs as Tuan notes, and is, rather, a nowhere, a flux of desires stuck between states. For the reportage artist, these spaces are compelling, providing a challenge in rendering the cacophony of human activity and meditating on the meaning of such spaces. As Dewey noted about 'mastering the unknown' in observation, such spaces provide an opportunity to engage with place in a profound way through the practice of reportage. Massey encourages this practice-based approach to place noting 'place, in other words does – as many argue – change us, not through some visceral belonging (some barely changing rootedness, as so many would have it) but through the *practising* of place, the negotiation of intersecting trajectories; place as an arena where negotiation is forced upon us' (Massey, 2005, p. 154). Massey's call for the 'practising of place' reflects what reportage drawing does well in its articulation of complexly layered environments. De Certeau makes a similar call noting 'to practice space is thus to repeat the joyful and silent experience of childhood; it is, in a place, *to be other and to move toward the other*' (De Certeau, 2011, p. 110).

Conclusion

What distinguishes reportage drawings from other forms of drawing is that it is actively responding to a subject in situ. The formulation of the drawing is happening either in real time or through a temporal memory of the subject. As such, it reveals its construction and thinking in a manner which often excludes pre-determination and artistic indulgence, revealing a palimpsest of direct perception. As Maynard notes, 'like depictive perception itself, it takes special meaning from being something that we are doing: from a present active participation, not just the evocation of something past' (Maynard, 2005, p. 195).

Experience resides in the reportage drawing in its total construction and attests to the artists' understanding and framing of the subject. This reflects the filter of experience through an artistic temperament and, therefore, represents a part of the artist's larger world view. Although the drawing is the product of observations made in situ, the resultant image equally contributes to a story of the experience, isolating a moment and inviting speculation. Taussig notes:

> What we mean by 'story' swarms across this boundary – and no wonder, because while that boundary (the boundary between fiction and non-fiction)

is one of the most fundamental ways by which we fix and figure reality, it is actually porous and, not be too cute, a lively piece of fiction itself. This is why style and voice are so important, for it is they that do the heavy lifting of analysis. (Taussig, 2011, pp. 147, 148)

For Taussig, the 'story' is a framing of reality and he champions the personal, vivid and even poetic responses that come into his fieldwork as an anthropologist. Relating to this book, the inevitable translations of experience in the marks of a drawing will be imbued with subjectivities but do not depart from the observed; rather, they are invested in the totality of experience and, when successful, move the viewer into, not out of, that same confrontation with lived experience. This is what the reportage drawing does that the photograph cannot; it delivers a vivified record of experience.

6

THE GRAPHIC CONSTRUCT – JILL GIBBON

Jill Gibbon's reportage drawing is defined by her belief that the act is a vehicle for a unique kind of political activism. Drawing in events that are largely unknown to the general public such as arms fairs and more widely publicized events such as political party conferences, she aims to document, through the act of drawing, the small human dramas which are unique to such events and become emblematic of troubling values within wider corporate and political structures and cultures.

Gibbon's work is marked by both an urgency which is evident in her quick, abbreviated drawing, done surreptitiously, and the contextual knowledge that these drawings are done in, for example, an arms fair in Paris. What might otherwise be perceived as a group of ordinary businessmen and women takes on greater meaning and their actions, both subtle and overt, are scrutinized more finely. As anthropologist Andrew Causey notes about the difference between looking and seeing:

> I have come to the understanding that in *looking*, our vision floats across the visual terrain without directed engagement, while *seeing* interpretively illuminates the visible, in many ways bringing it to being ... when that active engagement is made manifest by the hand's creation of permanent marks such as drawn lines that document what the eyes are perceiving, the seeing will be more discerning and more attentive to detail. That's because the marks made with the hand become the actual evidence of visual perception, proof that there is some concurrence between perception and representation. (Causey, 2017, p. 13)

Causey has drawn on ethnographic research trips and has found, as this book demonstrates, that the drawing done on location contains a wealth of information that enables him to more fully internalize and write about what he has seen and experienced. Like Taussig's drawing practice mentioned earlier, this is not drawing with an aesthetic aim and rather seeks to document experience through the medium of drawing, a medium that for both Causey and Taussig is revelatory and meaningfully attests to their own experience.

For Gibbon, this trace of perception which is evident in her searching and responsive line draws us close to these intimate moments of human interaction and isolates our focus, aligning our attention with hers.

The graphic construct of Gibbon is defined by the telescoping of aims in her drawing with her aesthetic inclinations, methodology and conceptual orientation focusing on the singular goal of exposing, through observation of real people, the darkly symbolic realities of players in the shadowy corners of global capitalism. Like the vast majority of reportage practitioners, her vision is validated by our understanding that these people were directly observed and that the drawings, irrespective of stylistic intent or flourishes, are brought to the viewer as the document of a witness and, in the case of Gibbon's work, are a rare glimpse into a largely unseen world. For Gibbon, our understanding of place is almost entirely void of clues other than the odd missile or gun and instead draws us into human interactions where, with the dual knowledge of their surreptitious capture and location, we formulate a new and distinct vision of these private and secretive events. With Gibbon's work in particular, that vision is highly personal and draws the viewer's attention to gestures and dramas which the artist feels are worthy of our scrutiny. Gibbon seeks to explore in her work not only the decadent nature of corporate capitalism but how we are complicit as people and nation states in tacitly condoning such actions. As Gibbon notes about her wider aims, 'How do you make *it* visible and in what locations is the weirdness of capitalism visible' (my own emphasis).

Drawn effects

Gibbon's drawing is economical and direct. It is not only directly related to the sketch in form, it utilizes the conceit of the sketch to emphasize the urgency of its creation. Gibbon's line can be seen as a trace of her perception and she notes the frantic hurry to get the drawing down, to capture the moment. She speaks of working in the 'here and now' and notes that there are awkward moments in the drawings which attest to this, identifying, for example, the long forearm of the woman in Figure 11. She does not see these inaccuracies as distracting and rather folds them into a wider understanding of her methodology and notes, 'there is a wildness which extends from that desperation to get it down'. She notes about her initial thoughts when looking at a drawing,

> first is the urgency of 'oh my god I've got to get that'. And almost a feeling of urgent panic. And, how the hell am I going to do justice to this. So, that's

> very often the feeling I have. The feeling of urgency. The feeling of anger. The
> drawings are very often driven by anger. Something like 'you creep.'

For Gibbon, the formal qualities of the drawing reinforce her impression of the subjects. The visceral line which has an immediate, bold and charged contour reflects with urgency her own moral shock at the subjects depicted. As Berger notes of the ultimate aim of drawing practice, to 'draw in order to discover' and 'to find effect and cause' (Berger, 2008, p. 102). For Gibbon, like many reportage artists, the speed and responsiveness of the sketch merge with conceptual and aesthetic aims and the artist is fusing both observed and rendered reality, presenting a wholly personal and subjective vision to the viewer. Although this process may seem to be a contrivance, by virtue of the demands of the act and the artist's own limitations to draw from the observed, what is rendered is within artistic perception and indulgences that exist are extensions from that vision. As Causey notes, 'your act of drawing, when done seriously and with focus, is evidence that you saw, and manifested it in *your* form: it is simultaneously a souvenir of your experience, a primary document, and interpretive remembrance, a concocted mnemonic' (Causey, 2017, p. 67). As Gombrich notes, 'if all seeing is interpreting, all modes of interpretation could be argued to be equally valid' (Gombrich, 1972, p. 298).

The following passage from an interview with Jill Gibbon about her most recent trip to Eurosatory arms fair in Paris highlights clearly how the drawings, through their immediacy and capture, draw attention to specific observations that the artist learns from and begins to organize in a taxonomy of gestures.

> This insignificant businessman is able to take on some of that seeing power
> of the military industrial complex (see Figure 9). But as you were saying, do
> I re-see or learn about places from the drawings? I think that one gains insight
> about the importance of gesture and respectability, I got that through the
> drawing … What I have begun to see is two sets of gestures: the required
> ones, the corporate ones, the ones that the reps are meant to have and then
> the ways that those are disrupted. There is always something that rebels in
> the body. So, like this bloke he is looking rather tense. He does not look like
> he is really enjoying his job at all (see Figure 9).

In Gibbon's work, we see a conflation of the two prominent uses of the word gesture in drawing: the guiding line of the drawing often brusquely dashed in at the beginning and highly responsive, and human gesture which is a key part of how the drawing communicates in figurative work. Gibbon cites Brecht as an inspiration for her approach to isolating gestures. Benjamin notes about gesture in Brecht's work: 'This strict, frame-like, enclosed nature of each moment of an attitude which, after all, is a whole in a state of living flux, is one of the basic dialectical

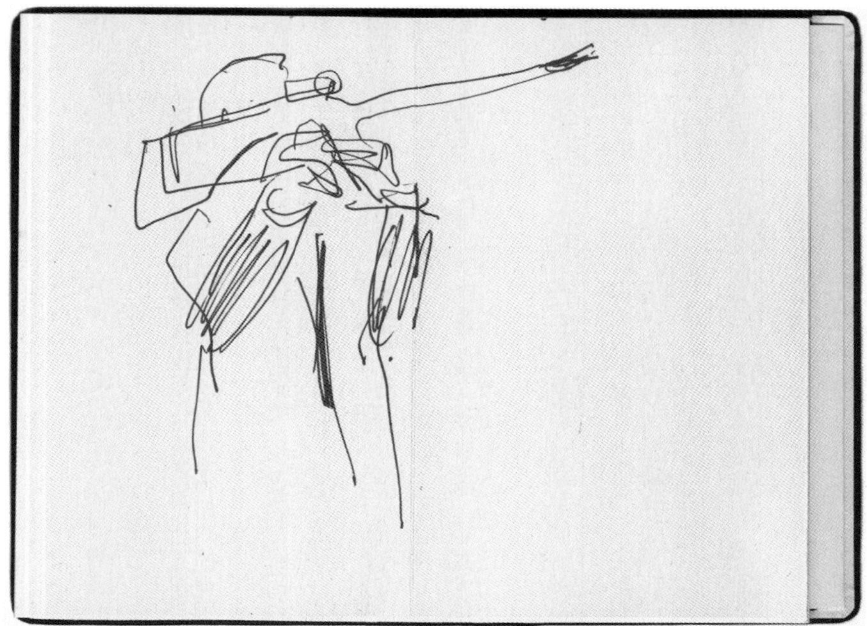

Figure 8 Big gun.
Source: Jill Gibbon

characteristics of the gesture' (Benjamin, 1998, p. 3). This extraction of gesture from 'living flux' is critical to Gibbon and allows the viewer to consider its meaning in isolation. In a further alignment with Brecht, Gibbon's intention for her captured gestures is to provoke questions from viewers about the wider significance of the acts as a metaphor for capitalist mechanisms more broadly. Benjamin notes that 'the gesture demonstrates the social significance and applicability of dialectics. It tests relations on men. The production difficulties which the producer meets while rehearsing the play cannot – even if they originate in the search for "effect" – be separated any longer from concrete insights into the life of society' (Benjamin, 1998, pp. 24, 25).

Gibbon's working methodology reflects the similar aims and sentiment of one of her artistic heroes George Grosz. Grosz noted of his own practice: 'I made careful drawing, but I had no love of the people, either inside or out. I was arrogant enough to consider myself as a natural scientist, not as a painter or satirist. I thought about right and wrong but my conclusions were always unfavourable to all men equally' (Lambourne, 1983, p. 40). In the immediacy of the sketch, which also formed the basis for Grosz's more refined work, Gibbon discovers the gestures and the nuances of gesture through the challenge of depiction and begins to classify them as behaviours which furnish our conception of place.

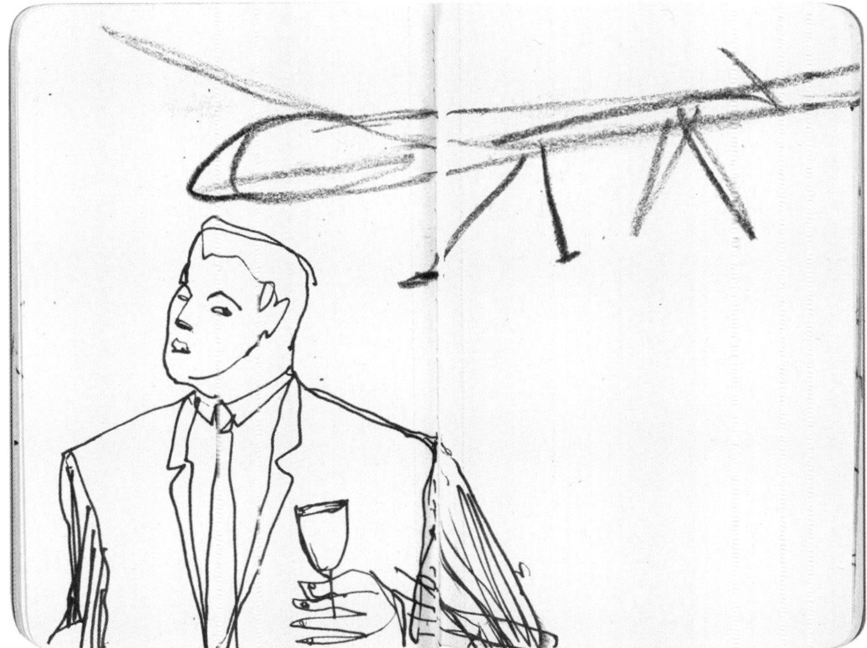

Figure 9 Predator drone.
Source: Jill Gibbon

Gibbon notes:

One of the things I am increasingly interested in is how physical and visceral
drawing is. That you are seeing but with your hands. Your hand understands
what the body does more than eye. So, it is a hand understanding of the
gesture a camera could never give. It is a delicate and complex thing. There
is something really magical about a drawing when it is your hard drawing it
and not your mind. And you are discovering through doing it and you can see
it in a drawing when that has happened. When it is not the head it is the hand
that has seen it. And it is very compelling when you see it. It is felt and seen.

The above neatly sums up how Gibbon, like many contemporary reportage artists,
submits to the moment of making the drawing and how the formation of the
drawing reflects the selection from a crowded field of stimuli and the scramble to
get that down. The mind is seen to be an interruptive presence in the submission
to the senses, particularly sight and, specifically, as Causey notes above, *seeing*
rather than merely *looking*. Maynard identifies a type of critical seeing and depiction
in caricature and notes that caricature's effects as 'secondary forms' are critical to
the full appraisal of the content of the drawing. He notes:

Caricature, when effective, combines immediate recognizability of the subject and an independently strong sense of wilful marks, lines, and facture ... it does seem that typically, in such drawings, all levels – drawn marks, picture primitives such as lines and enclosures, shapes and so forth – are usually not only salient but saliently at work.' He then notes 'often there is a special emphasis on facture, part of the effect being that we seem to see the visage taking form, *being* drawn. (Maynard, 2005, pp. 197, 198)

Reflecting what Gibbon has noted about looking at her own drawings and how observation in reportage reflects a different kind of intelligence of seeing, Ruskin notes, 'how much of all that is round us, in men's actions or spirits, which we at first think we understand, a closer and more loving watchfulness would show to be full of mystery, never to be either fathomed or withdrawn' (Ruskin, 1971, p. 120).

Tenor and topic

As noted previously, the terms 'tenor' and 'topic' are Rawson's attempt to explore the duality inherent in drawing, that is, the subject and the rendering of the subject in media. As indicated above, the 'tenor' and 'topic' for Gibbon's work are, like Embury, unified in the act of drawing. What distinguishes Gibbon from Embury, however, is a stated desire to comment upon what she is seeing through the work and present the drawings as an act of political activism.

To understand Gibbon's 'tenor' and 'topic' respectively it is important to understand her methodology and the way in which her infiltration of events such as arms fairs is a significant part of the content and activism of the work. For the interview for this book, Gibbon talked about a recent trip to Paris for the Eurosatory arms fair. Gibbon has attended many similar events in the past and has done numerous drawings, exhibiting many of them, even being featured twice by the *Guardian* newspaper. These are often fraught experiences dealing with overwhelmingly vast exhibition centres, multi-sensory distractions in the form of large screens, explosions, excessive alcohol consumption and the constant threat of detection. For the entirety of the events, Gibbon is dressed like a businesswoman and is imbedded with salesmen and women, dealers, prospective buyers from around the world and people staffing the event including scantily clad women displaying instruments of war. Gibbon is exploring in these environments the small moments when, as she notes, she can 'strip back that respectable veneer of capitalism' and even 'crack that veneer'. In the following passage, it is evident in the selection of subject how she isolates gestures through composition to draw our attention to a distinctly sleazy aspect of the arms fair. She notes:

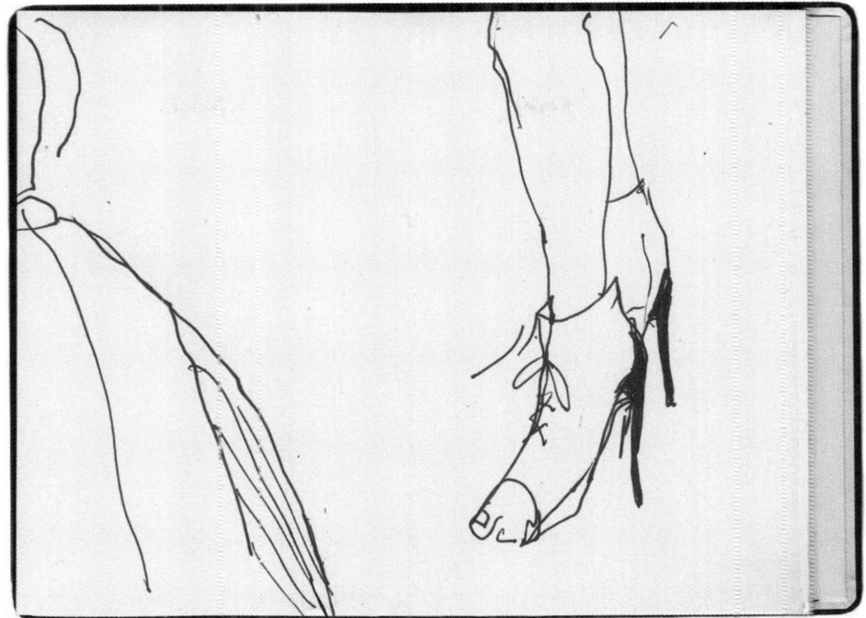

Figure 10 Sculptural heels.
Source: Jill Gibbon

I love this drawing of the legs. This is something that I have learned to do quite recently. The shoe is like a corset (see Figure 10). I've started doing this (severe cropping) because I am absolutely limited to tiny sketchbooks. Actually, they are largely informed by graphic novels. You can just get a detail. I think when I started I was always trying to get the whole scene in and to be honest, it was one of those aha moments I had talking to a student when I was looking at a student's reportage. 'When you look at this drawing everything is over there. Why don't you start changing the point of view?' I went home and saw the same thing in my own work.

Gibbon's graphic construct is shaped by her drawing and isolation of seemingly ordinary people and objects which acquire metaphoric intent in the context of their location. The tenor or the treatment of the drawing plays a significant role in shaping the implications of the image. The artist is both limited and liberated by their own representational language and Gibbon plays on this, exposing the construction of her images in the rawness of the sketch and emphasizing, at once, the circumstances of production and the nature of her subjects. The deformations allowed in the sketch allude to the deviant nature of her observed subjects. For Gibbon, tenor and topic are synchronous and as Rawson notes, 'the graphic types the visual imagination evolves will always seek in our experience of the outer world for tenors upon which to project themselves'. He then notes: 'we will see in nature the images the artist has prepared us to see' (Rawson, 1969, p. 248).

In the passage below, Gibbon notes of the unique properties of drawing and how its operative functions are distinctly compelling in the environment of an arms fair and how the small dramas and gestures become the subject. She notes:

> I mentioned earlier about Brecht being influential. Brecht talks about the gesture and Brechtian theatre is quite strange. Brecht will freeze gestures that he feels are particularly redolent in a social situation. Walter Benjamin talks about this noting, that he quotes gestures. And in so doing, in drawing attention to them, you stop their flow. Interrupt them. And so you interrupt their ideological function. You are becoming aware of what's going on. That's what I am trying to do. I am trying to show, like I was saying at the beginning with sales gestures and handshakes, or being poured a drink or the light conversation, the pinstripes … I am using drawings to quote the gestures that give an arms fair the aura of respectability. With the hope that by quoting them, you see how weird they are. I am also looking at all the many moments that that polite veneer is cracked by the vomiting, by the hand on the leg, by a manipulative hug, a snarl, despair, exhaustion. I am very deliberately looking for all of the cracks … A lot of it is outside of language … A lot of it is about bodily communication (see Figures 8–14).

The above identifies a critical aspect of Gibbon's graphic construct which is, namely, the isolation and depiction of the vernacular of human interaction in an arms fair, for example. In her drawing, she acknowledges the influence of artists like George Grosz and Otto Dix along with drawing conventions and motifs which she intentionally employs to give prominence or amplify what she has observed. What Gibbon witnesses in these arms fairs and attempts to capture in her isolated moments is closely related to Edwards and Graulund's point about the dualities that exist in the push and pull of grotesque things. They note 'the grotesque is disturbing because it incites seemingly incompatible emotions through its representations of abjection and possibility, limitations and becomings, compassion and rejection, attraction and repulsion' (Edwards & Graulund, 2013, p. 78). Gibbon notes herself that the Eurosatory could be depicted very differently as the glitz and glamour of the event is seductive and the party-like atmosphere could convince one that all is ok. For Gibbon, her identification and isolation of these small but poignant human interactions and dramas enable us to see something unexpected.

It is also important to relate, as above, the observed gesture and the drawing gesture. Ingold notes 'in the lines left upon its surface the handwritten page bears witness to gestures that, in their qualities of attentiveness and feeling, embody an

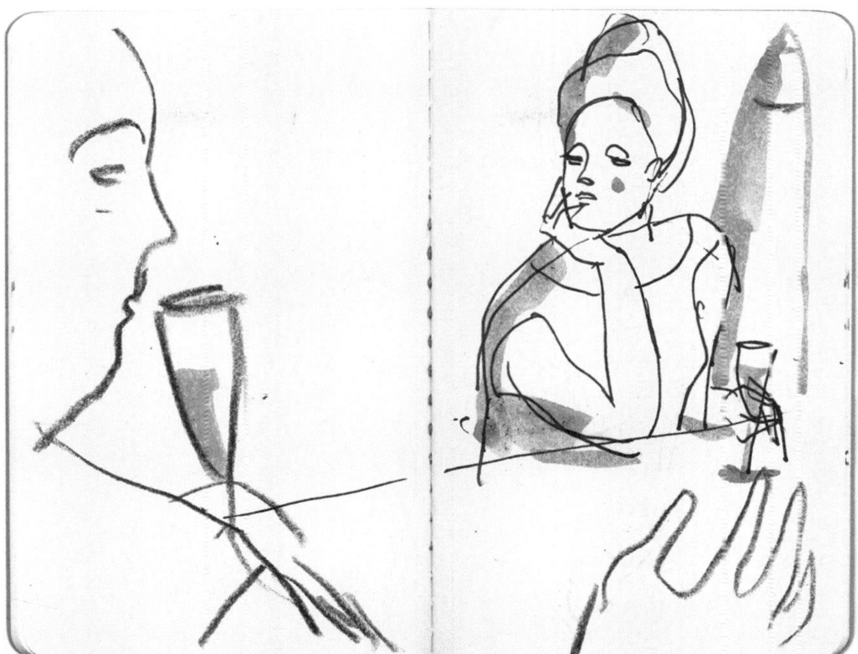

Figure 11 Wine.
Source: Jill Gibbon

intentionality intrinsic to the movement of their production' (Ingold, 2016, p. 147). In gesture drawing there is a correlative response to the gestures that are being depicted. Like the way in which Gibbon dresses up and infiltrates arms fairs, the drawing itself is a mirrored performance of what is observed. Citing a Tiepolo drawing, Rosand coins the term 'graphic momentum', defining it as 'the creating exploration of the draftsman's pen in dialectic motion, responding to the challenge of its own initial idea' (Rosand, 2002, p. 311). This momentum can be seen as the propulsive force of the drawing but also the way in which the drawing, particularly in reportage drawing, is working towards completion in a changing environment, often relying on tentative impressions or memory. Ultimately, what Gibbon is seeking to capture in her graphic construct and the ultimate destination of her tenor, the topic, is to depict these gestures and bodies and for them to highlight the observed and show the bizarre pageantry of corporate and political events. Taussig identifies in drawing an important aspect of the work of Gibbon, mainly the dialogue between her, her human subjects and the medium of drawing. He notes,

> What is important to me is what happens in the act of drawing or in the act of looking at a drawing and how that relates to thinking and acting in the world,

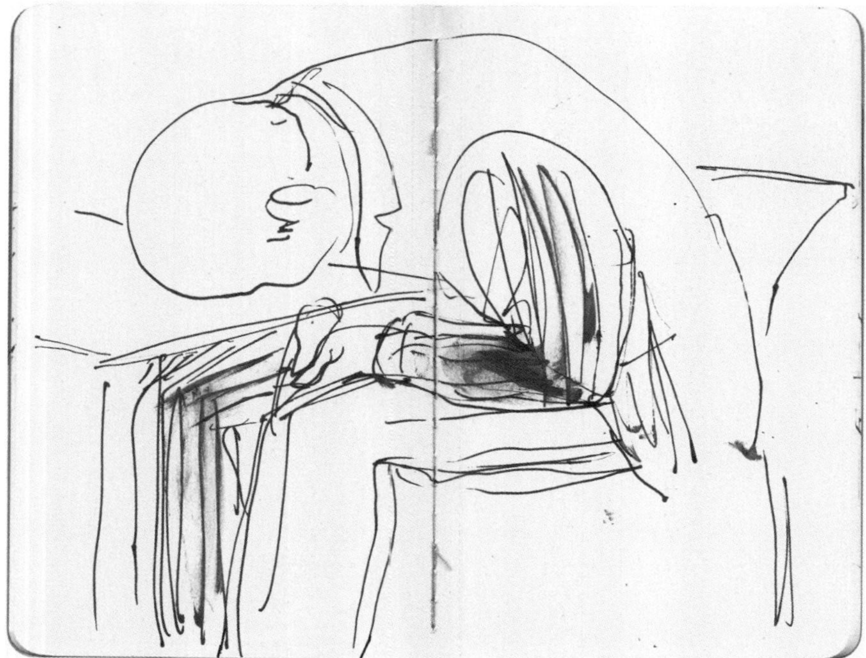

Figure 12 Head on table.
Source: Jill Gibbon

for if drawing is corporeal, it must be the mediator par excellence between body and image, and looking at drawing must have some of this as well. (Taussig, 2011, p. 80)

The passage below explores a specific drawing which for Gibbon encapsulated several important and worrying aspects of the arms fair. Here we can see the union of 'tenor' and 'topic' in the form and formation of drawing and her explicit intent to capture this sleazy encounter.

This was in a café in Eurosatory. What is motivating the drawing is the challenge of finding little moments that sum up a bigger issue. The bigger issue here being corporate capitalism ... So here, I was sat in a café in an arms fair in Eurosatory and at this point it was quite late in the afternoon. I was feeling really exhausted. This bloke I reckon has had a few drinks and was actually starting to feel a bit casual and relaxed. I think he is sat with one of his sales staff. They employ hostesses to stand on the stalls. And he is touching her leg (see Figure 15). So, I just went for it. So, it is a really scribbled drawing. Because what it's got and what I am aiming to get here is the suit, which sums up the corporate element of capitalism ... The hostess, the young woman

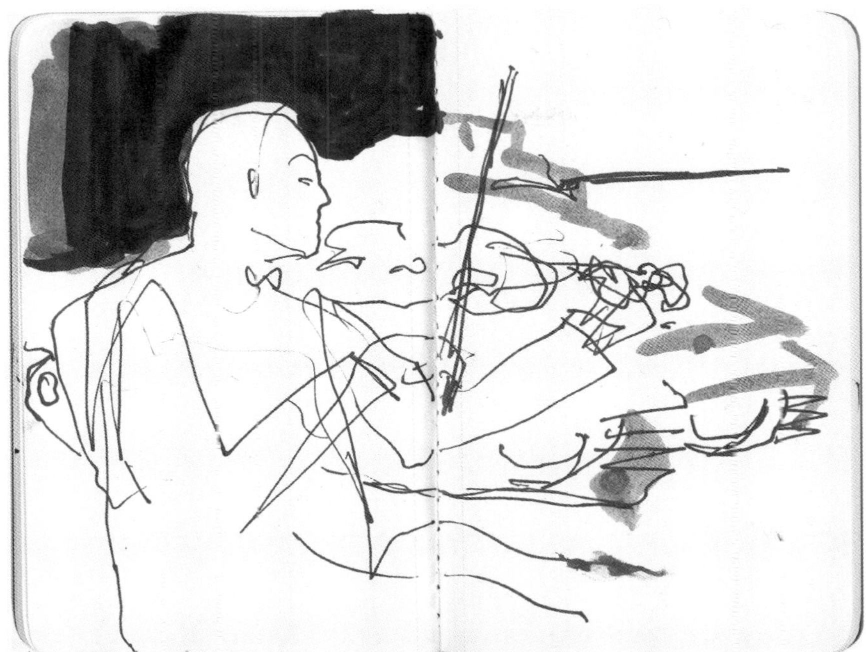

Figure 13 Tank and violin.
Source: Jill Gibbon

… that is all about the way that capitalism is sexualized … So, for me, the heels and the short skirt sum up that sexualization that's there to sell things. To make killing seem acceptable. Desirable. Seductive. It also sums up the seduction of an arms fair. The seduction of capitalism … But then the hand, right in the centre of the page, is about exploitation. There is absolutely no respect here … He kept going for her … I deliberately cropped it … I have been playing with it to get a sense of the violence. Well, both to zone in on something and also to get a sense of the dehumanizing aspect.

This drawing reflects the summation of multiple aims and the violent cropping accentuates the disturbing and audacious abuse of power that was witnessed. Gibbon notes that the compositional strategy to crop as brutally as this, looping of heads, is in part a result of a small sketchbook and thus limited room for larger tableaus. Gibbon is constantly pointing to the aim of the work and its political content, the telescoping of her intentions towards political comment and activism reflected in the same narrowed focus on these specific episodes. In terms of drawing, Gibbon displays here, like in her other drawings, a trace-like contour that is bold in some areas and tentative in others, detailing the narrative of its production. She is also identifying here the rituals and types that exist in the arms

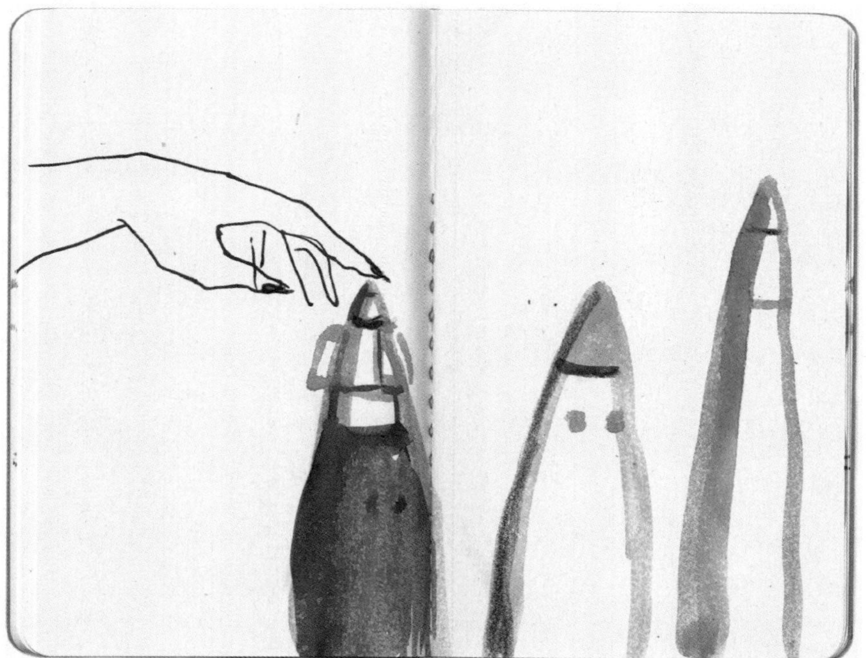

Figure 14 Hand on ammunition.
Source: Jill Gibbon

fair and these are rendered in the drawing as a kind of closed set of symbols, calling upon our own understanding of the presented types. Rawson notes, 'they (visual types) identify his topic for him and provide a vehicle for his structure and invention … but if he is a major master, he will develop substantial modifications of his types and perhaps add substantial type-ideas of his own from his observation and synthesis of forms and meanings' (Rawson, 1969, p. 254).

What Gibbon is ultimately doing in the merger of her tenor and topic is to reveal the grotesque in the seemingly banal. Edwards and Graulund note, 'the grotesque is often intended to disrupt the norm of a particular context, and the "frame" against which the "form" of grotesque takes on its bodily manifestation then becomes shapeless' (Edwards & Graulund, 2013, p. 136). In Gibbon's work the 'norm' is the normalization of greed and the acceptability of buying, selling, manufacturing and presenting instruments of war like any other product in a capitalist economy. The 'norm' is also in the small-scale performances in a sales convention and the power and consequence that has when the focus of the sale is deadly weaponry. The figures are not always vulgar but the drawings aim to make these small interactions metaphoric and grotesque with the contextual knowledge of their setting. As W. J. T. Mitchell notes,

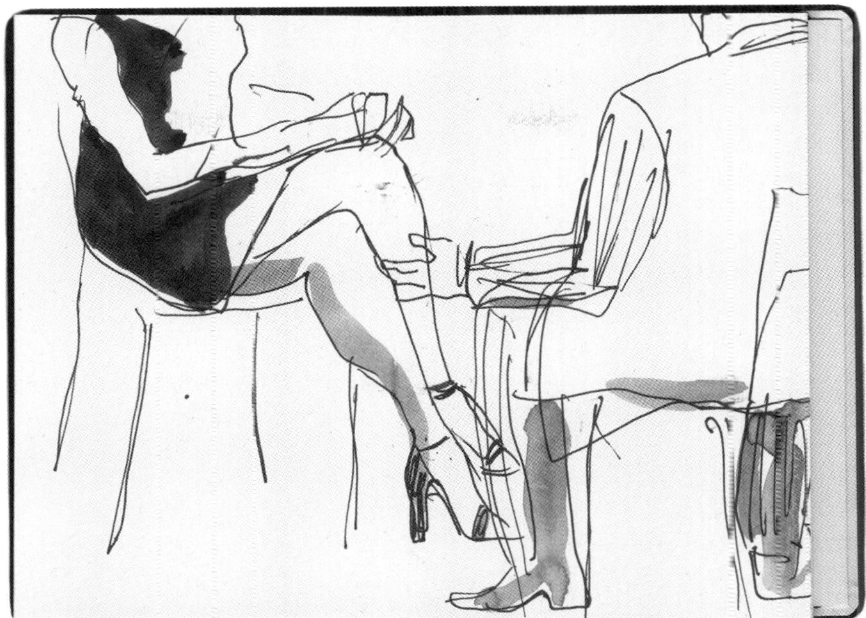

Figure 15 Hand on leg.
Source: Jill Gibbon

In this New World Order, freedom means the freedom of commodities (but not of human bodies) to circulate freely across borders, and democracy means an infinite proliferation of consumer choices accompanied by an increasingly narrow range of political choices. Before we celebrate the demise of imperialism, then we had better reflect on the disembodied utopia of the World Wide Web, we had better ask ourselves what things we will have to leave behind, and what the consequences will be for the real bodies and physical objects that remain. (Mitchell, 2005, p. 150)

Experience of drawing, experience of place

It is impossible to understand the power and implications of Gibbon's drawing without an understanding of the locations in which she draws. Presenting her work as a form of activism, we see the artist and her covert drawing as a performance, blending into the event disguised as a representative of her employer and using this access to bring to the viewer a largely unseen world. Although she has drawn in arms fairs for several years, she notes that there are always surprises and obvious fractures between the banality of a sales convention and the devastating reality of the goods on offer, imbuing even the smallest gestures with metaphoric subtext. She notes:

> What I have really begun to hone down on in the last couple of years, is, given what capitalism does, globalized capitalism … So, what I am focusing on more and more are venues where there are all of those tropes of respectability. It is a continual challenge to find these places but to an extent you can see it when people are coming home from work. If I was to identify an emerging interest, it would be that. The phrase I have been giving it is corporate work, corporate life. And I am interested both in the motifs and, particularly, a word I got from George Brecht, gesture. I think the gestures have real power in relation to the question how is capitalism made respectable. It is, I think, through gestures and rituals of respectability.

For Gibbon, her drawings are not rendering place from space and rather start off with a place which is the container, the set, setting and critical backdrop which is necessary for the total understanding of the images. Massey explores the notion of globalization, a term she feels has replaced capitalism in name only, and the way in which it has its own conception of space and spaces which it uses for its own advantage. She notes, 'the imagination of globalisation in terms of unbounded free space, that powerful rhetoric of neoliberalism around "free trade", just as was modernity's view of space, is a pivotal element in an overweening political discourse … it has its institutions and its professionals. It is normative; and it has effects' (Massey, 2005, p. 83). Gibbon's work exploits the impression that globalism, capitalism and our political structures are generally beneficent and finds in this hidden part of capitalistic enterprise a dark banality, a moral failure. Through drawing, Gibbon is able to process these spaces and capture the darkly banal rituals of the sales floor. She notes of her strategies in situ and the comfort she finds in drawing:

> A year or so ago in 2017 I went to Ideks which is an arms fair in Abu Dhabi and I was absolutely terrified of being caught because … to be caught in Abu Dhabi would not be good at all really … and I felt like I was drowning in the place … It is almost like I felt like I was drowning in aggressive technology if that makes sense. So eventually what I did because I felt I wasn't surviving in this place was I found a café and a place like this and I thought, okay, now I am totally safe with a tiny book on my lap and I did some rapid drawing and I felt fine and that was such an example to me of how central drawing is to me navigating situations where actually I feel very unsafe. It gives me a way of looking back at this intensely powerful military gaze. It's the slightest tool a pen and paper and yet it's so powerful I think in how it can ground you. It was

an aha moment in how much militarized capitalism how much contemporary politics how much the military industrial complex is based on looking. Really violent, phenomenally powerful, surveillance gaze. And that drawing totally subverts it … There is almost like a 'fuck you' in it. You've got all that kit but I can look at you just with this … What is it that drawing enables you to see? That you can't simply with the eye.

The above confirms Gibbon's interest in drawing as a humble but powerful mediator of experience. She notes in her recent book 'so why draw when you can take high quality images, instantly and discreetly, for immediate dissemination?' She further notes, 'drawing is a curious process, less accurate than photography, more ambiguous than writing, less substantial than painting. If hovers between seeing and feeling, experience and imagination, movement and image' (Gibbon, 2018).

Gibbon's methodology guarantees a responsive trace of her perception and she captures, with urgency, unfolding action which is revelatory even for her. As noted above, the comfort that Gibbon experiences through drawing is part of a process of finding meaning and making sense of what she is seeing. Causey notes 'the point of drawing to see is precisely *not* to settle for preconceptions but to allow delineation to act as the window into a lived reality' (Causey, 2017, p. 54). Gibbon confirms this, noting, 'we begin with a blank page, mapping our relationship with our surroundings. The process of drawing brings us powerfully into the present; it grounds us' (Gibbon, 2018). The sense of the present and presence itself are important aspects of Gibbon's work and although character types are identified and reflect a 'schematic restatement', containing elements of caricature, they emerge from the moments of their making and the feelings that charge them (Nisbet & Lauer, 1993). Gibbon is not rendering objective reality but her claim as a witness and all that it implies situates the drawings in the places they are made and are. as Gibbon notes, 'messages from this hidden witness' (Gibbon, 2018).

The graphic construct

Gibbon's graphic construct can be best described as a total alignment of aims which sees her methodology, aesthetic interests and commentary fused in the responsive act of covert drawing. She notes of the continual struggle to capture what she sees and experiences, saying 'the drawings swing between caricature and observational methods, never quite conveying the strangeness of the event. It is a frustrating process' (Gibbon, 2018). Gibbon, like Embury and other practitioners, is subject to the vagaries of her own self-imposed limitations and this can cause uneven results. However, as noted previously about Embury's work and my own, the value of the work is less about mimetic accuracy, as seen in the wilful and accidental distortions above, and is valued for its closeness to the artists' remembered experience. Experience, and the drawings evocation of it, is the one thing that myself, Embury and Gibbon all see as a critical gauge of success in a reportage drawing.

Gibbon's graphic construct is simple yet powerful and it reinforces her desire to challenge capitalism through exploring the vernacular of the bodies which operate on its behalf. Her reportage drawing is motivated by moral shock and deep feelings are threaded into her observation and activate the drawing through the perception that the subjects have been observed or witnessed and that the artist has something to say about them. Reflecting this seeing and feeling and the shock that motivates many of her drawings Gibbon notes, 'drawing is a "process of looking" that takes place in the stomach as much as the eyes' (Gibbon, 2018).

Gibbon's graphic construct can thus be mapped as in Table 1.

Conclusion

At the core of Gibbon's reportage drawing is the stark contrast between the activity of drawing and the machinery of capitalism. Her subjects are engaged in a dark commerce with lethal consequences and in the drawing, we see how this trade is packaged like any other product and sold using the same crass and seemingly inappropriate tactics. Exploiting the properties of the sketch and isolating gestures and interactions, the viewer is invited to see and feel what Gibbon sees and feels and this closeness to her vision accentuates the illicitness of her activity. Gibbon reflects on the power dynamics between the humble drawing and the seeing machinery of war. Read clearly delineates the two opposing forces and their properties as 'an empire is by definition a power-concept; art is born in intimacy' (Read, 1967, p. 27). Although seemingly contradictory considering the subject of Gibbon's drawing, the work is deeply intimate and a pervasive sadness and psychic trauma mark many of the faces. For Gibbon, capitalism is the invisible enemy in her drawings and the subjects are playing out its disastrous game. She notes: 'drawing while feeling nauseous, I realise I am not alone; there is often a disjuncture between arms traders' neat dress, and the uneasy figures within. There hunched shoulders, tense movements, contorted expressions.' She continues, 'a rep collapses into a chair, a sales assistant recoils from her client, a contractor snarls at a rival' (Gibbon, 2018). In witnessing the bizarre rituals of the arms trade and building this taxonomy of small acts in drawing, Gibbon's most devastating claim is that this troubling trade is in fact a deeply human one with wider implications for the state of capitalism and the normalization of such commerce. Referencing Celine's novel *Journey to the End of the Night*, Edwards and Graulunc note about Celine's vision of capitalism: 'the

Table 1 *Gibbon's graphic construct*

Drawing	Experience	Assessment
'Tenor' and 'topic'	**Experience of drawing**	**Fidelity to the observed**
• Fused in the act of drawing. • Some stylistic features are present which reflect commentary and have acknowledged features of caricature.	• Done covertly and the caution not to be detected. • Looks for certain types and interactions which expose the cracks in the respectable veneer.	• There is every intention to draw from observation and her own assessment of the success or failure of the drawing is tied to the capture of specific observational details.
Drawn effects	**Experience in situ**	**Assessment of intentions**
• Both a result of hurried and covert drawing and intentionally cultivated to align with aesthetic aims. **Aesthetic influences** • Influenced by George Grosz and Otto Dix.	• Dressed up in heels and pearls and intended to blend with the crowd. • This element of performance enables her to get closer to her subjects and catch them with their guard down.	• The drawings are valued for their capture of moments when respectability is shattered and for their evocation of the subject and experience in situ. • Although the aims are specific and clear, serendipitous moments are welcome and many drawings are motivated by surprise or shock in some way.
Aims and intentions	**Experience of place**	**Graphic qualities**
• The work is intended to bear witness to the sleazy underbelly of global capitalism and to document the way the body can be metaphoric and convey troubling truths about the arms trade, for example.	• The place and the knowledge that the drawings are done in them is critical to their appreciation and their impact. • Although there is little indication of setting other than a few missiles or a gun here and there, the people and their actions provide a compelling window into this hidden world.	• A continuous line contour reflects its quick production and distortions are present which are either a result of hurried drawing or caricature. • The aesthetic of the sketch combines with subtle stylization. • Exaggerations, whether intentional or not, draw the viewer closer to the aesthetic of the sketch and therefore make them evocative of the moments of their making.
Graphic Construct		

contemporary body politic is better represented by "contagion", by the oozing pus, dripping blood and the festering blobs of meat that have been infected by the fluid and grotesque power of the global financial system of a deterritorialized Empire' (Edwards & Graulund, 2013, p. 139). While Gibbon's drawing does not present a coherent metaphor for capitalism per se, her work subverts both the grotesque and capitalistic enterprise by revealing its banality, and only when we acknowledge the context and implications associated with it do we understand our own complicity in it.

7
THE GRAPHIC CONSTRUCT – MAPPING MY OWN PRACTICE

The graphic construct in reportage drawing reflects a unity of aesthetic and conceptual interests. Fused in the hurried act of drawing in situ, the two concerns merge in the immediacy of responsive thought and action. Artist Ben Shahn noted 'form is formulation – the turning of content into a material entity, rendering a content accessible to others, giving it permanence, willing it to the race … form in art is as varied as idea itself' (Shahn, 1957, p. 53). Rawson, whose use and definition of the term 'graphic construct' is critical to this book, notes that graphic constructs 'summarize and condense the psychological meaning of the graphic forms of which they are composed' (Rawson, 1969, p. 247). For Rawson, all forms of the drawing are a construct as they are a rendering of something, observable or imagined, into graphic forms, relating to, as Rawson notes, 'our experience' of the subject (Rawson, 1969, p. 247). Here, on a most basic level, the graphic construct of the reportage artist is beyond pure objectivity and even observation, and is better understood as a rendering, with distinctly individual concerns, limitations and desires. As Rudolph Arnheim notes, 'form must be invented; and since no form invented by someone else will fit an artist's own experience, he himself has to do the inventing' (Arnheim, 1954, p. 141).

My own graphic construct, which will be further explored below, bridges the concerns of the purist, observational branch of the practice with the more stylistic, commentary-laden practitioners. Like the history of reportage practice, these two concerns can be seen as complementary in my work as the sustaining interest in the drawing is always anchored to an observed subject, even when it departs into broader thematic commentary. What my graphic construct contributes to the larger exploration of the contemporary practice of reportage drawing is the wider narrative of production that is possible through my own reflective practice. The narrative of the selection of subjects and the range of intentions for the drawing can more vividly highlight the emergence of the drawing through a constellation of factors including but not limited to the weather, engagement with subjects through conversation, identification of subjects for their thematic potential and position of the artist relative to the subject.

Additionally, through seeing the wider narrative of a group of reportage drawings and how they reflect the experience of the artist but equally developments of the artist's thinking, the practice of reportage can be seen more clearly as the manifestation of a world view, relishing subjectivity and engaging the viewer with the unique potentialities of drawing for understanding our world. The feedback the artist can identify in the finished drawing is instructive to understanding how intentions were or were not resolved in the graphic marks and whether this is desirable or not, indicating the serendipity which pervades the act.

Drawn effects

My own work shares the aesthetic properties of the sketch although it is not a first thought necessarily, and through placement and composition, it is a deliberate construction. Because the vast majority of my drawing is done in situ, the work is hurriedly produced and this is reflected in the look and feel of the work. However, an additional aesthetic exists which is the refined, economic line which has a stylistic intent. Often referred to as a shorthand, this storehouse of graphic marks and strategies finds refinement through practice and becomes, to an extent, conventionalized. Related to Gombrich's ideas about schema and classification, my own reportage drawing can be seen to combine the 'universals' and the 'particulars' or the refined schematic approaches and strategies to form and the on-the-spot inventions, conceived through responsive observation (Gombrich, 1972, p. 152). The schematic shorthand can be seen in the approach to forms and, more specifically, similarities in certain features such as eyes, for example (see Figure 16).

These developed forms are part of refined perception and can be called schematic but additionally, they are informed by artistic inspiration from artists such as George Grosz, Toulouse Lautrec, Nicolas De Crécy and Jacques Tardi. In my reportage drawing, these forms are not purely responsive to features identifiable in the subject but are rather developed strategies to render those forms in a refined language, with intent. What results from this deviation from pure observation is the production of 'types'. Rawson's clarification on what constitutes a 'graphic type' is relevant. He notes:

> The typical and the individual may seem to be inevitably contrasted. However, in my use of the word 'type' in an artistic context individuality is not by any means excluded … But there are also arts of drawing which include into their type-images indications of individuality, symbols which serve to represent the idea of uniqueness … They are permitted by a kind of flexibility in the type, which allows latitude for variation within its construction. (Rawson, 1969, p. 251)

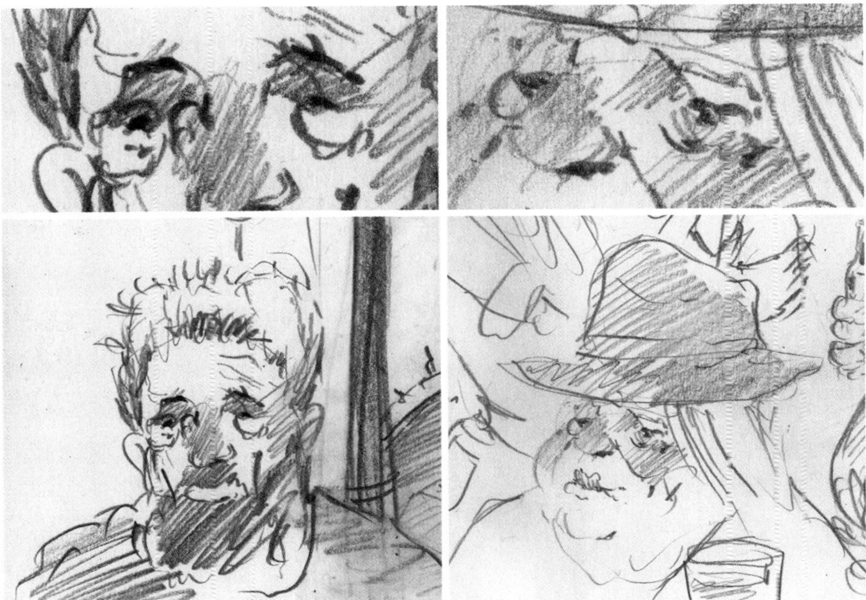

Figure 16 Approach to forms.
Source: Louis Netter

As Rawson notes above, it is possible for the artist to engage with 'types' as an exploration of a creative vision and avoid typical convention, achieved in reportage through some fidelity to the observed (no matter how tenuous). You could also see Rawson's words as permitting modifications on a conventionalized form such as differing features, clothing or accessories.

One such drawing and reflection from Portsmouth in 2016 is indicative of how the experience of the subject can be synthesized in a drawing (see Figure 17).

Walking back towards work I saw a middle-aged woman looking out of a window in a café right before closing. I noted the scene in my head. Taking several long looks I decided to draw it later in doors. Because of the cold and rain, it was near impossible to work on location and necessitated drawing it later. I also drew her on A2 paper which enabled me to re-experience the scene in the spontaneous manner that I typically work. While it would seem likely that drawing sometime after observing subjects would lead to greater deviation, on occasion, the impression of the subject and interest is so acute that the re-experience in drawing is vivid and surprising.

The above reflects a lucky re-communion with the subject in a drawing done sometime afterwards. It is of course difficult to determine whether the drawing

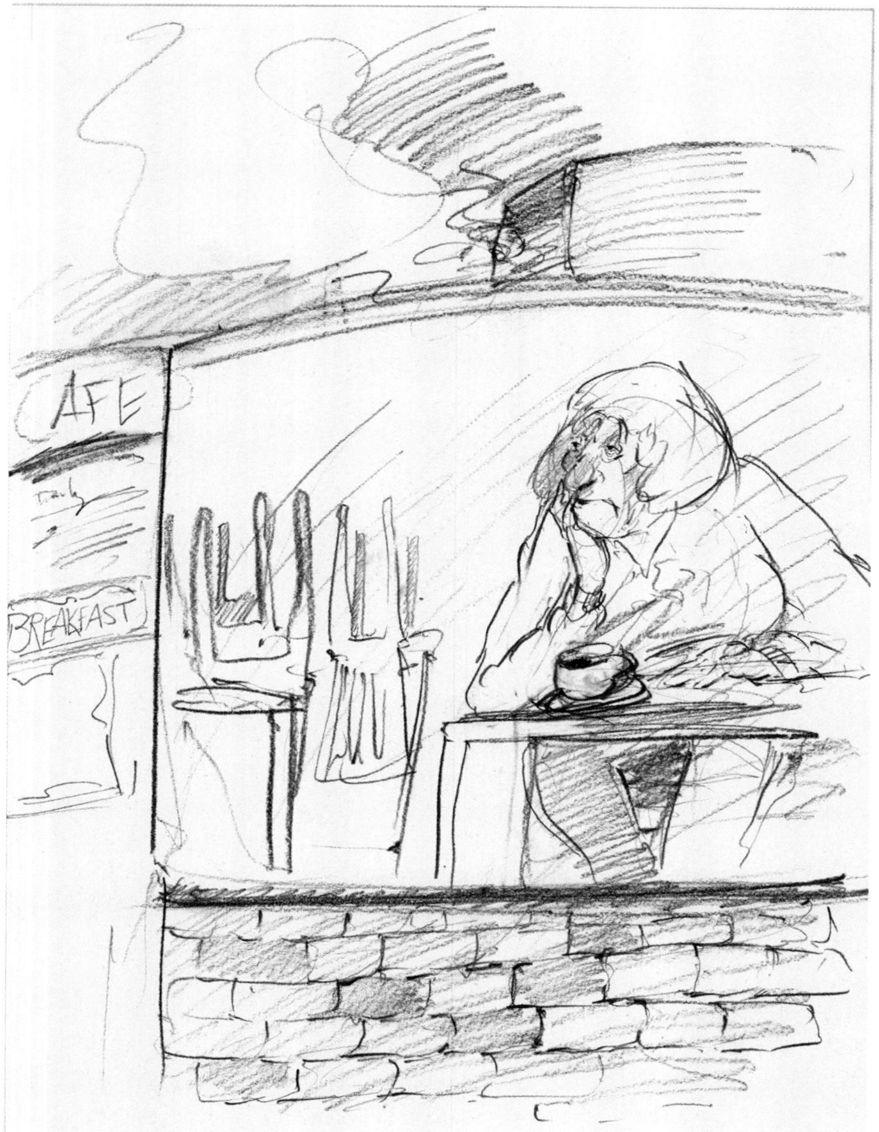

Figure 17 Lady in café, Portsmouth, 2016.
Source: Louis Netter

bears any close resemblance to the woman at the table but for me, the drawing evokes that moment on a rainy afternoon and her forlorn expression crystallizes something that I perceived on the day. Because of the nature of fluid environments, observation and the act of drawing, the capture of subjects can occur at different times, even when the subject is no longer in sight.

The conflation of observation and comment in my own reportage can be seen in the following passage. Here, the features of the sketch in the quick, reductive marks are also synchronous with the commentary sought and the way in which the subject relates to other themes and even drawings such as the drawings of George Grosz. This passage relates to a drawing trip to Hamburg in 2017 (see Figure 18).

The next drawing was done directly after the butcher shop as this man came around the corner. He was actually just standing there for a little while as I moved my drawing pad out of the way. I noted his features and immediately he reminded me of the Grosz drawings of fat businessmen. The head looked like a single bone and his dark sunglasses at once like skull sockets and long view telescopes. The glasses helped to avoid specifying him and he became, as I had hoped, more symbolic of a German man of a certain age. Overweight and somewhat gormless, he was perfectly formed as a stand in for the well-fed, successful German. I drew this on some stairs to a building of flats and I was sufficiently hidden. This drawing was executed quickly and the roving graphite stick managed to apply the right emphasis in the right areas, accentuating the shape of the head, the high trousers and thick arm.

What is also notable in the passage above is the way in which observational details are themselves laden with commentary and guide the image towards the refinement of a thought or comment. Here the 'half-created' world of the drawing is clear in the dialogue and musings that occur during its production. Berger's idea of the 'half-created' world of the drawing is extended in his claim that 'any drawn place is both a here and an elsewhere'. He further notes: 'each drawn place has all the particularity and local knowledge of a here, and, at the same time, the promise of an elsewhere … Here embodies necessity; elsewhere offers freedom' (Berger and Savage, 2008, p. 143). The negotiation in the drawing that occurs between the subject and the rendering of that subject results in a record of thought and action that manages two spaces: that of the identifiable subject and the inevitable symbolism of drawn marks which point to other potentialities. Additionally, those drawn marks can be, as in the drawing above, laden with commentary which are clearly representative of an 'elsewhere', the interiority of the artist's thoughts and intentions.

In the following written description, the drawing is described as an assemblage of observed people and in this particular case, the challenge of capturing such diverse subjects and action made the process of drawing and the perceived success of the drawing seem particularly engrossing. This drawing is also from Hamburg in 2017 (see Figure 19).

This next drawing was one of the more successful of the day. The man on the right with the brightly coloured vest was actually dealing with his young

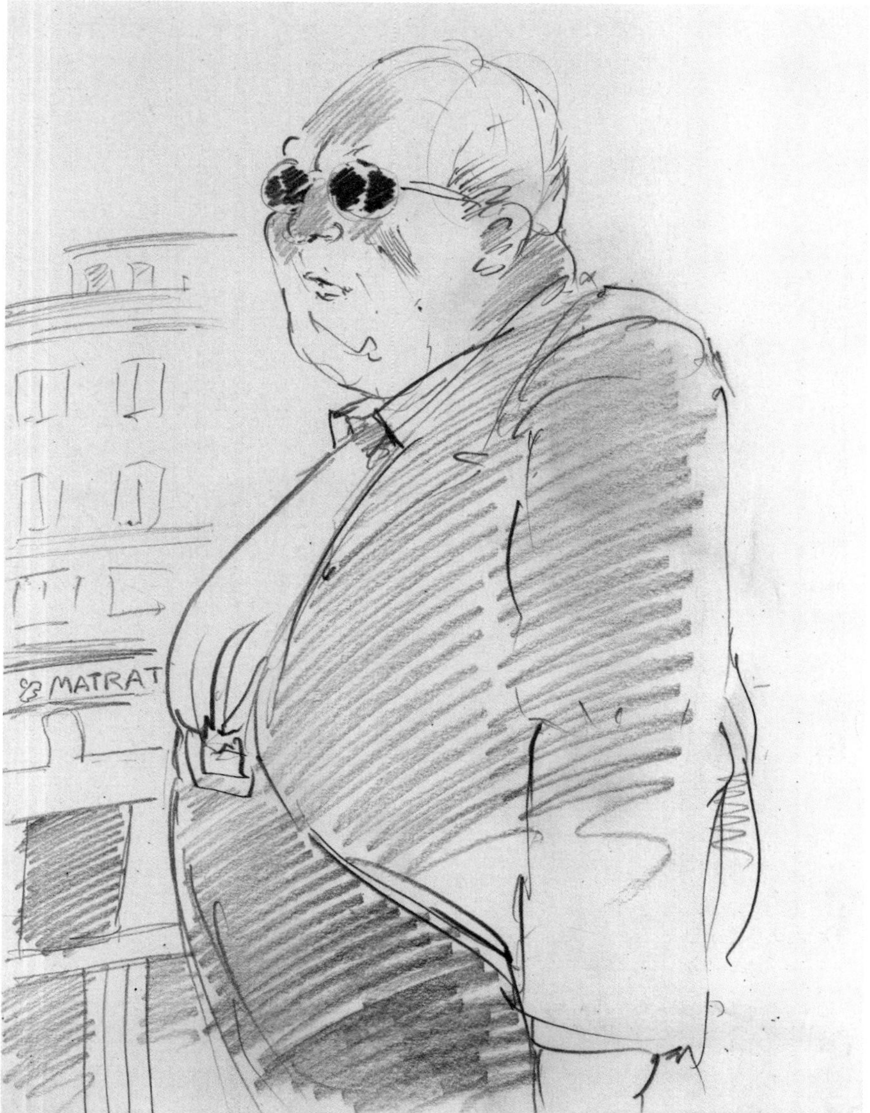

Figure 18 German man, Hamburg, 2017.
Source: Louis Netter

son when I captured him and his mullet, along with his drunk and bewildered expression, was well captured. Again, the speed at which I was working and trying to note down characters was enabling a more accurate and specific kind of depiction that, at this stage, was starting to pay off. The man with the hat attempting to kiss the woman was observed along with the larger woman in

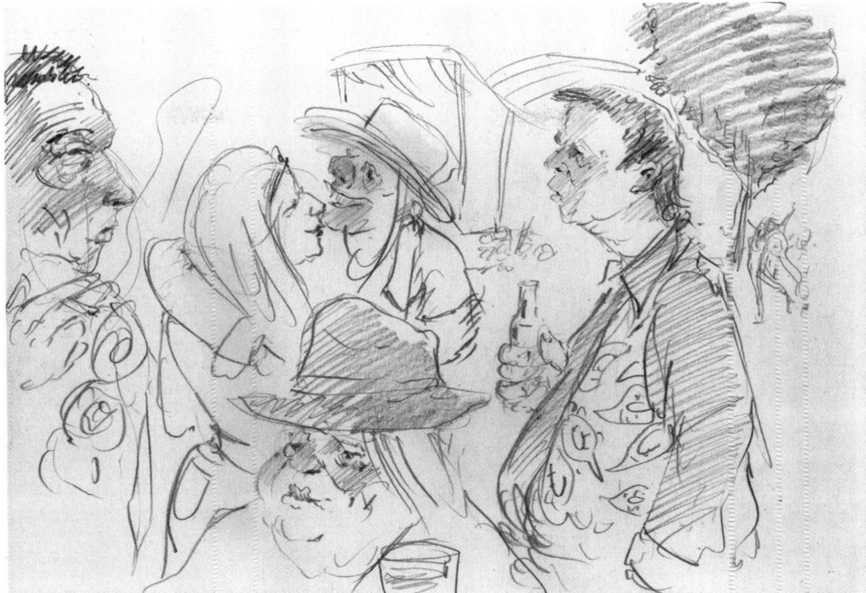

Figure 19 Schlagermove festival, Hamburg, 2017.
Source: Louis Netter

the foreground who appears to be walking towards the viewer. These people reflect quick selections from the frenetic environment on the day. Their capture is, I believe, successful, and I can remember these figures, and even smell their breath. The piles of spent booze were inescapable. These were the first casualties. The first group of people partied out as they had followed the first Schlagermove buses. Crowds dancing and singing are indicated in the background but I was conscious not to linger too long on any one drawing and I was desperate to catch the fluid action. It was a somewhat overcast day but bursts of sunshine came in intermittently. Many people were also smoking. The smell of alcohol and tobacco made me think of bad hangovers and I imagined the number of sore heads that would be lumbering around the next day. While there were many episodes of joyous dancing and singing, many quiet and somewhat sombre moments of drunkenness were visible. The figure to the right with the vest and mullet is the anchor of this drawing. He, like me, is a witness. This drawing, by virtue of its production, has a lightness of touch that connects the viewer to my direct vision more readily. I can't be sure that it reads as more or less constructed than others but for me, it feels momentary and raw.

In this drawing, the mixture between resolution and half-finished forms heightens the engagement with the drawing as an act of direct observation. While this was a constructed image, because of the demands on the ground, it was not overly considered and the choices made are quick and intuitive. These spontaneously constructed images have a compelling vitality for the artist and are more rewarding on re-viewing because they lack the logic and premeditation of other images, making them more surprising. Drawings like this that are a composite of several observed moments offer the viewer a greater sense of the totality of the experience, especially considering the complexity and cacophony of this event. The valorization of the sketch has taken many forms, but as artist and writer Deanna Petherbridge notes, 'the appearance of spontaneity' is critical and, she further adds,

> An engendering sketch has to be accomplished quickly because of the instability, incoherence and fleeting quality of conceptual images, which hover on the edges of consciousness like pale ghosts, floating away if approached too deliberately. (Petherbridge, 2010, p. 49)

Reportage drawing is a wrestle to give vision permanence and these visions occupy liminal and rapidly disappearing spaces in our minds.

Tenor and topic

Rawson defines 'tenor' and 'topic' as, roughly and respectively, the rendering of forms with intent and the subject, which is directly related to the choices made in its rendering. Rawson notes, 'the artist projects the image-containing forms upon the tenor, and hopes that we, his public, will be able to grasp his meaning from them' (Rawson, 1969, p. 5). The terms 'tenor' and 'topic' are instructive ways of seeing reportage drawing (and all drawing) as both a complex construction and a dialogue between the subject and the artist as he or she confronts their own intentions and renders those intentions in the forms of the drawing.

Extending this concept of 'tenor' and 'topic', it is worth thinking of the act of drawing as an act of thinking. Because of the demands of the act of reportage, this thinking is highly responsive and grounded by the task of rendering the observed but also the constellation of ideas that surround the subject and environment. The artist William Kentridge speaks of the playful and surprising evolution of a drawing and how the artist engages deeply with the essence of his or her subject. He notes about drawing a horse 'inside, there is a sense of HORSE, of horse-ness, waiting to be triggered. Rocinante, Bucephalus, the Trojan horse, Stubbs, the photo-finish in a horse race, are all there' (Kentridge, 2014, p. 18). This kind of associative process also occurs within my own drawing and extends 'tenor' and 'topic' towards an understanding of drawing and drawn choices as the conclusion of thought(s), like Shahn's contention that form and idea are essentially the same thing. The following passage from a drawing excursion in

Portsmouth in 2016 reveals this wider narrative which surrounds the images and my own feelings about the place (see Figure 20).

> I had no roadmap for this drawing other than to start with the circus sign and populate the drawing from there. I tried to capture the sign but something sinister crept in and it is a wild distortion of the actual sign, which was brightly coloured, cheery and hideously tacky. Again, this was a struggle with multiple erasures. It is odd that when I am directly observing and drawing, I am often too reliant on the subject. When operating from recent memory of an observed thing I often tend to not only be more confident but more accurate in my drawing … These two older ladies struck me as interesting subjects. They seemed like twins. The woman with the white hair had these strange eyebrows that shot right down. They were both dour faced and swiftly walking. I was interested in the way they seemed to walk like they were attached to each other … It is a common occurrence to hear women talking about the horrendous behaviour of their partners. Often expletive-laced tirades end with a chuckle and comment like 'cheeky cunt'. These are hard worn faces and more often than not Portsmouth forces you to see this side of itself … I then needed something on the other side of the sign to finish off the composition. I remember walking through the crowd on the other side of the fountain and seeing a middle-aged man with glasses eating a sandwich from a bag. He was also wearing a NY hat. What did that NY really mean? Has the place become a brand? Did this man acquire the hat consciously or was this something that was around, available to him at the time? Although he lacks the detail of the larger figures, I was pleased with his rendering. This drawing overall achieved what I wanted. With a scene like this and a very fluid environment, it is especially hard to make choices. Those choices are consequential as they shape an interpretation of the place. Those two ladies could have been replaced with a myriad of other characters. From what was on offer I can honestly say that this is quite a sympathetic vision of this area.

In the passage above, 'tenor' and 'topic' are attempting to move the viewer towards a nuanced view of the place, which is sympathetic and unsympathetic in equal measure. The commentary and the image are depictive of the same thing which is a psychic portrait of the Cascades shopping area in Portsmouth, a place of interior and exterior struggle. A drawing such as this reveals how observation is polluted or informed by the subjectivities of thought and ideas which swirl around the drawing process. What Rawson calls the 'numen' or the projected essence of the image can be seen as the cohesion of thoughts, observation and rendered forms which move the viewer towards the fulfilment of the artist's subjective vision in drawing (Rawson, 1969, p. 7). Like the drawing above, this can imbue the work with an overriding, pervasive sentiment. This

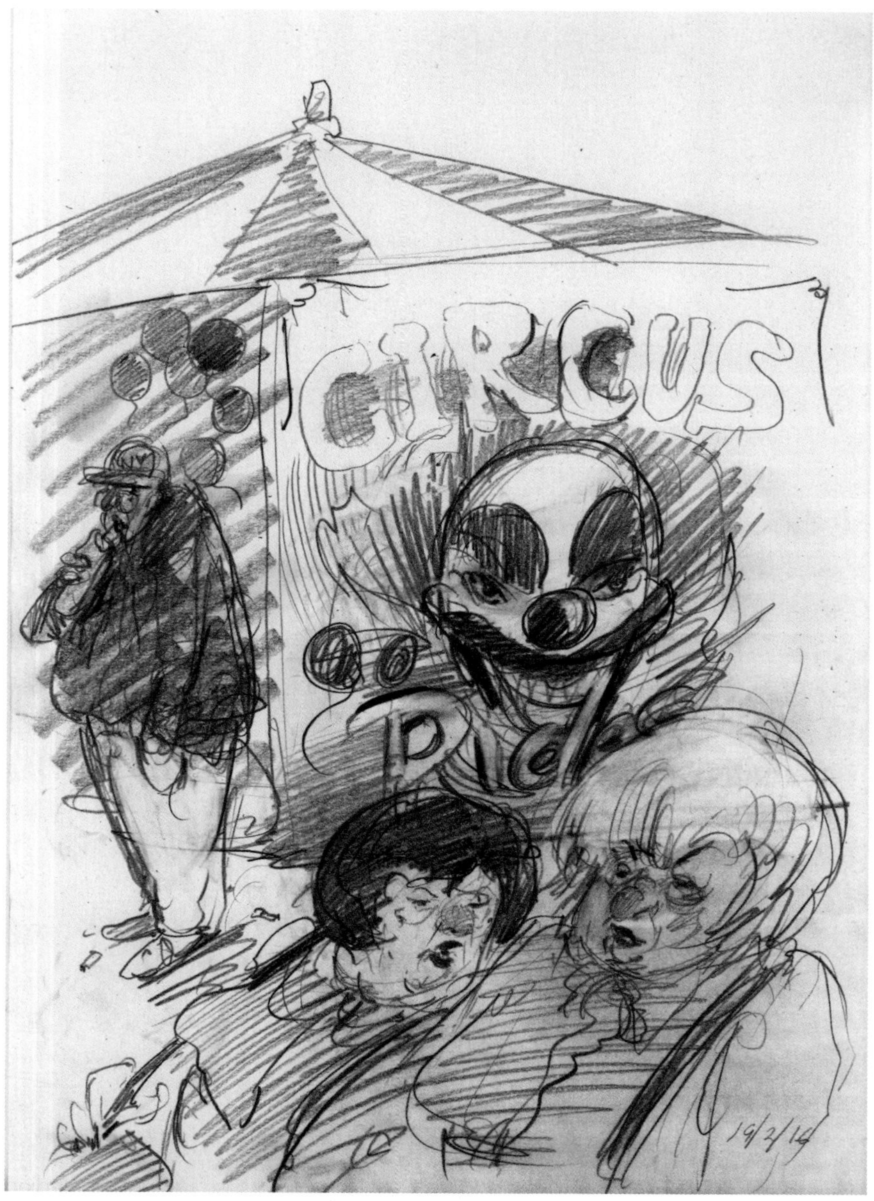

Figure 20 Cascades shopping centre, Portsmouth, 2016.
Source: Louis Netter

sentiment relates to an emotional connection to individuals who reflect some injury as a result of the unfortunate vicissitudes of life.

The commentary below directly followed the previous drawing and continues many of the same thematic concerns. Here the person as symbol is crucial and the 'here' and 'elsewhere' that Berger speaks of is apparent in this drawing and the accompanying dialogue (see Figure 21).

> The final drawing came from leaving my perch from the last three drawings and going beyond the circus ride to a row of benches. I was immediately hit with the line of people on the benches smoking despondently as the foot traffic passed in front of them. Any of these characters would have made good subjects. I kept looking … My hands were very cold as well. Walking around the benches and beyond them I noticed a large, ruddy-faced woman with what looked like a kid's hat, decorated with a cute cartoon kitten. She had a pleasant face and was chatting to another older woman. She seemed somewhat eccentric with multiple layers of clothing on (like the NY guy) and she had the same confounding headwear. This cute kitten hat seemed to be a commentary in itself about both age and culture and the breakdown of fashion that is a consequence of poverty. It was a difficult face to capture, as it was delicate and ruddy but also bold with the strong thrust of the nose downward. I also noted her jangling earrings, which were also oddly out of place. This was an odd case because the addition of the earrings and the hat would imply a conscious decision for wearing them but the items themselves clash so harshly against rational taste. Dashing in the cheap amusement ride in the background and the old woman smoking finished off the drawing. This was one of those drawings which comes together with ease and managed to imbed a range of compelling ideas through the capture of the subject's singularity.

What we can see in this commentary and the drawing is a successful conveyance of the textures of the experience of the subject. Although rooted in observation, the success of the image is less about accuracy than it is about the assemblage of character. What my drawing is attempting to hold is the presence of the subject. Berger reflects on this engagement with subject, noting, 'in my own very small experience the being or thing, which I'm drawing, never becomes defective, but often the drawing does. The drawing fails to embrace the presence.' He further notes, 'drawing is about a company which, beyond or outside the drawing, will very quickly or eventually become invisible' (Berger & Savage, 2008, p. 116). What is implied here is that the drawing and circumstances of its production, including the act(s) of thinking involved, reside in the drawings alone and that 'drawings offer hospitality to an invisible company which is with us' (Berger & Savage, 2008, p. 116). Relating this to my larger contention about the graphic construct of the reportage artist, drawing is more than rendered forms, it is rendered thought and

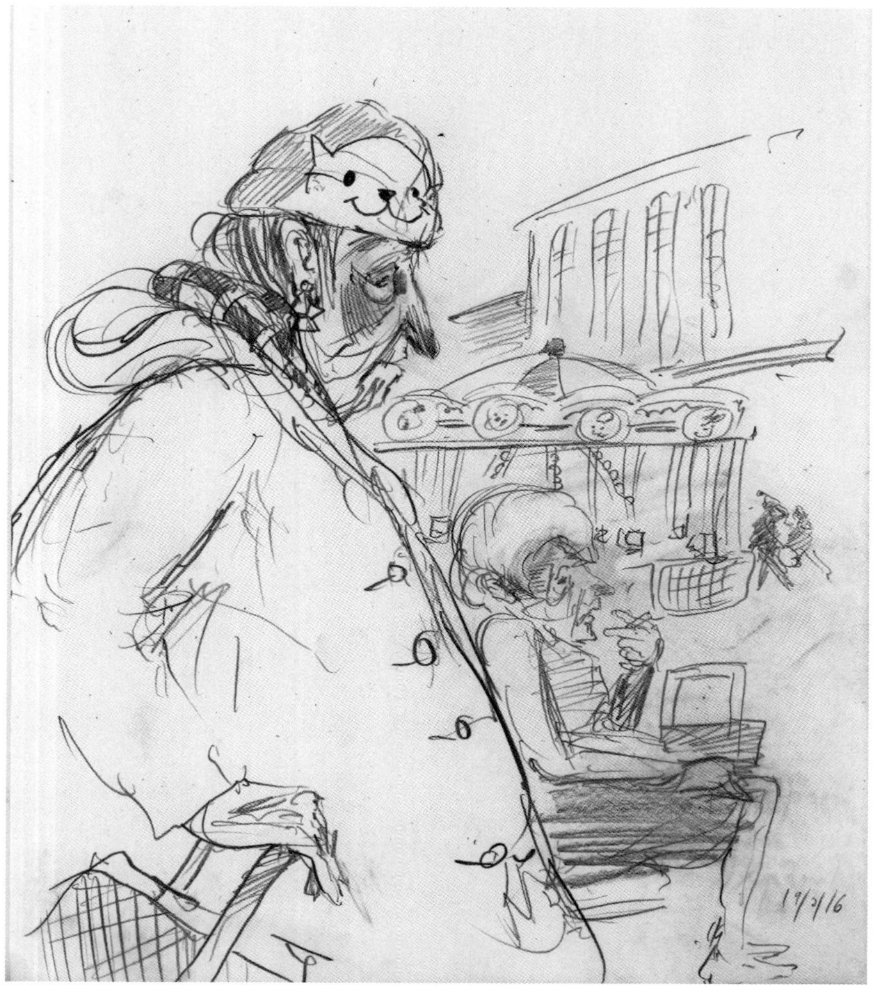

Figure 21 Woman with kitty hat, Portsmouth, 2016.
Source: Louis Netter

therefore it is as idiosyncratic and personal as the machinations of one's mind. It is also, as Berger has noted, as temporal.

Experience of drawing, experience of place

As established above, the act of drawing is essentially an act of thinking. What the reportage artist thinks, believes and projects onto his or her subject results in the ultimate shape of form. For my own work, as seen above, my own thoughts, prejudices and on-the-spot revelations infuse the work with subjectivities that come through in the stylistic flourishes which define the subjects. When I am on a more planned and considered reportage journey, such as my journey to Hamburg in 2017, I engage with my own ideas and preconceptions of place as a way of establishing and confronting what I already know or feel, or what I think I know or feel. This passage explores some thoughts I had as I flew over Germany and how this thinking sets the stage for the drawing to come.

> When we neared Hamburg, I looked down through the few clouds and saw the fairy tale pitched rooves of the large detached homes. Germany holds a unique fascination for me. I distinctly remember my first trip to Munich when I was a student and a serious fan of the work of George Grosz. Grosz distilled much of the German spirit and character in his work and confirmed my belief in drawing as a record of complex textures and character. I also thought of the German people as shadow dwellers. Under the darkness of their own violent history but also brave in confronting that history and learning from the past. I saw this myself in the museum at Dachau and the Topography of Terror museum in Berlin on the site of the former SS and Stasi headquarters. Both raw and unvarnished historical records were on display with appropriate context. The terror was real and it was a warning to the German people of successive generations and the world. These, I believe, are some of the most important sites in the world.

This very difficult history inevitably frames a view of Germany today but aspects of that shadow can be seen in the pre-war work of Grosz. The atmosphere of pre-Nazi Germany s captured well in Grosz's work and reveals that drawings can capture more than the specificities of people and places, they can capture, what Ruskin noted, where things are going. Where the photograph is historical, the drawing can balance itself between the historical, contextual moment, the universal and thematic, and the future, an implicit forecast of what is to come.

Here I am seeing Germany as I first saw it through the eyes of Grosz out also through the lens of its own history. I am also considering what drawing can do in the communication of place and how I might perceive this 'shadow' in my own work. This kind of musing is important to establishing one's existing feelngs but also in preparing for those feelings and presumptions to be challenged by what occurs in situ, which is often provocative and surprising, even in subtle ways.

The next drawing and passage from a trip to Gunwharf Quays in Portsmouth in 2017 reveal how the subject, an older woman, and her environment play off each other and form the true content of the image. Considering the lack of context in this particular piece it is near impossible that the wider meanings explored in the reflection could be surmised by a viewer. However, this passage reveals an intimate connection with the environment when drawing and how

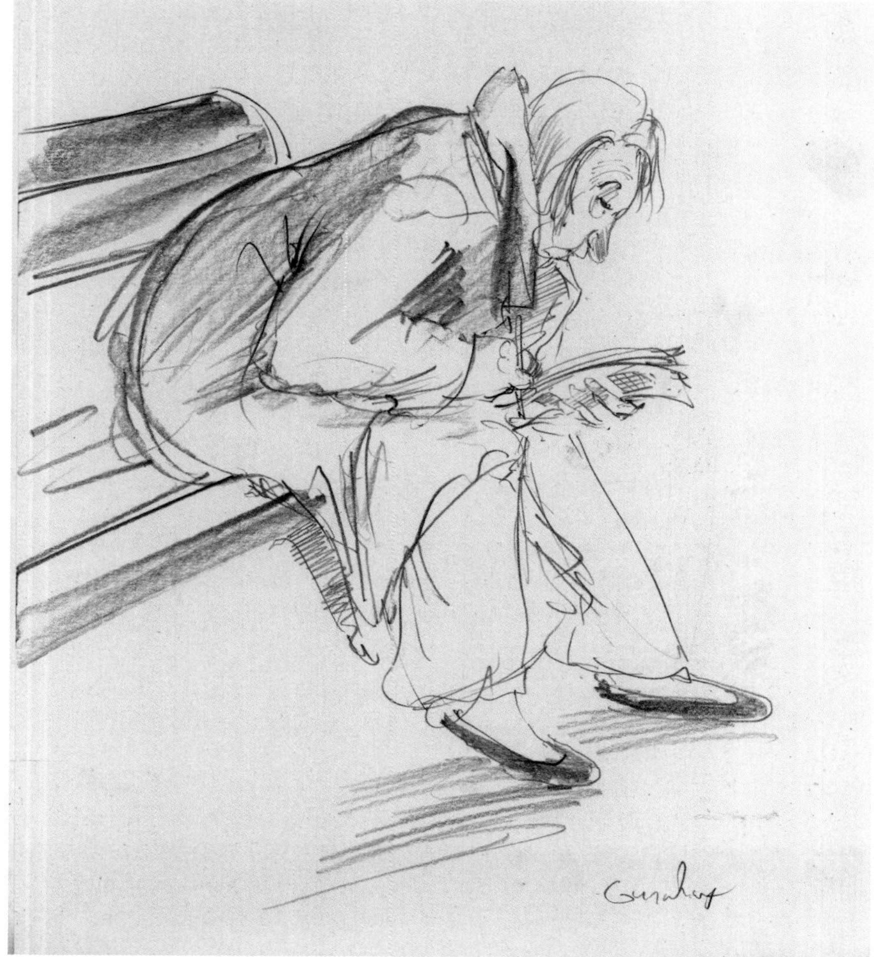

Figure 22 Gunwharf Quays, Portsmouth, 2016.
Source: Louis Netter

these musings, for the artist, cement the interest in sustaining a drawing (see Figure 22).

This next drawing was done near Spinnaker tower, a strange purposeless monument that looks vaguely like a sail but also, from a certain angle, as noted by several locals, like a man weeing into the Solent. There is a line of wooden benches right by a docking area in which some very nice schooner boats are moored. Behind the benches are the big bars and restaurants with large outdoor seating and beyond that, the retail stores of Gunwharf Quays. This woman on the bench was hunched over in this fashion and it appeared to me a perfect opportunity to draw. I was able to draw her almost directly from observation as she was engrossed in what she was doing and I was in a particularly good perch for anonymous observation. I was able to see and capture this large gesture that went from the top of her head, around her rear and under her knee. She could have been doing this on her kitchen table but instead she is out here, with the rest of us, being in the sun, being together. Besides her obviously characterful face, she was a wonderful oddity in that she was defying the expectation of the location that was, in some ways, to bask in the glory of the vista. They are little planned moments of observance and reflection. My instincts were sharp today and little observed moments like her raised heel (in concentration perhaps) on her right foot put together this narrative of urban bench sitting.

What is notable here is the way in which the central subject is defined by her location and her private activity and also other bench dwellers and the act of sitting at a bench as an activity that is itself meaningful. Related to these kinds of considerations is caricature and the way in which subjects are categorized and relate to each other through their symbolic function. Gombrich, quoting William Hogarth, noted his intention to 'learn the language of objects' and 'if possible find a grammar to them' (Gombrich, 1972, p. 349). This relates to the training of the artist to better understand people and forms for the flexible application of them in caricature but it relates closely to my own practice. The classification and assessment of drawn subjects as 'types' reflect a wider social categorization, sharing the method of the caricaturist but with less of the pure fabrication. Additionally, the caricature often contains an impromptu response to the salient features of his or her subject, very much like the reportage artist. Writer Werner Hofmann notes, 'When the artist, at the invention of caricature, first thought of the fascinating possibility of inventing forms in graphic improvisation and transforming them step by step, he laid the foundation for a process that is now the justification for the artistic act: the drawing that draws itself' (Hofmann, 1957, p. 55). The 'drawing that draws itself' can be seen in multiple ways but for my own reportage practice, it relates to the way in which a gesture (as noted above) unlocks a drawing and how a strong creative impulse (often inspired by an emblematic subject) can make for a quick rendering. The capture of a person in the simplest, most economical and quickest manner is often said to have 'practically drawn itself'. Beyond my own work, other reportage artists report that their interest in the act is on-the-spot invention and this is clearly related to the methods and approach of the cartoonist, particularly in the exploratory stage.

The passage below was the final drawing done during the Schlagermove festival in Hamburg in 2017 (although it was not the last drawing I did in Hamburg). It highlights a cartoonist's eye for identifying absurdities and reveals

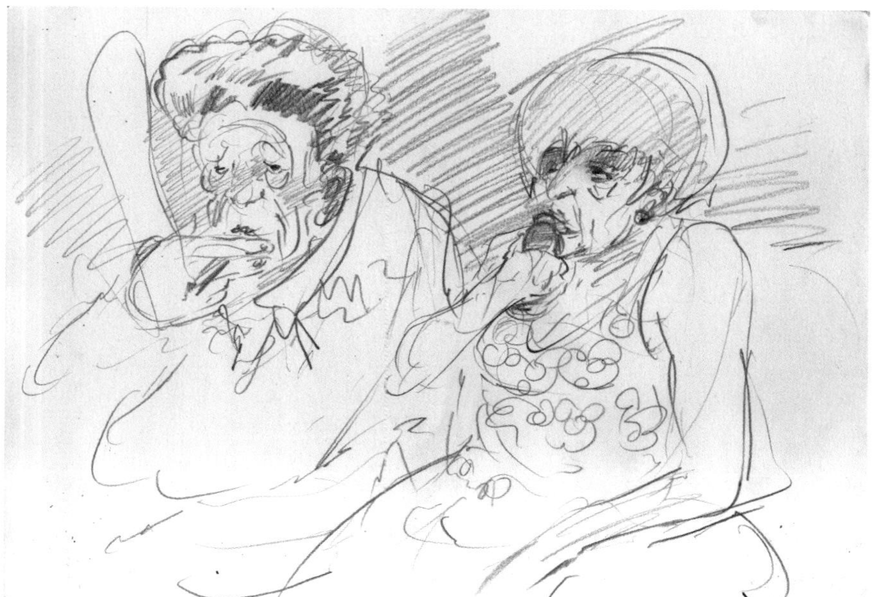

Figure 23 Worn out, Schlagermove, Hamburg, 2017.
Source: Louis Netter

my own interest in subjects as part of a wider narrative that is assembled, in a random way, in situ (see Figure 23).

I walked further up the Reeperbahn and saw more carnage. More exhausted souls who had indulged too much and looked like they were dreaming for their beds. I spotted this couple and was compelled to draw them. Unlike before, with crowds thinning in the closed off centre of the street, I was able to draw with somewhat less crowded interest. I drew this couple practically from direct observation and I feel like it was a success. He looked like a tired clown and his deeply lined face was full of character. Here the quick execution of the drawing enabled some strong abbreviation and his character and face was achieved with great economy. What is striking in such a drawing is how the face takes its essential form in so few lines. His strong cheekbones and deflated balloon cheeks reveal a man who is a heavy smoker and perhaps drinker. The lines of the face are deep and sculptural and the little dark dots for his eyes capture his hollow, drunken stare. She is more simply rendered with a beak nose and her arm seemingly supporting herself on her handbag. They were sitting on a curb like me and behind them the party was still in full swing in the bars. This drawing is an appropriate end to Schlagermove and I realized that although the day held such great visual spectacle and colour, I was, as usual, drawn to the human story. The human story inscribed on the faces in the crowd. Also, it felt like it took me the entire day to find this iconic couple that really captured the day. The absurd clowns washed up and spent.

What this drawing demonstrates, like many previous drawings, is that the tensions within reportage are key to its sustaining interest for the artist and the viewer. The primary tensions are between resolved and unclosed indicative forms, objective, direct observation, and indulgent extension, even fabrication. As noted above, these tensions are also reflected and exploited in the aesthetic of the sketch which, by virtue of its seemingly hurried production, is perceived as a correspondent image. Highly resolved forms (such as those found in my drawings) are often viewed by reportage artists as proof of departure from observation and the prettified forms are less honest because they hide the struggle of direct recording. For my own reportage drawing, the desire to resolve the image is not to depart into pure illustration, divorced of the rigour of direct recording, rather it is a struggle to achieve what I feel I have seen (a subject which has more than likely moved on or that I can't, for logistical reasons, draw directly). I am therefore more interested in the intangible properties of the subject, the emotive aspects, than the purely objective. For my own work, the reportage drawing is a proposition. It proposes that what I have drawn I have seen and hope to engage the viewer in the textures of that experience. The resolve of the image towards greater competior is a desire to exchange as much of my vision to enable the viewer's full participation in that experience. This experience, as noted above and as seen in the image of the bewildered revellers, is intended to express, above all, a sentiment. It is also a narrative moment. Baudelaire's appreciation of the art of Daumier sums up what I and many reportage artists seek to achieve in their work through a combination of an observational, subjective knowledge of subjects and applied commentary through stylistic means. Baudelaire noted:

> Look through his works, and you will see parading before your eyes all that a great city contains of living monstrosities, in all their fantastic and thrilling reality. There can be no item of the fearful, the grotesque, the sinister or the farcical in its treasury, by Daumier knows it. The live and starving corpse, the plump and well-filled corpse, the ridiculous troubles of the home, every little stupidity, every little pride, every enthusiasm, every despair of the bourgeois – it is all there. (Baudelaire & Mayne, 2006, p. 177)

For my own work, the selections in situ tell a narrative which is skewed by my own thematic inclinations. My own reportage drawings could never deliver a holistic impression of a place but they could, quite effectively, capture an aspect and exploit that aspect for deeper consideration. While objective truth is rarely a desire or possibility for reportage drawing, the material of art itself points elsewhere. Dewey notes:

> The imagination, by means of art, makes a concession to sense in employing its materials, but nevertheless uses sense to suggest underlying ideal truth. Art is thus a way of having the substantial cake of reason while also enjoying the sensuous pleasure of eating it. (Dewey, 2005, p. 269)

The graphic construct

My own graphic construct can thus be mapped as in Table 2.

Conclusion

My own graphic construct reveals that the demands of the act of reportage drawing make construction, fabrication and stylistic indulgence essential to the capture of all the textures of experience that I aim to impart. Because my work is less anchored to the purely responsive observational approach of other contemporary reportage artists like Gary Embury, my work explores more thematic material and the drawing s marshalled to depict provocative ideas as much as it is to attest to its own production. Like all drawing, the reportage drawing cannot be seen in isolation from its maker. As Tania Kovats notes, 'when we look at drawings ... we are witnessing something being created at no further than arm's reach, and can often see the moment passing or thought emerging, right there on the page' (Kovats, 2005, p. 8).

For my own reportage drawing and orientation to the act, a greater acknowledgement of individual artistic subjectivity is key and a move from the dogma of direct observation towards the merger of intentions and thinking that evolve in the act. As Kovats notes, 'drawing mediates between two states of mind' and the 'picture is the portrait of a process'. In referring to a Rembrandt drawing of a girl sleeping, she notes 'its subject's unconsciousness reminds us of Rembrandts own unconscious; that what we are seeing played out on paper is a fantasy. In a sense, the subject of *A Girl Sleeping* isn't the girl at all but Rembrandt's desire to draw her, with all that implies' (Kovats, 2005, p. 201).

Table 2 *Author's graphic construct*

Drawing	Experience	Assessment
'Tenor' and 'topic'	**Experience of drawing**	**Fidelity to the observed**
• Observation is laden with commentary and elements of caricature are employed to heighten and transform observed subjects towards symbolic 'types'.	• A reflective experience which condenses thought and action. • Wide-ranging thoughts about people and places occur. • The drawing occurs out of a felt attraction to the subject as a symbolic 'type'.	• Observation is key to success, however, not through direct recording necessarily. • Some drawing is done from memory but the success of the drawing is still anchored to strong impressions and the observed subject.
Drawn effects	**Experience in situ**	**Assessment of intentions**
• The sketch is the prevailing aesthetic but is refined. • Overdrawing pushes the sketch towards greater refinement.	• A desire to keep hidden and be highly selective of subjects who are evocative of place.	• Related to the rendering of what I feel were the most essential qualities of the subject. • Equally desirable if they point to a wider narrative about society itself.
Aesthetic influences	**Experience of place**	**Graphic qualities**
• George Grosz, Lautrec, De Crécy, Tardi, to name a few • Artists who are economic in their line and infuse their work with commentary. **Aims and intentions** • To communicate the sense of place and capture a sentiment. • My aim for the drawing is to render the emotive content of people and places.	• Drawn to the downtrodden. • Looking for people and places which challenge perception and confront the viewer with harsh realities. • An interest in people on the fringes but equally in the banality of everyday life. • Some politically motivated themes emerge.	• Looking for drawing that has enough resolution to connect to the specificity of character but equally has the economy and speed in rendering that attest to responsive observation. • The graphic marks should draw the viewer in through the impression (whether entirely real or not) of a directly drawn and experienced subject that reflects a social or political ill.
Graphic Construct		

8

THE GRAPHIC CONSTRUCT – GARY EMBURY

The reportage drawing of Gary Embury is identified by its immediate urgent and honest recording that looks and feels as if it has emerged from the moment or moments of its making. For Embury, his own graphic construct is about the merger of drawing and thought as they occur without premeditation and this results in a construct which actively avoids the prettifying stylistic aims and intentions. Of course, stylistic concerns exist (more below) but they are marginal to the larger aims of the work, which is the mirrored reflection of direct experience in the responsive marks of the drawing.

The experience in situ is key to Embury, as he sees the sketchbook page as a palimpsest, a record of the shifting activity on the ground. For this interview, Embury was filmed and interviewed at the protest against Trump in London on 13 July 2018. Watching the artist work, it was clear that his orientation to the place was as a conduit of experience. Susan Owens quotes the mid-twentieth-century artist Peter Lanyon assessing his work as 'a re-creation of experience in immediacy, a process of being, made now' (Owens, 2013, p. 174). This aligns with the aims of Embury who seeks graphic immediacy in his work and distinguishes the practice of reportage drawing from other more refined works in both form and function. For Embury, the desire to 'make good drawing' is a dangerous one in reportage as it detracts from momentary observation and response, and his assessment of the success or failure of the drawing is in its evocation of his experience and not some artistic valuation (although there are some overlapping concerns here and a self-awareness regarding the aesthetic approach).

Embury engages in reportage drawing for the connection to the first thoughts of the sketch and what that reveals of his own experience in situ. For Embury, there is submission to experience in his work and, inevitably, a submission to the whims of his own drawing. Art Historian David Rosand notes of the moving inclinations of line as 'the line itself begins to assert a certain will of its own, to challenge the guiding control of the hand, urging its own agenda. Out of that tension there can arise the most creative conflict, as the drawing hand, which may have become complacent in its purpose, is forced to decision.' He further notes, 'the options available to the hand may lie anywhere between enforcing representational responsibility upon its own course and yielding to the momentum of line itself' (Rosand, 2002, p. 12). This conflict and struggle are appealing to Embury who, while actively resisting the inclination towards artistic resolve and maintaining the rawness of the immediate sketch, is very much interested in the resulting qualities of the economic line in his work. Additionally, for Embury, the energy and rhythm of those lines encapsulate experience more than pure representation. What results in the seemingly representational form of reportage drawing is something abstract, the capture of the dynamics of people, architecture and movement in situ.

Extending the above, Embury's work can be seen to be related to ideational drawing, particularly as it is often defined. In a chapter called 'Ideational Drawing' in Steven Garner's influential book *Writing on Drawing*, Terry Rosenberg notes: 'it is in investigating the articulation of knowing and un-knowing, in the way they are jointed and through this jointing consequently speak, that one can begin to develop a critical appreciation of ideational drawing' (Garner, 2008, p. 112). The work of Embury is related to this 'knowing and un-knowing' as he avoids the crux of memory drawing and approaches the task with self-imposed fidelity to the whims of thought and action as one in his drawing. What Dewey calls the 'inertia of habit' is what Embury is seeking to elude and find, as Dewey notes of true artistic development and originality as being 'the quickened expansion of experience'. Dewey concludes: 'art departs from what has been understood and ends in wonder' (Dewey, 2005, p. 281).

Drawn effects

The sketch as an aesthetic property and as a methodology is key to the work of Embury. Because of the features of the sketch or first thoughts, the 'open form' of the sketch reveals, as Rosand notes, the 'character of the hand, the trait of the artist' (Rosand, 2002, p. 21). Because Embury's self-declared intention is to draw without artifice, he approaches his reportage drawing like an athlete, limbering up through practice to settle into more confident responsive drawing. The raw forms are vibrant, economical and even chaotic as they are laid on the paper and Embury works quickly and deliberately. Artist and art historian Stephen Farthing notes of the topographic drawings of Turner and his direct drawing method that Turner was 'set on automatic' and 'to draw in this way, the recorder must lock their hand into a perfectly calibrated relationship with their eye, so that as the eye works its way across the landscape, the hand and pencil automatically follow, leaving the pencils trace' (Garner, 2008, p. 146). The character of Embury's hand is a mélange of continuous line, short abrupt marks and overlapping action. Like the sketch itself, it involves us in its creation and it is participatory. Rosand notes: 'on a fundamental level, it (drawing) involves us, as viewers, in the kinesthetics of the act of drawing: its qualities of direction, velocity, weight, its rhythm, pace, and inflection stand as permanent trace of the movement of the artist's hand' (Rosand, 2002, p. 16).

Embury noted that he preferred Bonnard's concept of 'first sight' to first thoughts and relayed that reportage drawing for him was defined by struggle, the struggle to get what he sees down on paper. Embury noted that the reportage artist has to 'edit on the fly' and he notes, 'you must give into that first sight image'. Here he is talking about the honesty of the image and, again related to his desire to purge the drawing of contrivances, he is consciously forcing himself to submit to first impressions. What this reveals is a desire to both expose the direct aesthetic of the sketch and eliminate the interference of a doubting, commenting or indulgent mind. This can be seen in Embury's contention that 'the minute you think "is this a pretty drawing" you are screwed'. For Embury, the struggle and labour of working in situ is manifest in his drawing and he is consciously avoiding 'good' drawing for more direct responsive work. Embury has surrendered in his reportage work to the first thought and the unpredictable results, hence the reference to the athlete preparing for the performance. Embury notes: 'I don't like not doing a successful drawing but I am not sure what a successful drawing is anymore.'

The struggle for Embury is a critical aspect of his graphic construct. He notes the distinct separation between his more formal academic training and drawing and his reportage work. He identifies that he is actively resisting the concerns and traditional orientation of the draughtsman even saying he is 'schizo' maintaining two separate working methods. For Embury, the aesthetic of the sketch is not cultivated but more a direct result of the activity of looking and drawing. He notes about the avoidance of refinement: 'A good drawing can stop you from moving beyond that aesthetic. It can stop you from believing in the fact that it was done in the moment.' Relating this to my own graphic construct, there is a similar awareness of the impression of immediacy in the sketch and, equally, the extent to which that can, through overindulgence, take us further away from the moment.

The extent to which reportage drawing can, through its facture, transport us to the moments of its making is key for Embury and his own assessment of a successful drawing (avoiding the qualification of 'good' drawing). Embury notes:

Yeah, if I look at a drawing and it leaves me cold in terms of looking at the original event … it might be successful on one level, an aesthetic, academic drawing level but for me, as I've said before, I really love the work of certain artists who some people might say, 'that's not a great drawing it's a nasty drawing.' I quite like nasty drawings but they are more about the moment … I think a drawing that looks like that person was there, has done it on the front line.

Here the drawing is valued for its rawness, for its testament to lived experience as recorded through drawing. Taussig explores this aspect of evocation in drawing and how the drawing is doing something different than capturing 'reality'. He notes, 'the drawings come across as fragments that are suggestive of a world beyond, a world that does not have to be explicitly recorded and is in fact all the more "complete" because it cannot be completed. In pointing away from the real, they capture something invisible and auratic that makes the thing depicted worth depicting' (Taussig, 2011, p. 13). Embury's 'nasty drawings' can be likened to the abbreviated drawing Taussig speaks of here (his own amateur scrawls) and how we, as viewers, seek closure in the drawing but not 'completeness'. The delicate balance that Embury is trying to achieve is to render what he is seeing in the moment through direct means and get out of the way of his own drawing, avoiding the interruptive desire to refine. Chronicler of the caricature, Werner Hofmann's statement about how the caricature can be a 'drawing that draws itself' is relevant to Embury's work as the drawing has a kind of autonomy, reflecting the 'time-based' nature of the act and the unfolding, unedited, unmediated move towards resolution.

The identification of types and the navigation of the in situ environment is consistently of-the-moment for Embury, as he is assembling his images from 'first sights'. He notes: 'My kids in the past when we were on holiday would always play a game where they try and spot my muse before I spot them. It generally tended to be a fairly large male figure.' Embury doesn't see this as interruptive to an honest rendering of what he is seeing and experiencing and rather sees these types as part of a conscious effort to render something interesting in the seemingly mundane. Embury notes: 'There is always an element of caricature. It's just getting a balance of the two. A balance between figurative drawing and exaggerating certain qualities. Sometimes that comes from the figure moving. So, some of it is drawn literally from memory.' We can see here that even when there is an acknowledged departure into caricature, the methodology is consistent and direct observation is central to it. The elements of caricature can be more accurately described in the work of Embury as a form of condensation, an impromptu mark which through necessity (moving subject) or response departs from or accentuates what was seen. As Embury notes, 'I have a terrible memory. Yes, I don't want to draw it from memory. I want to be in it. To be part of the moment. Otherwise, you end up being very good at memory drawing but not being about what it was like at the moment.' As Rosand notes of a Rembrandt sketch: 'rapidly sketched; rapidly felt' (Rosand, 2002, p. 233).

Tenor and topic

As previously defined, the terms 'tenor' and 'topic' are Rawson's attempt to explore the duality inherent in drawing, that is, the subject and the rendering of the subject in media. For Embury, the 'tenor' and 'topic' are enmeshed as his subject and his rendering of the subject testifies to one encountering the other, in-the-moment. Embury's drawing and his orientation to his subject are aligned as he is not seeking anything in the drawing outside of direct observation and recording. This kind of unfolding is well illustrated in the following passage while Gary was drawing:

> At the moment I am just kind of interested in the rhythms within the crowds and then just … I think when you look at a scene even if you're not drawing it, you are picking out some things that you remember. I am doing that with drawing so it's not an accurate view of the scene for me it's just little cues I take. Like I just spotted a CMG sign and it strikes me as a weird sign in the melange. You have lots of signs and Trump puppets being held up (see Figures 24–27). And then this guy here in front of me, I like how he has suddenly got up. Right where you have someone literally blocking your way.

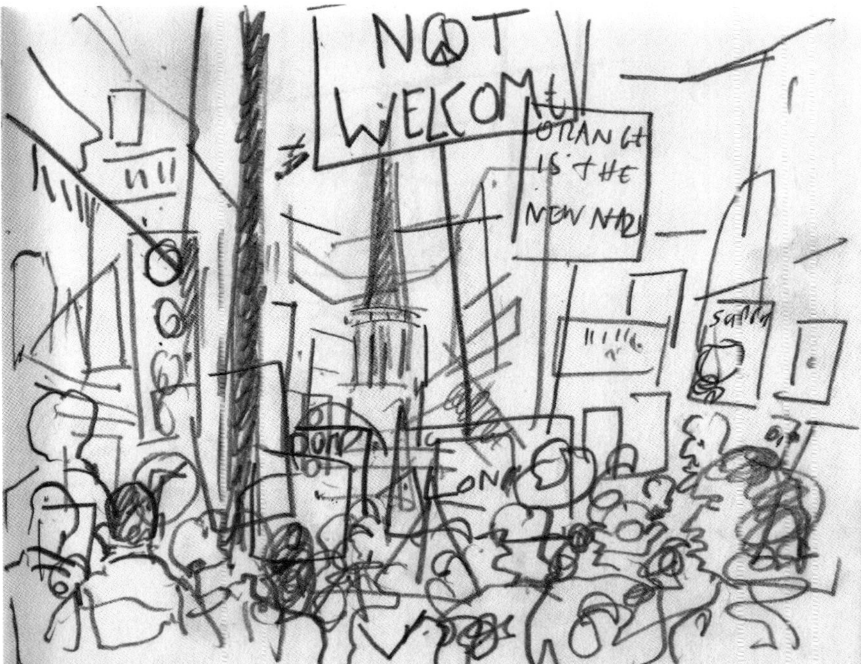

Figure 24 Signs at the Trump rally, London, 2018.
Source: Gary Embury

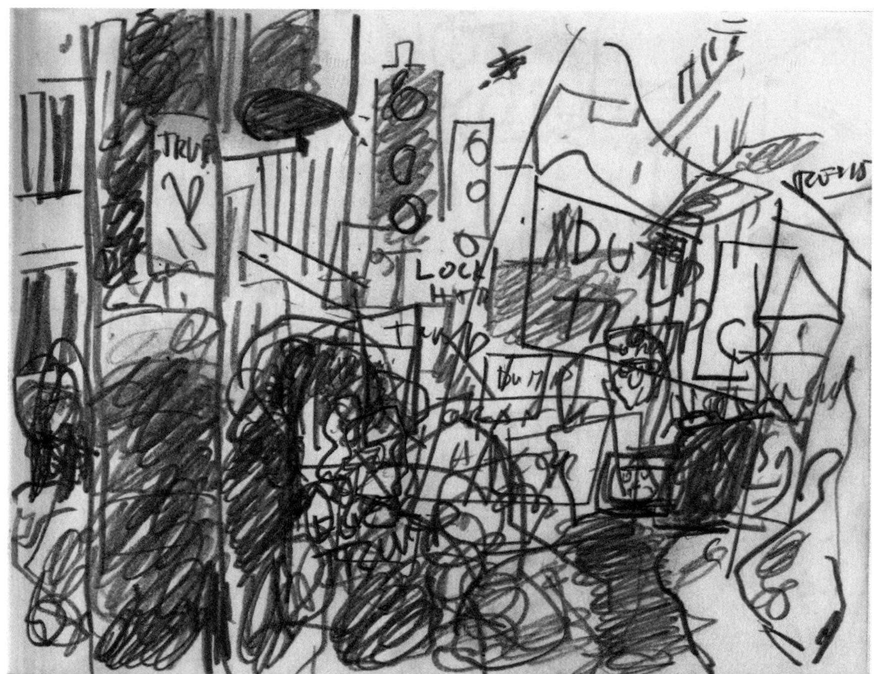

Figure 25 Trump rally, London, 2018.
Source: Gary Embury

Embury, while encountering the live environment, is making on-the-spot judgments about what comes into the drawing and what piques his interest. As semiotician Roland Barthes notes, 'the creation of the painter or the dramatist lies not in the choice of a subject but in the choice of the pregnant moment, in the choice of the tableau' (Barthes & Heath, 1977, p. 76). Embury is continually drawing and over-drawing so that his tableau is a record of overlapping lines and attests to his own 'sense of excitement' and 'sense of the occasion'. In terms of the 'pregnant moment', Embury likes to anchor his drawings to something to contain the 'spaghetti bolognese of people'. Still, the drawings and their intent (as expressed by Embury) is to snapshot all of the activity seen. He made a reference to the nineteenth-century French photographer Etienne Jules Marey and his multiple exposure images. Embury saw some affinity with that work and his drawings and noted, 'it's not about actual figures but it's about the rhythm of the event'. Here Embury acknowledges that his drawings are, due to the layered surface of his paper, caccphonous and, as a result, abstract to some degree. As Tim Ingold notes, 'indeed the apprehension of movement, and its gestural re-enactment, is fundamental to the practice of drawing' (Ingold, 2016, p. 132).

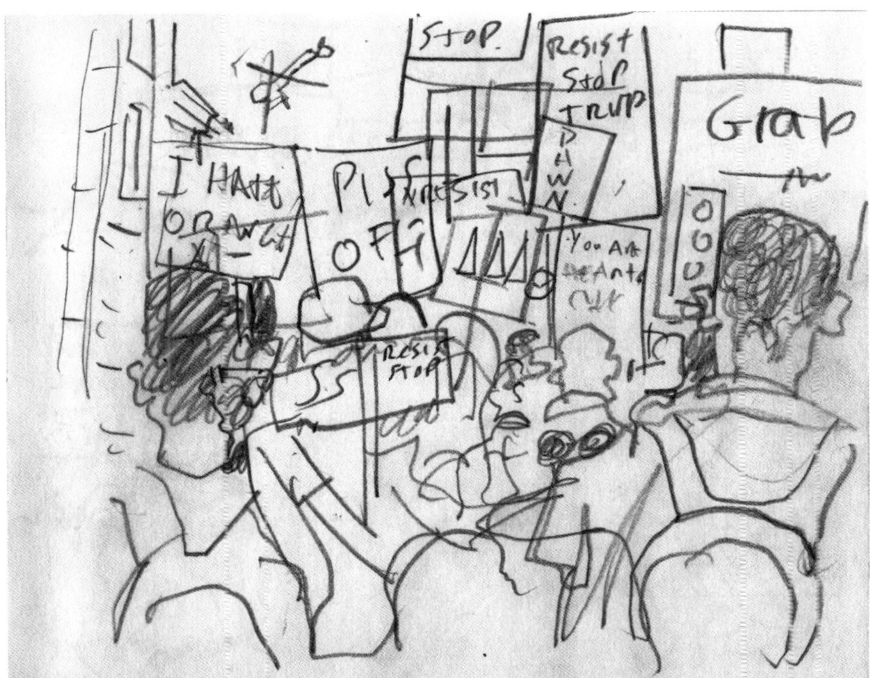

Figure 26 Trump rally, signs and people, London, 2018.
Source: Gary Embury

Ultimately, Embury's work reveals the struggle to capture fluid reality and the way in which marks abbreviate a variety of subjects. As Berger notes, 'one tends to forget that the visual is always the result of an unrepeatable, momentary encounter. Appearances, at any given moment, are a construction emerging from the debris of everything which has previously appeared' (Berger, 2008, p. 67). Relating to Embury's work, the subject in flux and the limitations of direct recording crystallize this view of the visual and make his drawing a vivid trace of in-the-moment perception, inevitably relying on past perceptual knowledge and developed strategies towards the rendering of forms.

Experience of drawing, experience of place

The Trump rally on 13 July was held in central London near Oxford Circus and I first met with Gary Embury at the Photographer's gallery just around the corner. For Embury, the demonstration was a chance to capture a 'spectacle' and although I know his political beliefs were aligned with the protest, his interest

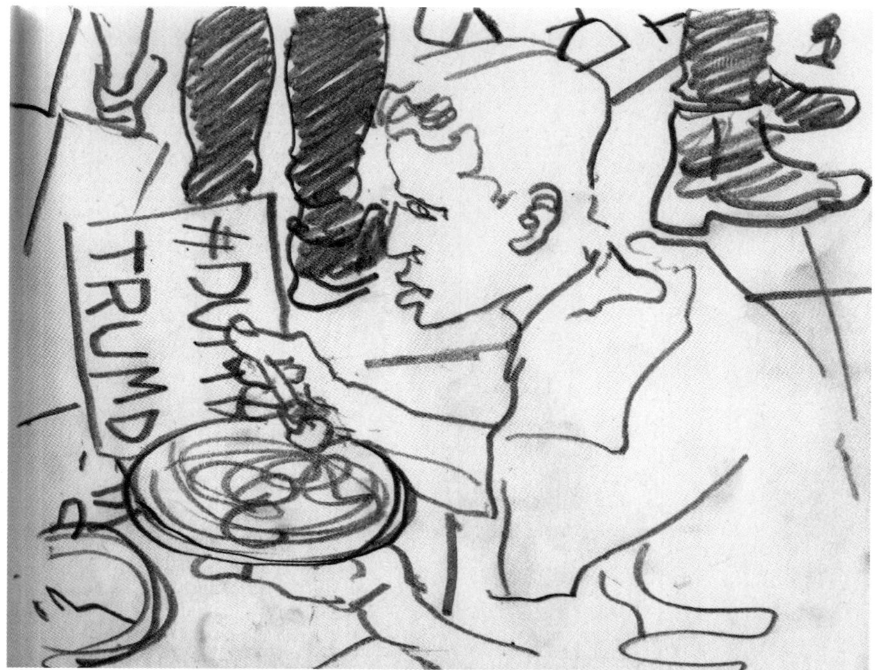

Figure 27 Sitting and eating, Trump rally, London, 2018.
Source: Gary Embury

in the event was to 'allow the situation to develop' and 'being forced into a position you are not familiar with'. Referring to a drawing some years back, Embury noted:

> I was drawing here a couple of years ago at Christmas during the mad Christmas rush. It was only afterwards I looked at the drawing because I caught a little bit of typography and instead of it saying hello kitty it said hell. And that was subliminal, I didn't realize it was happening. The text was on a bus and it was in fact hell.

The 'hell' that emerges from Embury's drawing relates to Tuan's (see Chapter 5) notion of time and place and how over time we develop a deeper understanding of place (see Figure 28). He notes:

> The visual quality of an environment is quickly tallied if one has the artist's eye. But the 'feel' of a place takes longer to acquire. It is made up of experiences, mostly fleeting and undramatic, repeated day after day and over the span of years. It is a unique blend of sights, sounds, and smells, a unique harmony of natural and artificial rhythms such as times of sunrise and sunset, of work

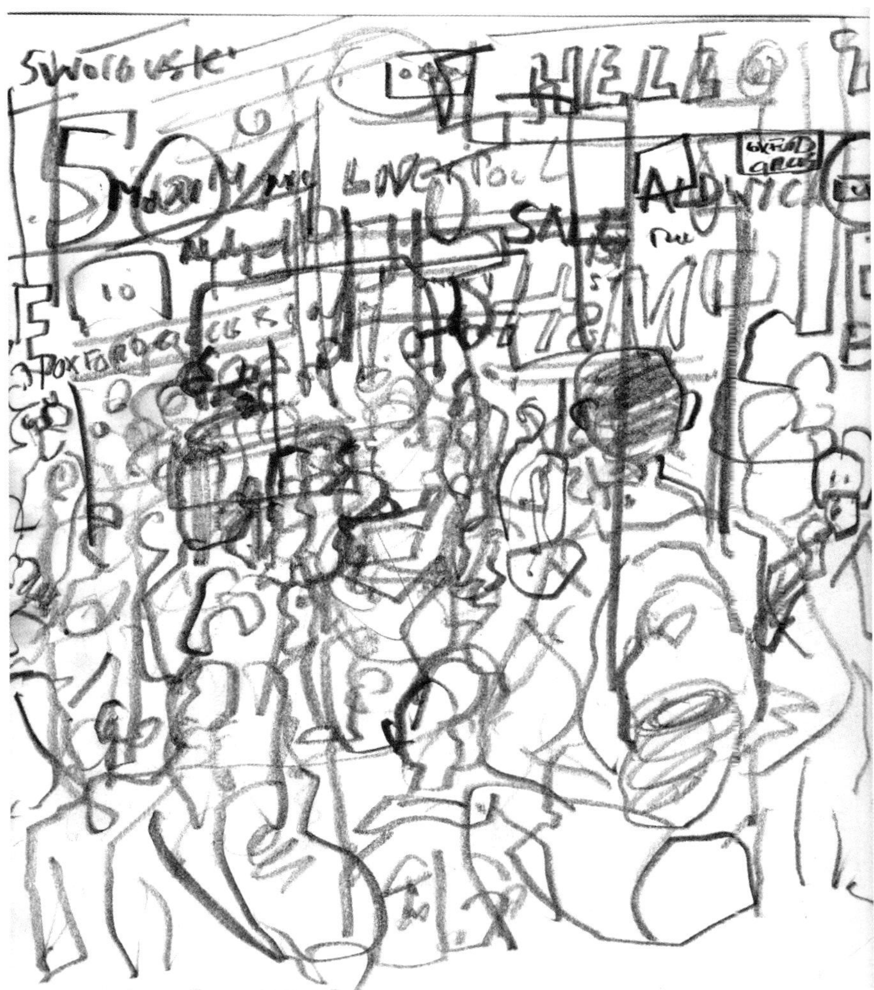

Figure 28 Hell, London.
Source: Gary Embury

and play. The feel of a place is registered in one's muscles and bones. Tuan, 1977, pp. 183, 184)

Embury's work, through his direct method, condenses many of these fleeting impressions and comprises a representation of place which can, when successful, evoke an intimate encounter and understanding of place through the punctuations of responsive lines and marks, themselves momentary and susceptive.

During the rally and our movement from Portland Street to Trafalgar Square, Embury drew quickly without stopping. He was responding to the ever-changing environment and his pace and output were impressive. Large signs with anti-Trump messages, bands, onlookers, filmmakers, costumed people, the police all blended in a noisy, chaotic but joyous crowd. Embury noted that he preferred an elevated vantage point from which to draw and survey but on the day, he enjoyed being within the tangle of people. Quoting Jill Gibbon, he said: 'Don't be a camera. The camera takes in everything. It's not editing anything apart from the crop.' While Embury states that his drawings are inevitably subjective, his aim is to project honesty and his self-imposed limitations enforce a fidelity to what he has chosen to record. Through this and through Embury's dogmatic approach, the drawings speak to the energy, chaos and noise of the event in a way that a more deliberative approach may not. What Embury captures is the direct response to stimuli that has the visual equivalence of jazz improvisation. Art historian Joshua Taylor, speaking of the Impressionists and how their vision was a challenge to the public, notes:

> There is a vast difference between knowing the form of an object from past experience and extended examination and seeing the object in its momentary environment as if never seen before, affected by the particular light and surrounding shapes and colours. The artists, (the Impressionists) fascinated with this immediate perception, tried to push memory aside in order to see everything with a fresh eye. (Taylor, 1957, p. 149)

Embury calls his drawings 'accessible', and his aim is for them to be read, as they appear, as a direct response to the environment. He also acknowledged that the roughness or 'nasty' quality of his drawn record can challenge notions of 'good' drawing and therefore create a barrier for reception and reading by the wider public. Gombrich, quoting Roger Fry, notes:

> The message of a work of art is generally immensely complex, summarizing as I believe a whole mass of experience hidden in the artist's subconscious. And this complexity renders it probable that each receiver only picks up a part of the total message ... many people possess only very imperfect receiving instruments, instruments that can only respond to extremely violent emissions of a crude and elementary kind. (Gombrich, 1994, p. 56)

Embury's intention to deny comfort, indulgent artistry and memory drawing has resulted in a method which, somewhat ironically, makes for a heightened confrontation with his own aesthetic. His professed desire to purge all prettiness has resulted in a graphic language that presents a greater challenge (albeit a rewarding one) for the viewer and a more abstracted sense of his subjects. Embury acknowledges the positive qualities of his on-the-spot drawings but regularly alludes to the need for greater context and a sense that perhaps the drawing is not enough. In the 'thoughts from the chair' section in the Falmouth University publication *Witness* which compiled selected writing from a forum on reportage drawing, Embury noted: 'However, a purely visual descriptive approach to drawn reportage may not be enough to expose underlying issues inherent in subjects or locations … drawn reportage, documentary illustration, reportorial drawing or visual journalism all describe the practice of "artist as reporter", author, or subject as storyteller and doesn't just rely on direct "on the spot" observational drawing' (*Witness*, p. 15). Embury furthered this in my interview saying, 'In the future, I am really more interested in researching an event or going with a writer or journalist and producing projects which are maybe multidisciplinary that involve drawing but they really inform people to what the issues are. I think otherwise they are too impenetrable maybe. I think they need context.' Embury's use of the term 'impenetrable' may reveal his awareness of the difficulties among some in the reading of his images and the necessary participation required to decode or unfurl the immediacy of his approach. Embury clearly feels a need to further contextualize his work but this is possibly less about the work itself and more about his aims to move towards more journalistic work.

The graphic construct

Embury's graphic construct can be seen as both a conscious and self-aware move from his more academic approach, and a cultivation of the here and now in his drawing which relates to both an interest in honest imagery and a move aligned with broader trends in drawing practice to challenge notions of 'good drawing'. Artist and writer Deanna Petherbridge identifies this trend in contemporary drawing as, in part, a focus on 'process over design'. Petherbridge notes a move from tradition as a 'breakdown of traditional hierarchies of practice. In their place, looser, hybrid and personalised ways of drawings have become the norm, associated with a suspicion of skill and technical considerations and a fear of literalism, and an avoidance of drawing as a study or interrogative practice rather than an expressive medium' (Petherbridge, 2010, pp. 412, 414). Embury would not reject drawing as an 'interrogative practice', but his suspicion of skill or rather stylistic indulgence is clear, and his practice reflects a methodological move from the intention and design that marks traditional orientations.

At the core of Embury's work and his own professed struggle to rid his drawing of contrivances is the notion of expression and honesty. Expression in art has typically been associated with the expressive characteristics of the work through the artist's rendering. Gombrich notes: 'the work of art as such in other words, was valued as symptom of the artist's state of mind, as an "expression of personality", and this, at once, raised the issue of the genuine *versus* the false expression.' He then notes, 'but have we really a right to equate artistic truth with truthful communication?' (Gombrich, 1994, p. 25). Here, Embury's claim for honesty in his approach to direct recording is challenged by the inherent expressive qualities of his work, intended or not, and that his method highlights the graphic mark and therefore the expressive potential of those marks. These graphic marks are, however, as Embury has intended, stripped of planning and consideration, and stand alone as a reflection of their immediacy. Petherbridge notes of the reappraisal of drawing and appetite for authenticity as '"bad" drawing, *dysgraphia*, in this context becomes a framing semiotic of authenticity that readily signals urban protest or general disaffection, and also acts as the (in) formal envelope that accommodates the multiple material borrowings, mal-juxtapositions and insertions that deliberately flout rules of traditional pictorial organisations' (Petherbridge, 2010. p. 419). While Embury's work is not as wildly transgressive as Basquiat (an artist Petherbridge makes reference to prior to the above quote), there is a stated intention to alter one's approach to drawing and present that drawing as authentic, raw vision. Gombrich noted of the Impressionists that their work 'stands on the watershed between two modes of satisfaction'. The 'pictorial symbol' is 'matched ever more closely with appearances' and marks 'the beginning of an openly regressive art, of primitivism' (Gombrich, 1994, p. 41). The methodology of Embury, in rejecting the indulgence and stylistic flourishes of more refined representation (which would also take him further away from the moment and his subject(s)), creates work that, like the Impressionists, testifies to the operations of vision and the material means to render it absent of expressive flourishes. The 'regressive pleasure' of Embury's work is his conscious desire, as manifest in his drawing, to deny his own capabilities in favour of the limitations of direct observation, resulting in raw, direct forms which guide us through the active process of looking and drawing. Embury notes:

> You've got to be prepared for people to see warts and all really. I think as soon as you start worrying about if it's a good drawing um … and you know there are other people that are so good with this kind of drawing, so good with it, so slick with it, but sometimes you can be a bit too clever.

Embury identified several artists who he sees as maintaining this perceived integrity in their work and relishes the way in which those drawings might be deemed as 'nasty' by some. He identifies Topolski's drawings of the Harlem riots as a good example of difficult drawings that are 'hard to read' but are vividly evocative. In terms of fellow reportage artists, Embury also identifies Linda Kitson and Robert Weaver, both artists who have a seemingly immediate, deliberate and economic line that, particularly with Weaver, feels like traced vision. Embury, seeing his work as part of the historical practice of reportage, is interested in what drawing does that the camera does not and yet, he also seeks to retain, as

Table 3 *Gary Embury's graphic construct*

Drawing	Experience	Assessment
'Tenor' and 'topic'	**Experience of drawing**	**Fidelity to the observed**
• Merged through the in-the-moment rendering in situ. • 'Tenor' and 'topic' are methodologically bound.	• The drawing process is an unfolding of observed action. The sketchbook page is a palimpsest.	• Self-governed. Some elements of caricature develop, largely through necessity. • While there is no claim to accuracy, truthful recording within the means of immediate drawing is held to.
Drawn effects	**Experience in situ**	**Assessment of intentions**
• The aesthetic of the sketch reflects the immediacy of the approach. • Highly refined, economical, deliberate, even continuous line pervades the work.	• Typically seeks elevated perch but likes to be a part of the action. • Seeking to make the seemingly ordinary interesting in drawing. • Ultimately, open to what crosses his vision.	• If the drawing becomes too 'pretty' or if it departs into indulgence it is deemed a departure from aims. • Drawings are valued for their evocation of place and the experience of the field of the vision by the artist.
Aesthetic influences	**Experience of place**	**Graphic qualities**
• Reportage artists like Topolski, Weaver and Kitson are most evident influences. • Other influences include London School Painters like Auerbach.	• Place is rendered in the drawing as observed. • Assessment of the location is through the record of the drawing and how that encapsulates the artists' experience on location.	• Artist is aware of the qualities of his drawing but is also courting the unexpected marks that occur as a result of his methodology. This relates to inventive forms as a result of the act and do not weaken his broader methodology. • The graphic qualities are seen as a result of his direct recording process and not a deliberate supplement to his drawing.
Graphic Construct		

much as possible, some element of objective recording in his work. For Embury, his graphic construct is about the act of drawing in direct engagement with one's environment. It is about drawing and vision equally and it seeks to explore how vision is mediated through drawing without explicit artistic aims and through that how we may see the affordances of drawing in the capture of our world.

Embury's graphic construct can thus be mapped as in Table 3.

Conclusion

Embury's graphic construct is the result of his refined methodology which renders his subject(s) through the most direct graphic means. Robert Weaver, who taught at the School of Visual Arts in New York City, was a proponent of observation in his artwork and teaching. Former student and now professor of illustration at Kutztown University in Pennsylvania, Kevin McCloskey remembers many profound utterances from the 'Weave' as he was known. One statement which stuck with McCloskey was 'The artist is the uninvited guest. The kid without a penny and his nose pressed to the glass of the bakery window. Isn't he the only one that really knows the significance of what's inside? Don't you see? You've got to put yourself where you don't belong to have any hope of making art' ('Illustrationclass', 2017). This directly reflects Embury's own contention that 'it is easy to draw things that are in your comfort zone. I want to fight that. Otherwise you end with all of your drawings the same.' He also notes: 'For me, it's an activity for which, like any physical activity, the memory of it comes through having suffered. I quite like the idea of, well, not suffering but the fight and the struggle.' Embury's graphic construct is therefore the expressed desire to seek something new, both graphically and experientially, in a chosen environment and challenge vision and academic training to render something new, honest and evocative.

9
ARTIST SPOTLIGHT – MARIO MINICHIELLO

It is quite difficult to introduce Mario to a wider audience as I know him, respect him and was so significantly influenced by him that I feel our destinies are intertwined. I am sure I am not alone in feeling this as a former student of his and someone caught up in his infectious enthusiasm and dedication to the craft of looking, with every fibre of our being, at the world around us and coming to a greater understanding of our place in it. Mario is larger than life and as you read this interview, you will see the clear alignment in thinking with my own about drawing, the observable world and the steadfast belief in the power and potential of art to make this a better and more humane world.

Mario is a world-renowned artist and academic. He is a widely published illustrator and created reportage drawings for the BBC and *Guardian* newspapers. Additionally, he has produced illustrations for the *Financial Times*, *Amnesty International*, the *Terence Higgins Trust*, *Longmans*, *The Times* and *ITN News* (and many more). He is a professor of the creative industries at the University of Newcastle (AU) and has helmed multiple successful research projects around improving the care and health sector through design and the arts. Mario has a rare and valuable combination of talents and there is no discernible gap between the intensity and passion he puts into his teaching and research, and that which he puts into his charged artwork. His contribution to reportage drawing is twofold: firstly, he has been a highly visible practitioner of the act in the late twentieth century, producing evocative, aesthetically and conceptually challenging work that never plays it safe or relies on convention. As a teacher, he has inspired countless contemporary practitioners and has had a measurable impact on arts education in the UK, fighting to put drawing back in the curriculum and persuasively managing to keep it there. As a former student, I feel immensely lucky to have had a teacher like him and to have found the clarity in my thinking about what the simple act of drawing can tell us about this confusing and brutal world.

What Mario demonstrates in this interview is that reportage drawing (or drawing in general) is not an isolated act outside of other acts of thinking. It is a manifestation of deep thought and looking, it is a uniquely human multimodal process.

Mario

In my experience Drawing at its height of engagement forces us to develop and apply our own philosophical 'angle' or 'take' on the world we see (what academics call ontology). My philosophical approach is as a 'pragmatist and relativist'. I am aware that my work reflects my individual experience of the world (my 'habitus' interpretation). Each person's individual reality (René Descartes's 'I think therefore I am') is socially constructed and reflects the subjective nature of the individual's experience (no reality without a mind as per Creswell & Creswell 2017, Atweh et al. 1998). Within our reality is the search for truth and meaning (no one wants to lead a meaningless life). For me, drawing is a means to seek 'meaning and truth'. I am conscious of how my own bias gives me a particular view (what Gray and Malins termed 'a modified objectivist' and 'subjectivist' epistemology) (Gray & Malins, 2016) and that my work is a continuation of the Dadaist tradition of questioning the status quo and perhaps even advocating for change. Due to the authors' assertion of the primacy of the subjective experience of individuals, experiences that would be outside the realm of the authors' understanding if not for the valuable contributions of others to the research process are considered to involve co-designers or collaborators (Atweh et al. 1998).

It encompasses a range of thoughts and feelings and can bring many new insights and revelations about the observable world and what symbolic referents can be gleaned from being wholly open to the act of seeing and feeling. The primacy of the drawing process is its ability to allow the artist to absorb the subjective experience of individuals, experiences that would be outside the realm of the artist's understanding if not for the interaction and understanding of others and different experiences. Somehow the drawing process of constant looking, 'layering of many moments' (John Berger) goes beyond surface appearances and into the nucleus of a subject (Minichiello).

This expansive view of drawing has been noted by other reportage artists, notably Felix Topolski, arguably the twentieth century's most visible and prolific reportage practitioner. He noted about Americans after spending a considerable amount of time drawing them:

Americans seemed (only glimpsed then) utterly different: the strut of ostentatious manliness (in dress and manner) compulsive to all – always in 'combat', if not with the enemy, in competition to outdo one another (the

English – at the time – relaxed within their station.) ... they had to sustain themselves building up resentments, hate – love – abstractions – bending towards hysteria. These would be white Americans. (Topolski & Riddell, 1988)

Drawing comes with it a whole collection of other revelations. In this fast world, we have forgotten that there are riches in front of us and that this moment in time, its complexity and confusion, can be better understood by stopping and looking. When looking becomes seeing and seeing become thinking and feeling, we can understand art as not merely a mirror, it is a psychic probe and physical things (including humans) move from the real to the symbolic in the act of drawing. Mario noted in a conference paper entitled 'On Drawing in Mass Media Contexts':

Drawing does this (connecting thought into action) through the artist's selection of different mark-making tools, tonal levels, intensity, the choice of single or multiple narratives, composition, dimension etc, as the basic rules of engagement. At root, the purpose of making drawings is to mediate between perception and physical realities. In making a drawing an artist utilises a way of incorporating the observed world into intuitive as well as a systematic intellectual process. (Minichiello, 2012)

Mario noted in our interview the distorted state of contemporary art and the role of the practitioner-maker:

It seems that the thing that makes for an effective artist today is seeing the possibilities of your ideas separate from actual making. I guess at one end is Jeff Koons who might be seen as a kind of Jeff Bezos for the arts, in that he has structured a business empire on a well-tried capitalist formula of branding and outsourcing production. Indeed, this is not a new approach, the renaissance artists had their workshops and it carried on throughout art history. The difference is the scale, reach and the ability, like supermarkets, to drive out or subjugate local traders. It's a value chain that has one winner and lots of losers. The next logical step has to be NFTs which are purely digital. So instead of getting an actual drawing or painting to hang on the wall, the buyer gets a digital file. It is quite a shift, a system for systems theorists to study for many years to come, where the concept is everything The danger is that those who make stuff are just dumbos with clever hands, who could be replaced by a machine if anything ever gets made at all. It's all exciting stuff. But I cannot help thinking of that scene from the TV series *A Hitchhiker's Guide to the Galaxy* where all the makers and other useful people are gone from planet earth and we are left with marketing, sales and account executives ... pathetic.

On the diminished appraisal of drawing that Mario had to contend with in his career as an academic and artist, he notes:

I guess it's hard to separate myself from the art I make. I sense that I am a bit of an anomaly now, the last of the Mohicans. A large part of my career was as a witness to, or to comment on events using my drawing language. This was an act of disruption of the status quo. In particular, the hierarchy of two elements in news media; the word and the photographic image. I develop the relationship between two distinct languages – the written or spoken word of the editorial and the response to this through my drawing language. I view drawing as a 'language' as it offers the possibility of using a different set of tools to express alternative perspectives, in often taken-for-granted or absent contexts.

This is also contrasted with the photographic imagery that often inhabits the same designed graphic spaces as my work. My reportage work, which has been produced as a direct response to eyewitnessed events, is used in visualizing a range of experiences. It is an area that I have helped to re-establish in contemporary illustrative practice in Britain. As Pat Kirkham has explained, much of this imagery 'takes us to places we fear to go and forces us to confront issues, sometimes directly through what we see' (Rhodes 1999, p. 28). Again, I wish to suggest that the immediacy and directness which can emerge from the overt 'authorship' in the direction and representation of a 'point of view' in the drawing is one of its most significant qualities. Going out of the studio into different situations to be the witness and translator of events is both exciting and challenging. You have no one to edit or censor your work, you are thrown onto your resources and wits. I had a put down for many years by an academic in fine art who said 'you're not really an artist, you just have a good facility'. It's a bit like telling a footballer, 'you're not a footballer you just have really good skills'. It was meant as a put-down but being capable of making pictures in a picture-hungry world that gave some form to the editorial ideas and added some insights required many tools and making and thinking skills. I never claimed to be a Fine Artist because I think it's now a meaningless term. Perhaps at University Fine artists have become the creative world's philosophers. Which was laudable in some ways but disastrous in others.

Drawing pictures is key to my practice because we increasingly live our lives vicariously through pictures. I believe that traditional forms of drawing, because of their directness of response and process, still hold an important place within media forms. Drawing should be seen as a visual communication language, not merely as art, but as a strategy for social representation, questioning and provocation, and as a means of providing alternative forms of narrative and communication. Does this role offer both the maker and the audience the possibility of 'seeing' differently and potentially developing different kinds of (conceptually charged) visual literacy?

In other words, narrative drawing offers different codes of making, new systems of representation and an alternative visual grammar that can challenge orthodox methods and outlooks.

In the Art Schools programs I have written and helped to deliver, we have used reportage projects often because we did not have access to a life room. Sometimes a school of art had stopped drawing and moved to purely conceptual ways of working. But then discovered that students in Illustration, fashion and all forms of design needed to learn to draw if they wanted to be useful to the industry and have a career. It's the core mechanics of things. It seems reasonable to me that if you wish to become a writer you would be expected to have learnt grammar and use it in your work. So, when we didn't have a studio to practice in, we went out into the world and used life, reportage and location drawing to be reborn. Much of these issues are part of the neo-liberal exercise of turning universities into factories where every inch of the space had a value and cost and we pretended we hadn't paid for the space. It was and is nonsense. It made me adapt to the situation to rethink reportage drawing and reinvented it for a new generation.

I asked Mario about the relationship between the sketch and reportage drawing. He spoke of his practice:

Having been paid to go and produce reportage drawings that will be used in a newspaper or on television or film, you are working as a visual journalist. This work is concerned with a particular kind of 'message-making' through narrative drawing.

The drawings are also providing a means of remediating the experience of being at a particular location or event or in time they provide a visual article published by the act of making them, and then distributed by the media outlet that commissioned them.

I often sketch thumbnail images that might become some of the ideas developed in these pieces, this process helps shape a definition of the media contexts I am exploring about drawing.

In the end, I must provide a formal piece of visual communication work. Where the sketch might come in is before I completed the reportage piece. The sketch will be several pieces that can be experimental, a personal record of my thinking process. In some sketches, you can see where I have made notes. I am looking for a way to find the true story, one that is not premeditated but rings true. I often have two drawing books with me, one for sketching out ideas and the other for more finished drawings.

I asked Mario about his art training and the influence of a more traditional artistic training on his development as an artist:

My art school education was a mix of things. On one hand, I went through a very traditional art school training; drawing, painting, printmaking, history of arts, visual psychology etc. On the other hand, I was part of the new wave, the move from film and print media to digital and the empowering nature of new technology was not lost on me at the time. It struck me that combining traditional skills and insights with the new wave of technology presented a fantastic opportunity. I also benefited from my tutor's knowledge and wisdom. Wisdom and lived experience seems greatly undervalued, even treated as some cynicism, which is a shame and a loss to all. Winning a place at art school was very special to me. I thought I had died and gone to heaven, it was a life-changing experience and would love to do it all over again. I practised for thousands of hours. I was in early every day, came home late and often kept working. I think I was always aware of taking any opportunity that came my way. I recently saw a social media clip with Elon Musk (unchallenged and overconfident as ever) saying that you don't need to go to college – there's no need for a University or college. You can learn everything from the internet. This is such rubbish, the academic literature that studies these things shows a rise in misplaced over confidant people thinking that they can do all kinds of things. The crashing and burning of people failing to achieve their goals end in damaged people. Commitment to 3 years of intensive education and training is still the best way to find out who you are and what kind of future you can make for yourself, it is a life-changing experience but only if you are going to be committed to it.

Mario talks about a drawing that stuck with him on an early trip to Australia to document the APEC conference:

Reportage is a means of taking opportunities and facing up to extraordinary things – Another life-changing event was my first artist residency and commission in Sydney Australia at the Sydney College of the Arts (SCA) by invitation of Prof Colin Rhodes, its director, and my commission by the Sydney Morning Herald in 2007 to draw the APEC, the conference of the world's richest nations.

I was drawing in the street every day (Figure 29). There were protests and unrest, the city was fenced off there was a surreal feel to it all. The cheerful and welcoming attitude of the local population made my stay easy as was staying with Colin and his family. One night, we were driving home through

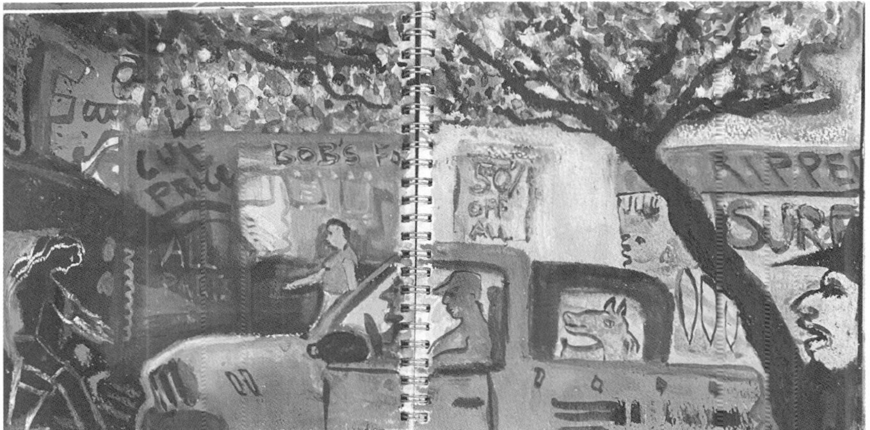

Figure 29 Man barks at a dog in a Ute, Woolgoolga, Australia.
Source: Mario Minichiel o

bush fires, it was a terrifying experience. You can see me looking startled in the drawing (Figure 30). I started the drawing in the car and completed it while it was still fresh in my mind. The experience was like being immersed in a nightmare, a mix of lights, shadows, heat, flames and smoke with dark ash in it. What added an extra element was the shadow thrown by the headlights of a car driver smoking in his car as he recklessly overtook us on a b ind bend in the road.

I was and … we were all shaken up … I sat in my bedroom and completed the drawing using soft graphite and an eraser. I then went to sleep and woke up the next morning and thought perhaps I will refine this in scme way. Because I draw a lot with the eraser to create lines and halftones, I was concerned that it would lose the immediacy of the event. But then I thought no, and fixed it, ready to use for the newspaper.

Mario elaborated on what compels one to make a reportage drawing. What moment demands to be drawn:

Yes, the composition isn't just about placing elements geometrically to make a pleasing balance, it is also like music. You need to take it to the bridge, to create staging posts for the eye that reveal more of the story and the key moments. That there is something there that makes you go 'Ah-ha' 'that's it!'. I guess my work should be understood as positing drawing as the work of a professional practitioner, using theory to enhance my practice and then adding to the body of knowledge in the field. But mainly I am motivated by looking deeper into things that excite my sense of visual narrative. W ll it make an engaging picture?

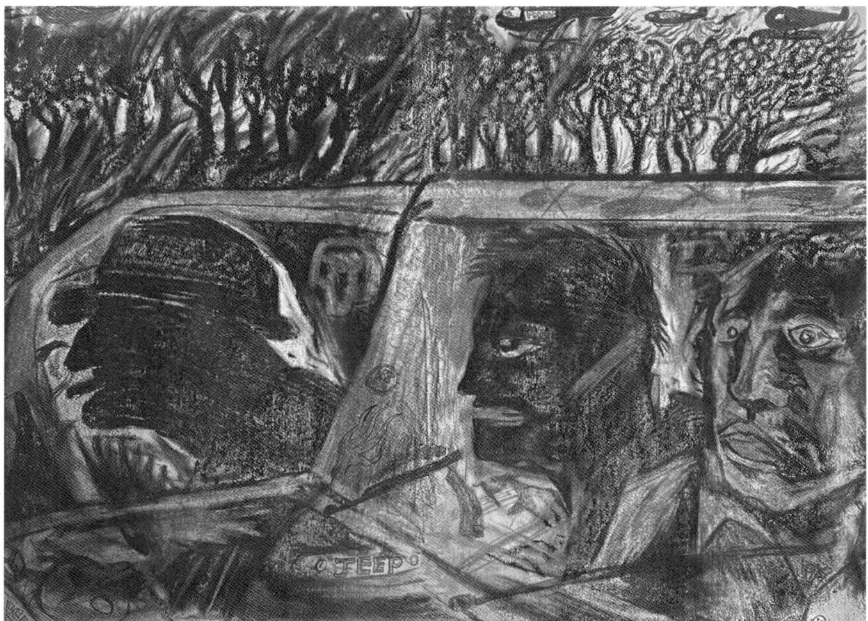

Figure 30 Overtaken by a smoking driver and bush fires, Australia.
Source: Mario Minichiello

That process becomes second nature, it is how I work. To me, there are similarities to other forms of design, gardening or cooking. I cooked a nice meal last night. I didn't look at a recipe. I just thought of how the elements would combine to make an experience that I could share with my wife – I have done it so many times I don't have to think that hard. Practice creates your nature, the real you. So, it is annoying to young people if they don't have the hours of drawing time that they need. My work is on Instagram and I enjoy staying in touch with some of my graduates now doing good work – but I am also struck by the banality of so many formula drawings, particularly the imitating of the Manga comic style. Instagram is becoming a visual version of the amateur talent shows. People are hoping to get lucky, rather than learning to play.

I asked Mario what role speed plays in his drawing in terms of enabling a spontaneous or inventive formal approach:

The life room was a kind of visual training gymnasium. It was there where we strengthen different sensibilities and visual muscles and techniques – but above all memory. I agree with John Berger, Betty Edwards and others who say that almost all drawings have some element of memory in them. When Gary Embury and I undertook the research for our book Reportage Illustration (visual Journalism) it was clear how often aspects of memory in many different sensory ways formed the drawing process for many Illustrators. This ranged from remembering things, events, smells, feelings etc. Memory was a key creative element in the broader creative industries, as Prof. Craig Hight and I found when researching our book, *The Elephant's Leg*. Memories are both personal but have enough shared elements to connect us through our work to others. As the song *I am the Walrus* (The Beatles) states: 'I am he as you are me. And we are all together,' and so we are.

So, I have always varied the pace of drawing, which is challenging. Thinking and decision-making rates; it's hard to decide and to then commit to a mark or a statement of what you see and how truthful it really is against the reality of the human form. Learning that you must get your eye in quickly serves you well as an artist. Learning about the poetry and power of the human form is essential to dealing with human stories. It also forces different thinking styles. This was explored in David Kahneman's Nobel Prize-winning book, *Thinking, Fast and Slow* (2011), which provides real insights into human behavioural traits. How we make decisions and how we have judgement issues which are common in almost every field. How we might improve these processes in our minds. The time to undertake formal research is one of the advantages of having worked as a Professor at several national and international universities. It helps me understand my discipline across several cultures, and how it relates to other disciplines.

So, in the studio, you must get your worst drawings over with. This is especially true with people who are new to drawing informal settings, i.e. studios, projects and life rooms not just doodling at home. I must remind myself that this is how it felt when I started as an undergraduate. None of us learns to ride a bicycle without falling off it. And that fear of falling or even starting can become overwhelming. So, speed is important because it forces us to decide and work on instinct, to switch from the left to the right-hand side of the brain and go into 'flow'. That fear of the white piece of paper that people have is real and is often reflected in other parts of their lives in things that hold them back. I was reminded of this when I taught drawing just recently. In the class, this person said she was having a panic attack because the paper was too big and too white. At first, I found it hard to believe her. I am so old I have forgotten that sense of foreboding – but then she went on to draw an engaging work in under an hour. I think anyone at the start of their practice in drawing, art or making pictures is concerned about the following things:

- Eye, hand, heart and mind coordination and conversation? (basic Kinetics learning)

- What's my reason or motivation (inspiration, rationale) for drawing? My subject or concern?
- What materials and surfaces? How does that change in digital?
- Composition, where do I stand? What's in the frame? (overcoming the influence of the photographic culture or selfie culture).
- Where and how do I start and when is it done?
- How do I find a style? (I prefer to think of it as <u>your</u> language) What's my work going to look like?
- How do I start to take and give constructive critical feedback to myself and others?
- What are the steps and systems to improve my work in the future?
- What elements do I use to communicate or tell stories to others?
- How do I learn to see and think about the world differently?

I asked Mario what he intended for his reportage drawing to be or do? And if the unfinished qualities enable a kind of investment in the closure of the drawing and encourage greater participation or investment on the part of the viewer:

My job as a professional practitioner is to engage the viewer. In some way, there must be shared, almost autobiographical, elements to drawing practice that is common to it and come as a natural part of any form of intense visual enquiry. By drawing we are really in the act of what Bolter and Grusin call the 'remediation of experiences', i.e. attempt to 'achieve immediacy by ignoring or denying the presence of the medium and the act of mediation'. (Bolter & Grusin, 2000, p. 11)

My work typically sits in a publication or in a broadcast that is surrounded by other news. So, I guess it is there to be the authentic human witness. You are elbowing your way in and saying this isn't about a corporate ethic. It is very much an authentic take and something humanizing beyond the corporate. It is the ghost in the machine, or, the Dadaist moment of disruption from being inside of the status quo; you cannot do much from outside. But there is a kind of historical continuum in that all mediated forms simultaneously borrow from previous models of visualization but innovate through personalized applications of making and through a range of media technologies.

I asked Mario what his orientation was to his subject:

Firstly, I am not a machine so most people's experience of being turned into a picture is through a machine. I think we have all forgotten that there is another way – in drawing a person you are having a dialogue with them. The dialogue gets converted into an image of them. And it is not the same as having a moment stolen through a mechanical device that might be misleading and irrelevant but now that the picture is taken, it exists forever. How many people are going to live to regret that selfie that is still on social media thirty years later? So, I am not a machine. I am not a computer. I am this biological, empathetic thing that understands their story. It reveals almost everything about why we can't be replaced by machines. They can take an image. They can take a likeness, but they can't co-create what the person is or represents in the same way that drawing as a process can – nor can it help them to reflect and reimagine the orientation of their lives. It is my contention, however, that the drive to photorealism has in some way 'naturalised' the way in which 'reality' is now perceived, and it is the primal, directness of expression through drawing that revitalizes 'the gaze'.

I am not engaging here with issues of aesthetics, however, but the ways in which this facilitates narrative. In making narrative drawings in journalistic contexts, my work is orientated or operates as a means to 're-observe', unobtrusively, what might not be able to be captured by photography (or if captured photographically, somehow remaining 'unseen' through its everyday familiarity).

I asked Mario about the political, social and emotional layers within his drawing and how commentary gets embedded in the work sometimes without fully realizing or intending it:

The editorial area have worked in provides many alternative forms of communication. In my role, the written word is helpful to me. I can work with the written narrative and visualize the text. On the other hand, photography is a rival and is often the first choice for many editors over drawings. Often an editor will ask me to draw or illustrate a story if they cannot find a photographic image or a photographer. Some art directors and editors have commissioned me because they want the qualities that they sense my work brings to the page or screen, particularly for covering political issues. I have great admiration for documentary photography and the way the best photojournalists deal with the impact of power. The best work reveals a great deal about the political mud that humans must run through. The best photographers have a great eye for the moments when humans reveal their inner thoughts or feelings. One of the greatest and bravest is Lu Guang, whose work let the world see the social and environmental impact of the Chinese communist party's policies and that they had not been an unqualified success. He was arrested and has not been seen since. His work is incredible, he has many of the qualities of Don McCullin, with the sensibilities of Nan Goldin. I admire and respect documentary and photojournalism but I try to do something different with my drawings. Art directors and editors use my work as a hybrid that resides between the written word and the lens. Crucially, my drawing is not merely about 'recording' a moment, but 'recalling' a moment; it is as much about what is known as what is seen. This is the space where drawing can 'still' life and re-mediate the constant waves of information. This is a collaboration of many moments and ideas, not one distilled moment. These two images work as examples of comparative reportage.

It is important however for the artist to breach the role of 'journalist' and engage with authorial agendas.

I asked Mario if he thought those insights that can reside in a drawing are planned or if they happen spontaneously on an unconscious level:

I try to remind myself and impress upon students, probably bore them, but somehow you must see the world in the abstract, trick your mind from the conformity of normal life. So if you have been asked to draw a flower you need to move beyond conventions and the received images on the internet of flowers, often captured badly as images. You have to take responsibility for how hard you look and see it as if it's new. As if You are visiting 'planet flowers'; noticing colours, hues, reflected light and different shapes and topologies. That's making art out of the everyday.

I asked Mario to identify his artistic influences and how they impacted his approach:

As a general attitude, my work is an extension of Dadaism's line of cultural questioning. I have never really fitted any mould so I don't have to accept traditional structures and conventional models of society or what is accepted as cultural norms. I have learnt that revolutions don't work, and that change is achieved by adding new elements and disruption from within to advance a better model. What we see and how we see it forms the way we can imagine the future. The music we listen to has a great impact. I have a music system in my studio and I select the music to suit the work I am doing. I write about it in the Book *The Elephants Leg*. Like so many people in the media world, I have been listening to Radiohead's Ok Computer a lot lately. What does that say about our collective subconscious?

When I was a boy, an undeniable influence was the art in the Roman Catholic church. As a boy, I was taken to church by my parents. The Catholic church is an interesting mix of eroticism and terror. On one hand, you have Bernini's sculpture of Santa Teresa having an orgasm and on the other you have St. Lucy's eyes plucked out and in a bloody mess in a dish that she offers you. Then there are saints shot through with arrows, whipped etc … It was and is extraordinary.

Then there was the work of Hogarth, Grosz, Goya, Rockwell, Duchamp, Sutherland, Nash, Hockney and others. There's also the writing of Golding, Shakespeare, PK Dick and many others. Literature and reading fires the imagination. I guess I take my influences very broadly. I listen to music and get obsessed with it because I think it relates to drawing.

I asked Mario about reportage drawing's claim to authenticity and what he thought about that term:

Drawing allows the maker to purpose an idea or translates what is seen and how they understood it into an executive summary of communication. Drawing can do more than put the viewer in the same space as the objects viewed. Drawing, like writing, enables the viewer to internalize the experience contained in the visual narrative. It also enables you to imagine something that does not exist and bring it to life. This link between imagination and creating something real in the world is facilitated by drawing.

I asked Mario if he thought his drawings capture these experiential elements like weather and other circumstances on the ground:

I think in drawing you are always experiencing. If it works you can use it or you just keep it as an ongoing experience. That's the joy of a sketchbook. An example of this is the Boxing reportage drawing from York Hall, Bethnal Green, London (Figures 31–33). I tried to convey the nature of boxing: the physical impact, the limits it took those taking part and even the sound of the crowd. I tried to use anything (mark, tone, image) that gave a sense of meaning, or authenticity, that adds to the special circumstances of that event, the atmosphere that surrounded the boxers. Looking at the drawings again I remember that it was almost surreal, a kind of blood lust cauldron of excitement. The sounds and smells as well as the noise and sight of it all resulted in the almost pornographic spectacle of violence. I wanted to contain the visceral nature of the experience in the drawings. In many of the drawings, the sweat and blood pour off the boxers. One of the boxers had a head cut which produced so much blood that it sprayed all over the ring and on those seated in the front rows. People sitting at home viewing television would have no idea. The visceral sense of it all is missing. That is what I was trying to capture in the drawings. At some point I lost myself in the drawing process I felt that there was an opportunity to do something that words or lenses could not capture. It's a long shot but worth taking.

I asked Mario if he saw reportage drawing as capturing purely objective experience or if he thought there was a kind of bridge between the subjective and objective in a drawing:

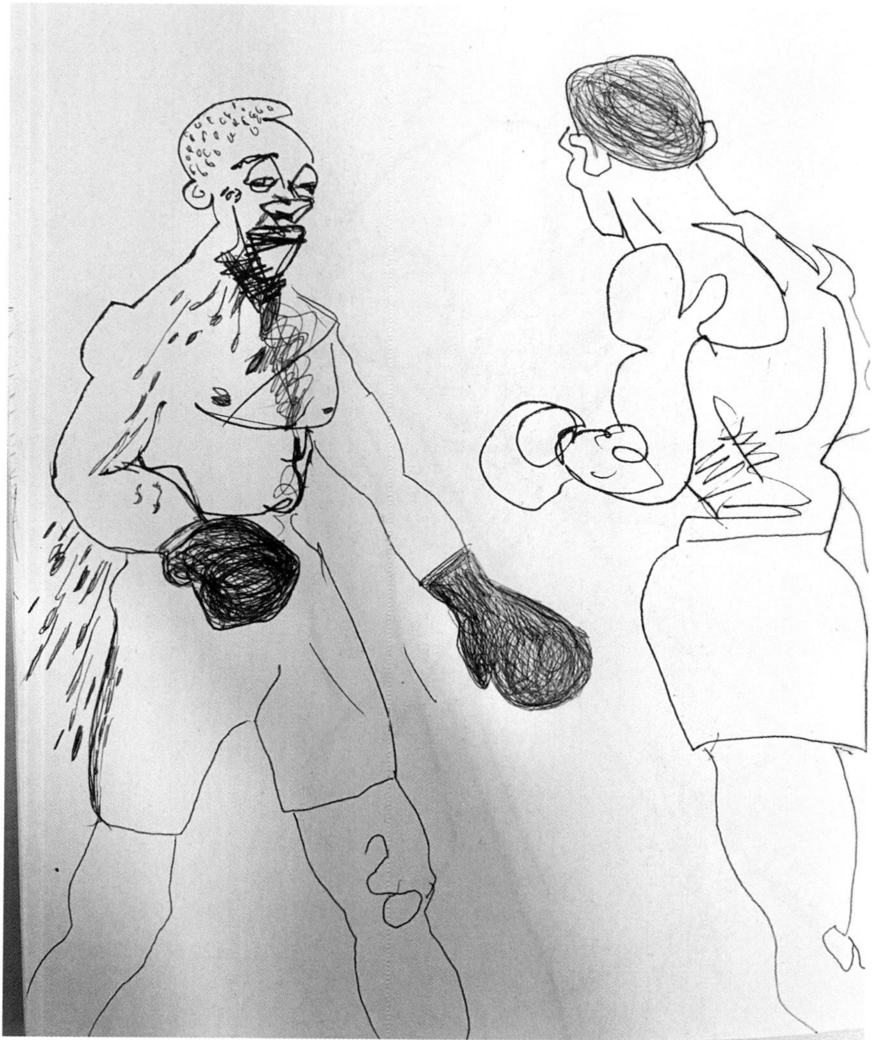

Figure 31 First blood, Bloodthirst Boxing Match, London.
Source: Mario Minichiello

It always starts in the pursuit of the objective to get the location and topology of the thing you have been sent out to document or report. But then increasingly, you're telling a story through your interaction with objectivity and your experience. In the end, you see the world through your mind's eye. The use of materials and the hand-drawn imperfections are crucial to remind the spectator that this is a drawn image and therefore, inevitably uses a series of different visual codes to those found in digital media, photography, or film. My

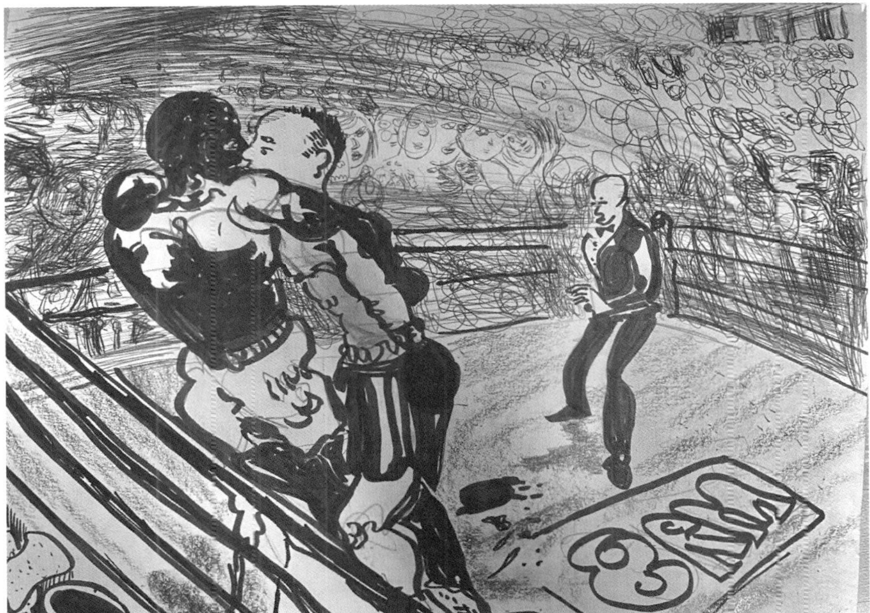

Figure 32 The sound of the crowd, the weight of another, London.
Source: Mario Minichiello

work, in the end, is my account which is not one single captured moment but is the result of layering of many moments of seen and felt experiences.

I asked Mario why he thought reportage drawing was still popular and if he thought it was because it was a conscious response to this hyper-mediated world:

That could be the end question.

The exposure to reportage through a range of media and galleries has allowed it to develop its audience and for them to learn the visual language embedded in drawing. My work has taken a 'journalistic' stance that seeks to promote a better understanding of the often problematic social, cultural, political, and spiritual challenges of our time; the existential crisis that is facing us all. This approach is later reinforced by 'artistic' contemplation, the way the work is made and its aesthetic qualities.

The overwhelming speed and the sense of being contained in a bubble of similar opinions have become a feature of our media. My art is slow art and like slow food, it's better for you than fast food. It allows for differences and for people of opposite opinions to meet. We all know that to achieve peace and happiness you will, in the end, have to embrace your enemy. I am old now and

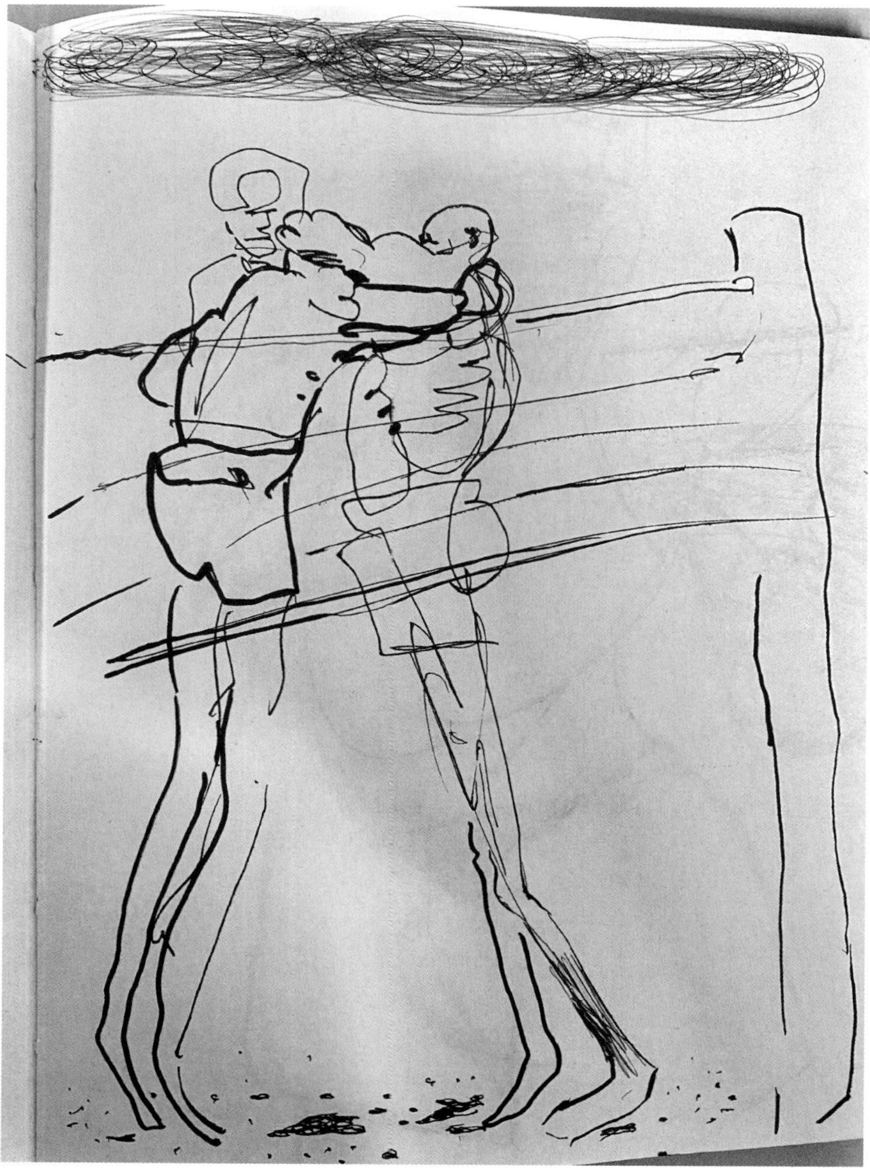

Figure 33 Last Legs, London.
Source: Mario Minichiello

I do have some limited wisdom to chew on. I have throughout my career tried to actively re-define my role as an artist and a draughtsman in the service of the truth and a better journalistic context. I have, in turn, defined and re-defined 'narrative drawing' as a model of reportage and as an art for my own form of practice. I think this approach has helped others. My students that have kept in touch seem to have benefited or reflected on this. This is partly because of using 'drawing' as an essentialist and determinist tool. In the end, making a drawing utilizes a way of incorporating the world into psychic processes which is shared by no other method of reflection. Drawing does not come out of philosophy, mathematics, linguistics, or scientific method. It is measurable neither by language nor numbers. Thus, in a world which places such a high value on the word and accountability, it appears an imprecise and vaguely defined method. Yet, this is also its strength. Drawing – the drawn image – remains resistant to other forms of analysis, and its singularity forces the viewer to engage with it on its own terms That is my conscious and considered response to this hyper-mediated world and all the distractions and confusions it brings to us.

Conclusion

Mario's work fits Berger's concept of drawing as wholly autobiographical. His work has an exciting and excitable quality. It is emphatic and chasing down vision and experience like a hungry dog. Mario's reflections above demonstrate that the journalistic function of reportage drawing need not be overly concerned with objectivity and must, for a truly radical embrace of the act, vivify individual experience and furnish the drawing which experiential knowledge only he can provide. By making lazy comparisons between drawing and photography and their journalistic functions, we are comparing apples to oranges. As Mario has noted, the emotionalized content of reportage drawing is not only a strength, it takes us beyond representation towards a communion with experience. Because experiences are multivariant, reportage drawing fixes the experience of the artist in a specific context at a specific time. The value of the drawn document is that this experience is re-lived in a new language, with new rules, and a primary or even secondary pleasure of viewing a drawing is to uncover and decode that language. Thinking of Mario's image driving through the bush fire (Figure 2), the reading of the image uncovers many layers of experience in the manner of its execution and the pushing and pulling of the paper to render the drawing. Unlike the specificity of the photograph and its depiction of identifiable people in specific circumstances, the drawing connects us to a psychic event of the artist. We are not only in the car driving fast through a dangerous burning landscape, we are in Mario's head and nervous system. We believe the drawing less because it is comprehensively 'true' we believe it because we can feel it. The artist has made an effective bridge from his experience to ours.

10
ARTIST SPOTLIGHT – LOUP BLASTER

I first came across Loup's (Louise Philia Druelle) work in 2014 with her film AL HURRIYA (Freedom, Liberte). The film explores the plight of migrants in a Calais camp called 'The Jungle' where lives are in a holding pattern waiting and seeking transit to the UK. The animation has many reportorial elements in the manner of drawing attention to the landscape and depiction of people. It utilizes a vibrant mix of drawing, painting, photography, film and sound. It was clear from the film that Loup was not only a highly skilled animator, but she was able to capture a wide range of tone, texture and metaphor, revealing the human story often overlooked in the noisy political debate around their (migrants) circumstance. What I learned afterwards was that Loup was from Calais and has been a consistent and vocal supporter of the migrant, displaced community through her own art, music and activism. She is not a distanced observer, she is imbedded in the lives of her subjects and through collaborations and activism, she has fused her story with that of the migrant community, seeing their destiny mixed up with her own. This distinguishes Loup's approach to reportage drawing as something inherently personal and comprehensive. She does not, however, overly sentimentalize and prefers a naturalistic approach. She notes: 'My responsibility is to accept the role of being deeply rooted here and to do whatever it takes to go wider and build a stronger community. Tell OUR story, because the dominant story is extremely oppressive, stigmatizing and literally breaks people's life.' In an interview with *Varoom* magazine in 2017 she noted in relation to what she thought was the most important aspect of a work of narrative: 'I think it's the honesty. Simplicity can tell you a lot more than a blockbuster. It's not the one that's louder that is wiser' (Blaster, 2017, p. 23).

Loup is a dynamic example of contemporary reportage practice which sees fluid boundaries between artistic and creative approaches and shifts towards media in a serendipitous, improvisational and intuitive way. Collectively, her work manages to avoid the burden of intentions. It does this because it emerges from such a close and intimate connection with her subjects The subjects themselves have a unique agency in the work, like collaborators, and

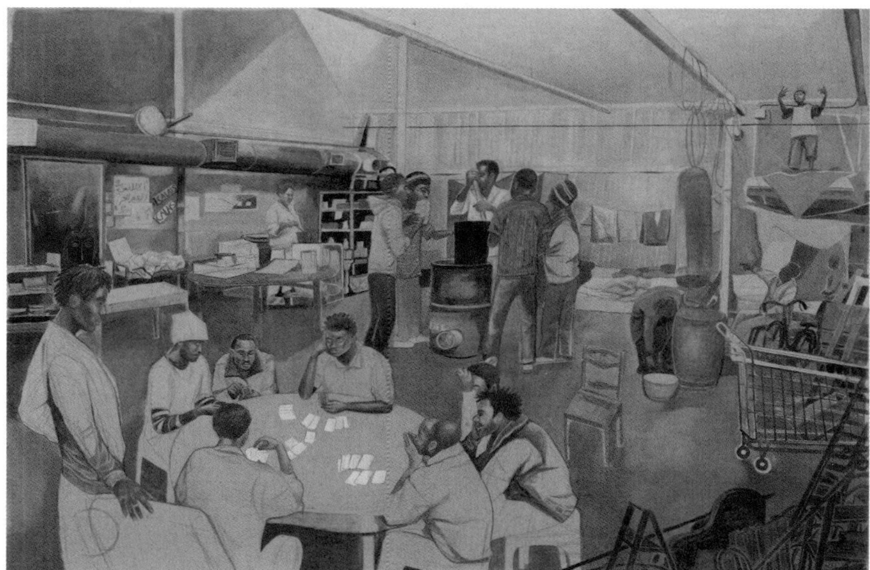

Figure 34 Playing cards, Calais.
Source: Loup Blaster

the drawings, music, murals and other media read like a diary of closely lived lives and compassionate understanding. In this sense, the work lends itself to activism. It counters negative messages in popular media about who the inhabitants of the 'Jungle' are and their identity beyond their circumstances. Like many reportage artists, Loup's work exploits the humanity within the contested narrative of the camp inhabitants and flattens the hierarchy between subject and artist through the open dialogue of artistic practice. As author Siri Hustvedt notes in relation to looking at drawing 'my perception of the lines, the shading, the figures or things is created between me and it (the drawing). And what I see there is also felt, not only for its content, but as an artifact of the living hand that once moved over an empty space and has left behind the marks of that intimate encounter' (Hustvedt, 2013, p. 280). This feels like a fitting description of Loup's work which chronicles her imbedded and invested journeys with a people that she cares deeply for.

See below for my interview with Loup and her insights into her own work.

How familiar are you with the term reportage drawing?

I've met the term when I started to work in Calais in 2014 and document the situation of people in exile at the border. I started right away to share my drawings online to tell people what was going on. Drawing was (to

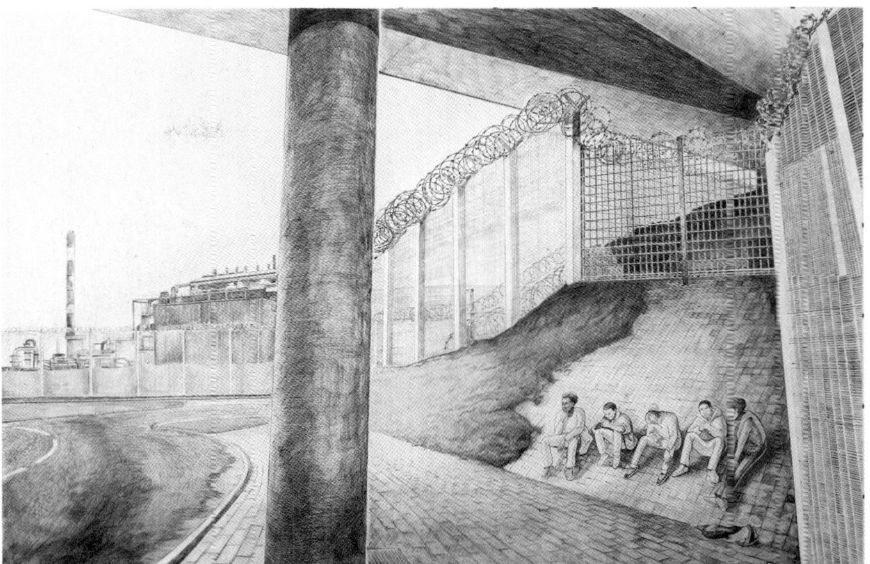

Figure 35 Under the bridge, Calais.
Source: Loup Blaster

me) a more sensible way to communicate than photography. Also people in exile do not often appreciate to be taken in photo, and drawing allowed me to communicate without words with them. After that, my work has been featured in newspapers (Libération), or magazines (Revue Bout du Monde) also in travel sketchbook festival (Festival du carnet de voyage à Claremont-Ferrand, Le Grand Bivouac à ___)

Where did you get your art training?

I started art classes as a kid when I was five and until I was fourteen years old.

Then I went to a public art high school specialized in design in Roubaix (E.S.A.A.T) and got a degree in 2D animation at the same school. I did a final year of training at the university of Volda in Norway, which was an incredible experience. I finished school at the age of twenty-one but since I never stop learning and experimenting with new things.

Lately, I have been back to my childhood art school in Calais, working at the fanzine – comics workshop of Frederic Fleury. I often miss being surrounded by peers, and people who can provide resources and different points of view. I'm currently looking for residency opportunities and a workspace. Feedback is so important to evolve and flourish!

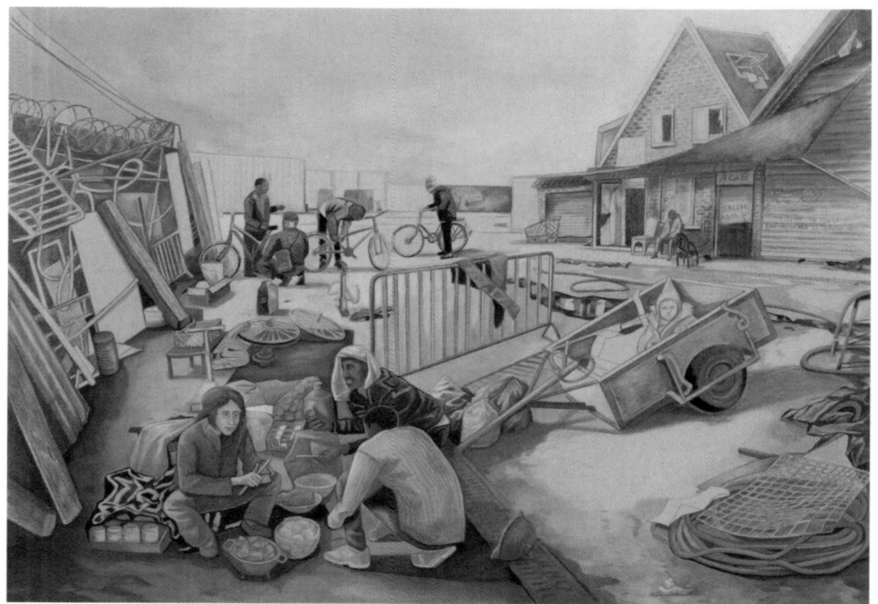

Figure 36 Squat, Calais.
Source: Loup Blaster

You have been working in the migrant camp in Calais for some time now. How did this happen and what keeps you returning to the people and place as a subject for your artwork?

I first stepped into the camps to direct my first short film Al Hurriya Freedom Liberté for the Late Night Work Club. It was for an anthology of self-produced short films on the theme 'Strangers'.

I would say this encounter changed my life and I have been more and more involved with things happening in Calais on several levels as a person, as an artist, activist and even involved in local politics.

The fact that I have a long-term experience with Calais gives me a lot of understanding of the conflicts and dynamics. I've seen things change since I was a kid, so I try to explain this in the project I'm working on now, which is an edition of my drawings; mixing sketchbook drawings, more detailed art pieces, newspaper samples, photography, etc. … I hope to print a series of fanzines as soon as possible.

Was your original migrant camp work self-initiated or commissioned?

So, as I said before it started with a commissioned but self-produced short film.

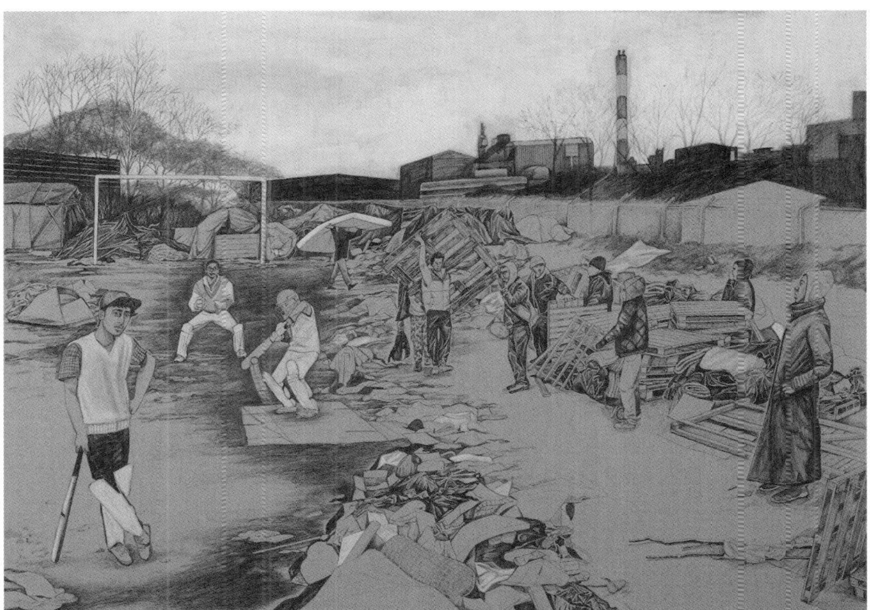

Figure 37 Community, Calais.
Source: Loup Blaster

But then I had so many drawings, because the film was based on documenting on the field, and I never stopped after the film was done, so I had a lot to show. In 2019 I won a grant from Foundation de France to initiate my edition project. I've been able to make some exhibitions and create new pieces for them.

How did this work get noticed by the press and become so visible?

I think drawing is a rare way to approach documentary. People connect with it in a more personal way. It doesn't impose reality but gives room to the imagination.

Also I don't push to be featured, it happens because my name spreads and people hear about me and think that it's an original point of view maybe?

But I can't wait to print the work and exhibit it so it can reach more people.

Do you see this project as connected to the tradition of reportage or journalism?

My older sister is a journalist, and journalism is so interesting to me. But journalism is about facts, I try to express the emotions, feelings, internal

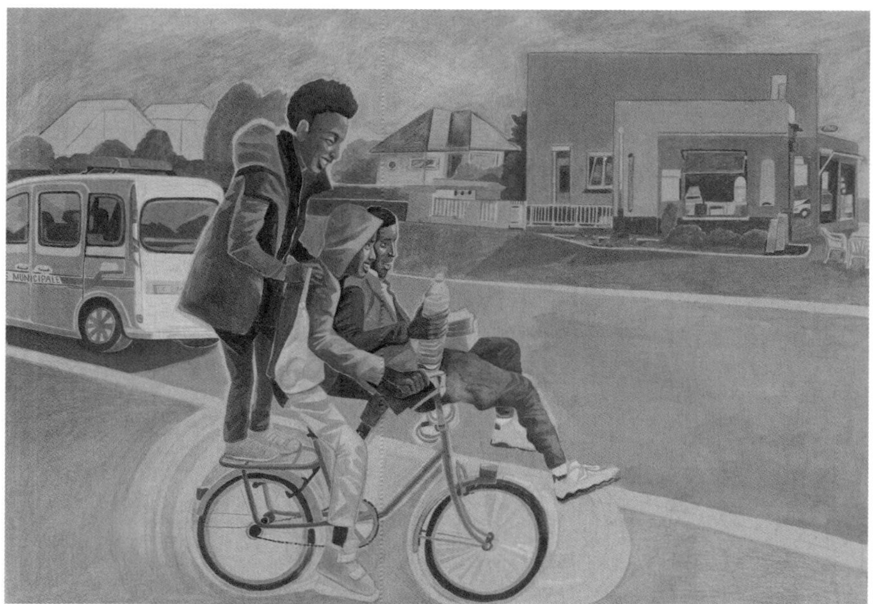

Figure 38 Oromo and my bike, Calais.
Source: Loup Blaster

thoughts and experiences that make you change when you're in a situation like here. I'd say I focus more on what's felt and personal, beyond facts and events.

Also the part of the personal story and fiction is important. That is, what's happening in one's heart and how character is built to overcome and transform sadness into power and action.

Do you see yourself functioning as a visual journalist or artist? Or both?

So, definitely an artist because of the reasons I just said above. I'm also a singer and performer.

You seem to be working across media these days (including music). Do you think boundaries between disciplines is relevant today?

I never stop jumping from one media to another. I stopped asking myself why. I think they all express different things. Maybe I'll need to organize a dance party and maybe I'll have to draw it to tell what happened.

Also, my edition project I will include animation, photography, field recordings etc. … I think having a diversity of outputs open more doors to people to enter the work and understand it.

Can you tell me about how your Sudan project came to be?

I fell in love with Sudanese people and their culture. I've known it very well across the years in Calais, Paris, and had the opportunity to travel with my husband who's from Khartoum. I really needed a break at that time, so it was really just a holiday. But to me it always feels nice to draw when I travel so I can share it later. This was the only 'work' I allowed myself to do there.

How do you see your drawing practice? Do you feel that drawing is your primary expressive medium or do you see drawing as a part of all of your artistic practice?

Drawing is definitely my first language. But sometimes I don't feel like sitting at the desk for it, sometimes I need to play music. So, with time I accepted to balance and go with the feelings. But at the moment I really miss having a proper workspace and really diving into drawing. Put drawings everywhere on tables and the floor. Maybe work on bigger scale too.

Do you feel any responsibility to your subject in terms of representation and narrative? Do you think reportage drawing (or reportorial art in general) creates a democratic space of understanding even though it is ultimately subjective?

I think, about Calais, things have rarely been told with a personal point of view.

At the same time, my way of drawing is quite realistic and contemplative. I just try to tell my story, because a lot of volunteers and people from Calais relate to it. My responsibility is to accept the role of being deeply rooted here and to do whatever it takes to go wider and build a stronger community. Tell OUR story, because the dominant story is extremely oppressive, stigmatizing and literally breaks people's life.

Do you think the image dominates text in this world? Do you think that is a good thing?

My images totally dominate my words but I don't think it's a good thing in my art. But in general, it's logical that an image hits the brain faster than a text. But I think the real poetry and the great meaning comes from a great combination of text, image, and composition (design). That's why I strive to experiment in my new editions.

In your work as a whole, do you feel there is a link between art and activism?

Sure, my art tries to speak with truth about injustices, violence and humanity struggling here. And my activism is based on writing, music, poetry and performance. But it's all about the impact. Though I try to not always be revendicate with art, sometimes I just need something refreshing too. But in general both are very close together.

Can you tell me a bit about what you are doing now or planning on doing?

I want to print, self-edit, screen print, and create several little books and a diversity of formats before to reach bigger publishers. So if anyone reading this is willing to support me on that you're very welcome to get in touch or invite me over!

Conclusion

What struck me about Loup's work when I first saw it was that it felt different than most depictions I had seen of the 'Jungle' (a once popular place for visual reportage. See Threads by Kate Evans among many others). Loup's drawings felt more intimate. They felt like they had more local knowledge than other depictions and they felt closer, more trusted by her subjects. This is the strength of her work and speaks to the way that reportage drawing can have a long relationship with a setting and context. Because people and narratives are so endlessly complex and shifting, any location can offer fertile ground for the visual reporter. The visual reality or, as Rawson terms it, realia is the new representational space of the drawing, defined by the propositional language of its formation (Rawson, 1969, p. 33). For Loup, this realia is less about the evident production of the drawing in the image than it is about an accurate portrayal of life for the migrants and a sense of individual experiences through identifiable people. For Loup, the images need to be richly detailed to understand the inhumanity of these spaces and the human will to thrive no matter what the circumstances (Figures 34–38).

11
ARTIST SPOTLIGHT – MERCY KAGIA

Mercy is a Kenyan born artist who is living in Germany. She studied in the UK and has a PhD from Kingston University (UK) in reportage drawing. Her work is remarkable for the confidence of her line and the comprehensiveness of her vision. She is very interested in travel and how drawings can capture not only intimate moments but also moments which are often overlooked. In her many travels, she finds herself drawing around the areas of primary tourist interest. She seeks out the narrative surrounding such locations and finds these observed moments to be emblematic of contemporary society in surprising and, sometimes, disappointing ways. In this free-form interview, Mercy identified many aspects of her practice and her drawing more broadly, covering the many contexts with which she has worked.

Mercy starts talking about the experience of drawing in the Kisumu region of Kenya during her PhD.

An early response that I got from people encountering me drawing was 'oh what are you doing? Oh drawing. A woman doing drawing. Oh, and you are doing a PhD? A woman drawing and doing a PhD!?' It was a challenge. It kept a dialogue going. It was always a good challenge. That is why I chose to go to Kisumu.

In Kenya my drawings are received very differently. People will say 'wow! It looks like a photo' and that is a compliment. If it comes close to the photograph it is good work. But I do enjoy drawing in a more gestural way. If I am seeing someone dancing, I like getting that in three lines. For me that is also important. But someone will say 'hmm … maybe you can take a photo and draw from the photo.' There is a very different cultural view on drawing.

More gestural minimal drawing is just as important as more classical detailed drawing. And that is a difference. It has been going on for much longer in the West and it allows for more diversity in the marks that you make.

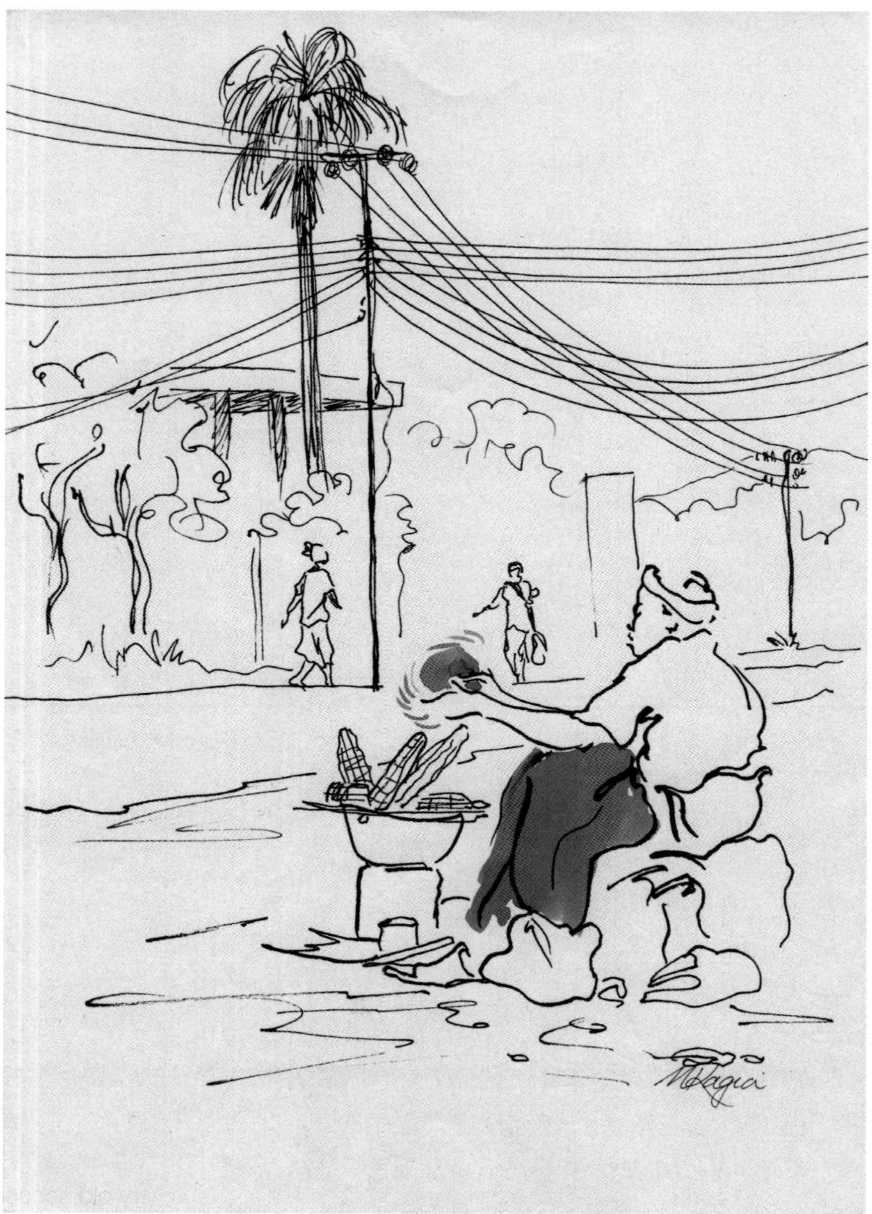

Figure 39 Roasting Maize, Kisumu, Kenya, 2010.
Source: Mercy Kagia

Whereas in Kenya, the aim is to get as close to reality and then you have achieved something.

I found when I was in the UK, a lot of people were too shy to interact. It is like there are lot of people who don't go to an exhibition in a museum because they feel that they need to understand the work. And that they must have an opinion and there is a fear of saying the wrong thing. Many people have said when they encounter me drawing 'I am sorry I am not an expert.' I tell them they don't have to be an expert. I found this to be the case often in the UK. The people who would engage with what I was doing were people who would go to art museums and so on. Or children. They don't have the same reservations.

In Kisumu (Kenya) it was always men. A lot of men standing around in a huge crowd around me. Then someone would stand right in front of me and when I asked him to leave, he thought you didn't have to look and draw. He thought you could look and then spend thirty minutes drawing it down on the paper. This speaks to that culture of looking. And then again, it is a different kind of conversation because they don't feel like they need an artistic opinion, they just want to know what you are doing and why you are doing it. Or, say 'you missed that bit'. 'Look, look, you forgot to put this man here.' It's refreshing but also very annoying. Having people correcting you and telling you, 'oh when I was very young I could really draw.' Many people also will watch you for a while and then come up and say 'I always wanted to do art but I wasn't so good.' You find people who have something in them that really wanted to go down that artistic path. Or they know someone who is very good and they want to introduce you to them. Many people wanted to be artists, but parents didn't allow it. Some also didn't know you could do a PhD in art. Some also said that their schools have no art. It was always a sad conversation to have.

Talk a little bit about how you get such rich detail in your work. Do you use any photographic reference?

I generally work on the spot. How I got into drawing maybe informs it a little bit more. When I was an art student studying illustration at West Herts College in Watford (UK), I had a wonderful history of art lecturer who told me after a lecture one day that if I wanted to do anything in sculpture, graphic design, or anything, that I needed to know how to draw and should draw every single day. She also said I needed to draw from observation. It was very old school and important. She said I needed a sketchbook and a pen so you don't try and rub it out and make it look pretty. And I took the advice and for a year I did draw every day. So, I did this and did some okay drawing but many attempts weren't good at all. For some I would start but not finish them. But then, it opened my eyes to the whole idea of observing and looking and learning by looking. The more I looked the more I learned about people. I started with just people. I had no buildings, no structures it was often just a person floating in mid-air. As I did this, I got more interested in anatomy. I wanted to know what was underneath the skin that holds the body up that makes it look like the body. So, I would crash a lot of life drawing classes that I wasn't really a part of. I went to the Wellcome Trust museum. I wanted to learn more about anatomy, how the flesh and muscle and sinews come together. It was all about how to draw people properly. I do remember at one point wanting to go into the medical illustration field. I went for an interview and it was very austere, very posh, a huge building in central London with wood panels and serious portraits of great doctors that have gone before. It was an interesting experience bringing my drawings and being told they were a little too loose for what they were looking for. But this interest continued, and it was much more interesting for me to draw from life. I hardly ever went back to work from photographs because I then got bored very quickly. I liked the idea of capturing someone or something before they disappeared. When I was learning to draw people, I would go to St. Pancreas and stand above on the restaurant level and just draw people. They would stop, look at where the train was and go, so I would have to capture them in those few seconds. I remember this stayed with me and informed how I draw now. I know I need to work fast to capture those quick moments. Now I include more like buildings and so forth if it so hits me. The sense of place is just as important but when I started, I was just focusing on people. And I would ask permission to go to mums and baby groups so I could learn to draw babies. I would go somewhere and find children and ask if I could draw them. I think in those days it was much easier to do that. So, it built from that. Now if I travel or go somewhere new, I have a dedicated sketchbook to record my experiences and do a drawing or two a day rather than take photographs. Whatever I have at the end, that is my experience. When I was in South America for three months, I had worked it out to a page a day to collect my experiences. It wasn't about capturing the most beautiful or the most touristy or the thing that stood out the most. Because everyone knows what Machu Picchu looks like, it could be a woman making smoothies with a new-born baby behind her.

Because that is the kind of everyday life that interests me. That has remained quite core to how I work. It is important to just sit there and draw even if it is just five minutes. Photographs come in if I have an exhibition coming up. The sketches stay in the sketchbook and rarely do I think I need to work that up into a larger illustration. But when I have had exhibition like one in Nairobi which was about street life in Nairobi, some were from life but a lot of it was from a road trip I did around Nairobi and I'd spot things on the side of the road in markets or people doing interesting things and I would stop and photograph them. And then the photographic reference becomes important at that point because I think I am not going to go back there and sit for that amount of time. And then I would edit the image. Pick out the things that stood out for me. And with a gestural approach I would make it like I was there. I would limit the amount of time I would spend on the drawing. So, I would try to create the moment of me sitting there. I treat the photograph as a kind of live thing. If I was here what would jump out at me. I would pick out bits and try and retain the sense of movement or immediacy. I think observation has remained key. And some of it is informed observation. Having seen the same scenes or been there before when I absorbed that moment. I then say go in with ink, trying to recreate the immediacy of being there. I never first draw with pencil. I always go directly with dip pen and India ink which is waterproof. Whatever comes out stays. If there is a mistake, I just draw over it. Other times I use photography. It is only because on those occasions I couldn't draw. I remember in Argentina at Iguazu falls, everything was just wet. It was like the heavens were sneezing at you and it was impossible to draw anything. Or even photograph anything. In a few fleeting moments I was able to take a photograph and work on it later. But when I look at the photograph … I don't know it doesn't do it for me.

Do you think it is possibly because reportage drawing isn't about these kinds of collective moments? Shared moments? It's about something that is more specifically interesting to you? Like the Falls or going to Disney World and drawing the castle, well … everyone has seen the same castle.

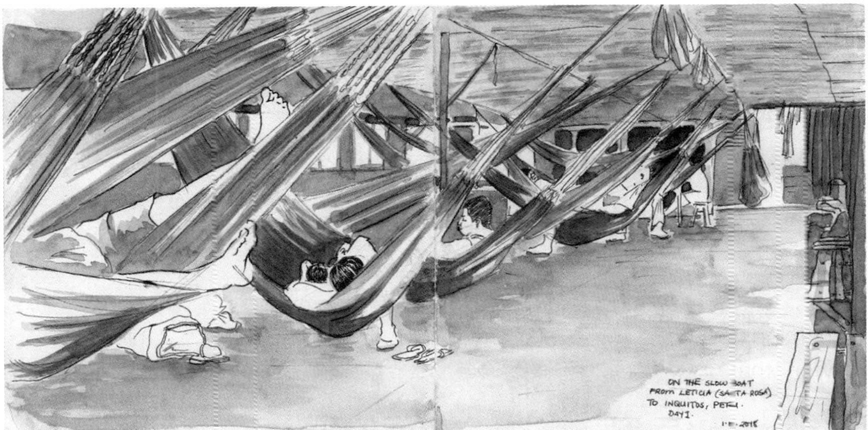

Figure 40 Cargo boat through the Amazon, Colombia to Peru, 2018.
Source: Mercy Kagia

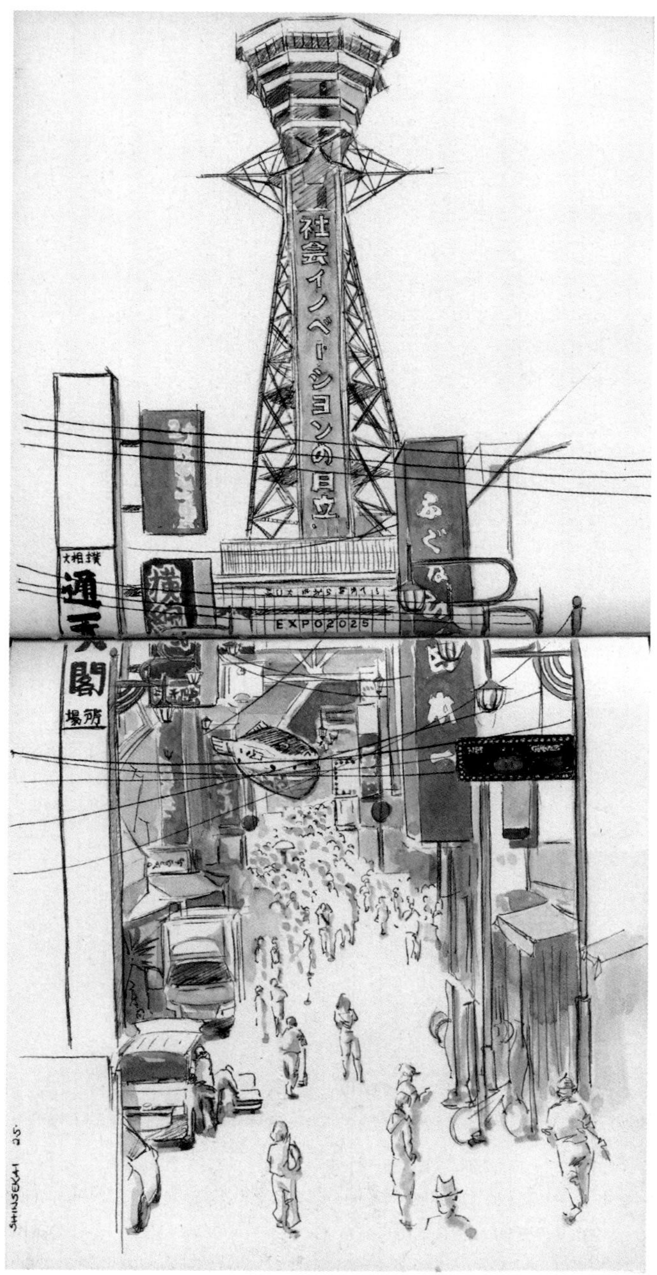

Figure 41 Shinsekai, Osaka, Japan, 2019.
Source: Mercy Kagia

That's true and I don't want to dissolve into a kind of stereotype. One of the things I found quite interesting was in 2019 when I was in Japan and I was drawing and there were so many people at this temple. And I really hated it so much. The actual place was really beautiful and interesting. They were these old and wooden structures. I just hated the people there. And then I found myself looking at the people. Where there is this huge temple and people are putting their hands up right in front of your face with their cameras trying to get the perfect photo and then looking at the photo to see if it was good and then taking another. Not actually looking again at the building. And then I became interested in the people's behaviour. I thought 'that's very odd. You are all so brash and rude.' Sticking your arms in front of everybody else who is trying to see the same thing. And then I do find that that happens. When I am in a place that is supposed to be quite interesting, I then tend to look at the people around me and what they are doing and how they are responding to it. And then I have to stop because then you just get a lot of people just looking at their phones. It becomes the same thing. In Kisumu I had to stop drawing groups of men because they were always doing the same thing, sitting and talking. I always have this same issue at a famous building or site. I feel it has been photographed so much, drawn so much … but oh, look at this person here and how they are not even looking or talking loudly on their phone or someone has fallen asleep under the shade of a tree. I think, 'that is actually more interesting. This is a place for them to take a nap rather than be in awe.' As an artist that is always observing, your eye is caught by the thing that maybe nobody else is noticing. And that I find interesting. It is interesting to capture the other things in that moment.

These peripheral things become more interesting.

I think a lot of places can be well captured by looking at people. And people are places. Even if you draw people in Disneyland, big fat Americans with their bratty kids with ice cream cones melting down their shirts and big teddy bears under their arms. That is *actually* Disney World.

Yes, without people it is just a load of brightly coloured buildings. I find that is interesting in cafes and waiting rooms. Waiting rooms … I have sketchbooks of waiting rooms. You get the people just waiting. Nowadays unfortunately everyone is on their phone. And this is something I have noticed since drawing. I remember as a student, people would be in the park lying in the sun or chatting with someone because mobile phones were not as evolved as they are right now. It is such a distraction from life. Even if there is nothing to look at, you will look at the nothing. So, it has been interesting seeing that change in my sketchbooks from people having a snooze in the park or

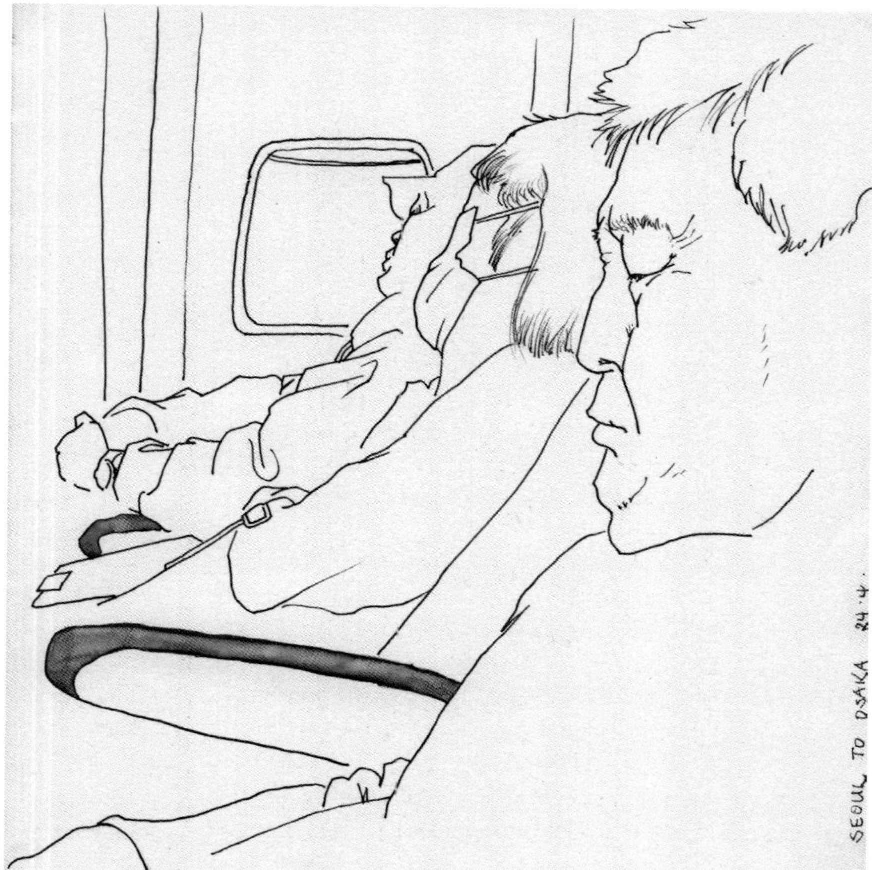

Figure 42 Seoul to Osaka, 2019.
Source: Mercy Kagia

just engaging with something somehow to everyone always on their phone. Like they can't wait to get on their phone. It has now become the universal distraction. I think that is the core of reportage for me. The mundane that no one even thinks about at some point will become a historical reference to how people live. It will become a social investigation. It becomes like a reference to how people lived. I love looking at Topolski's drawing and I think 'that's interesting.' The streets of Paris or whatever. I am drawn by his line or drawing but for him he was just capturing what he could see. But at some point, it crosses over to historical reference. And you can use it to look back and see how people lived and so forth. And I think that is the beauty of reportage. The most uninteresting situation while you are in it, in the future, will become some sort of archive. When you add a few more years to that moment it is very interesting. People used to sit at cafes and talk. And look at Covid now.

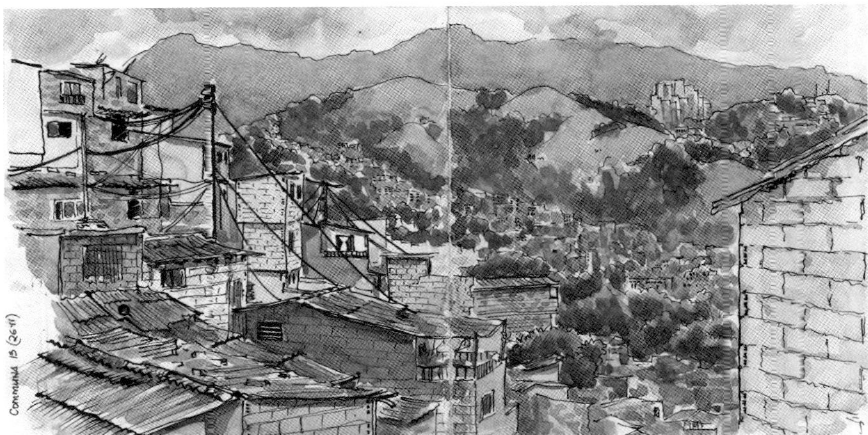

Figure 43 Comuna 13, Medellin, Colombia, 2018.
Source: Mercy Kagia

People used to share drinks with friends and sit and touch each other. And now this distancing. And last year that was strange for me. I am so used to being around crowds and seeing people interact and then suddenly the streets are empty. People don't touch each other anymore. Now it is just isolated individuals. Or, one person on each end of a bench talking.

What do the drawings bring back for you as opposed to looking at photographic snapshots from a holiday? What do drawings give you that is distinctly different from that?

The fact that I invested ten to twenty minutes on the drawing and really looking at one thing, I tend to remember that much more. I have a very bad memory. It is actually quite embarrassing. I have introduced myself to people I have met before.

That is actually quite surprising because your drawing contains a lot of information. I would have thought that you have a very good memory.

Well that's the thing. I have to draw right there in the moment. The minute I get up and go, it is gone. My detail comes from observation, definitely not from memory. Sometimes I need to leave a drawing and I say to myself I will finish it at home. When I get home, I look at it and nothing. I can't remember what I need to put into the drawing. Sometimes I make notes on the side to add this or that. But I just don't remember it. But I remember what I've drawn sticks with me as a memory. As you said I remember Machu Pichu and when you get there it is like cattle being herded from one point to another before they can get to wherever they need to go. And there are so many people that no one tells you when you are done you are not able to go back to a point you thought was interesting. You are standing in a place and the guides say this is a great place for a selfie. And you get these girls with their boyfriends to take a photo as they revel in being alive or something like that. And I just hated it. I absolutely hated it because I was interested in the history of it, I was interested in so much more. At some point I did get a drawing of a ruins which had the light hitting it in an interesting way but I stopped after a little bit as I was fed up with the crowd. But when I look at this drawing, I think about how simple it is and it doesn't capture the vastness of the place. It is such a small section of the place but it says a lot to me. Of my time being there. It was overwhelming and beautiful but it was also a bit annoying. So many people and so much pressure from the guides to go as fast as possible. The drawing becomes my memory. I remember doing this bit and I remember being tired. But I have zero memory to recall, to finish a drawing.

It is interesting that the drawing becomes the sole document of experience. The drawing exists independent of your own recall.

The drawings I have not enjoyed making are when I put pressure on myself to really capture something because it is really unique or rare. Especially when

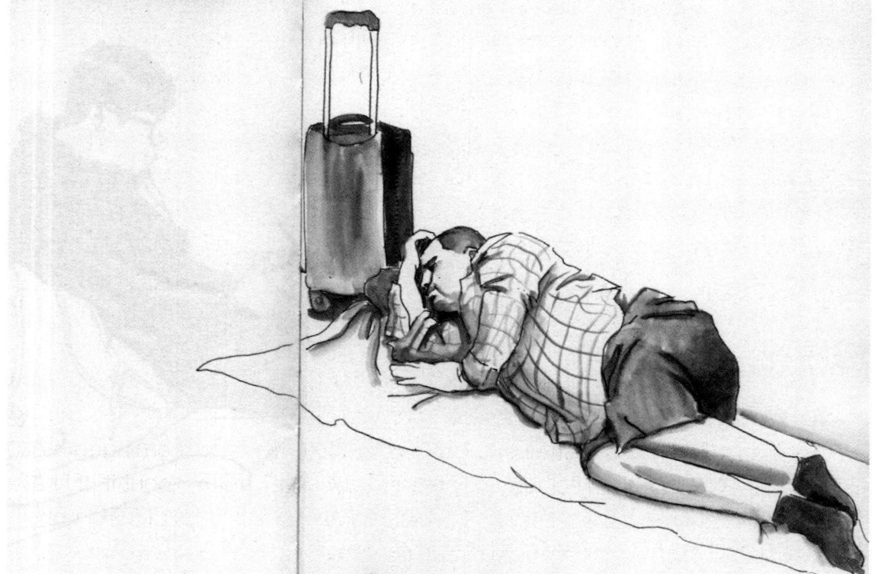

Figure 44 True airport despair, Doha, Qatar, 2017.
Source: Mercy Kagia

I am travelling. When I travel, I am aware that there is all of this new experience and things I haven't seen before and I need to capture something from it. If I think I must get this detail in or capture this moment because it might be good for an exhibition. I put this pressure on myself and I tend not to enjoy it as much. The minute I put pressure on myself to put colour in or capture some light. The minute I put pressure to get this because I won't be able to again. That is the moment I get disappointed. Whereas if I am just sitting there and think 'oh that's an interesting perspective … lets start' and never think about the end result. Let me put my pen down and see where it goes. Those drawings when my brain is empty and I have no expectation of myself, those are the ones that I find work … it doesn't mean they are beautiful and it doesn't mean they capture everything but they work. They have captured something of that moment. If I have a plan before and think I have a lot of information that I have to put together, then I am not very happy with them. Later I look at the sketchbook and thing 'ugg' is that what I have done? That's not the memory I wanted. And I always feel a little bit … I wouldn't say resentful, but I hold it against myself. I look at it and think I could have done much better if only I hadn't switched my brain off. On that note, I think the drawings that I think work better are the ones that I haven't over analysed. Or haven't planned through. Ones I have a goal for the drawing it doesn't work out. A little like life. My life philosophy is well, if you just start and don't put any expectation and don't over plan and things will work out. I find the drawings that work for me have that attitude. Go with the moment. You need a lot of trust in what you are doing and that allows you to switch off. I've spent years and years working on my observation skills and my line work. I find that when you start off you have so much you need to work through you are thinking about everything. Now, to be honest, if I just have a dip pen and my India ink that is sufficient. I don't need fancy paper. I don't need fancy water colours. I do use good quality materials now but then there is a sense that I have invested so much in building my sense of observation and building that eye and hand coordination that I trust that. I can switch off. And some of the more interesting drawing I have done I have had an audio book on. So I have really switched off. I am listening to something interesting and letting my hand follow through. When I was starting off I was very conscious. When I was drawing people I was trying to remember all the shadows around the eyes and the sockets and where the teeth are and how the lips come out from … I am trying to put together all of the information I have been learning to make this work. Now, subconsciously it is there. Now I don't think about it. If I have to make a quick drawing I am not thinking about how to do it I just know it. I also trust the eyes of the viewer. Even in a minimal drawing, there is so much memory and information in people's minds that they will fill out areas that you haven't included. In the end there is an element of trust in yourself and in the

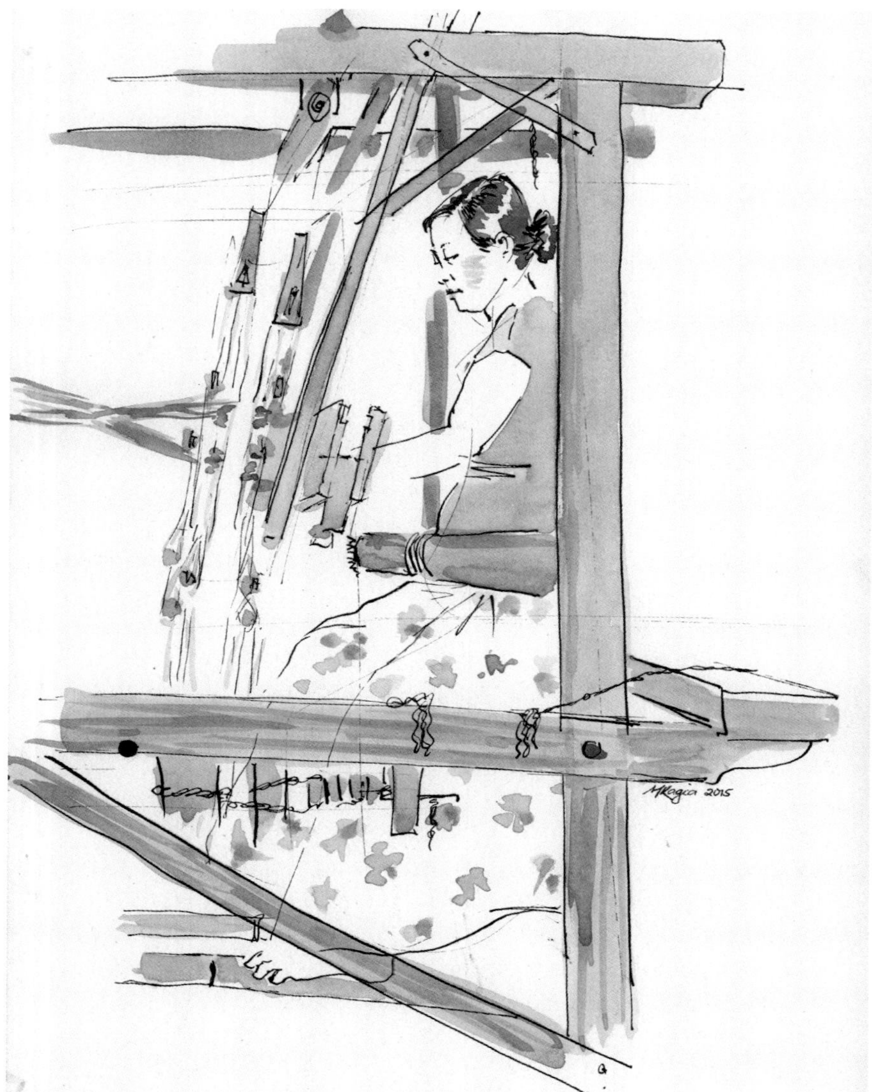

Figure 45 Weaving lotus and silk, Inle, Myanmar, 2015.
Source: Mercy Kagia

viewer. They will get it because we all have this collective memory. If I drew a horse in six lines, people know enough that it is a horse and not a dog.

How do you disseminate your work? How do you share it with the public?

It varies a little bit. Last exhibition was an illustration exhibition in Germany. It was an illustration show. I do find a little bit of a difference between reportage and illustration. I know there is reportage illustration. These works were more about things people could relate to. Travel destinations in Germany, Spain and also a sketchbook that had life drawing in it that I thought wouldn't go on sale but someone did want an image in there. The last exhibition I had in Kenya was based on travel and it was sketchbooks. Tons and tons of sketchbooks. From the sketchbooks that I keep you can learn a lot more about what I think is important in drawing and reportage. And I wanted to present them. The work that was on sale was a lot less than the sketchbooks. I would never want to sell a sketchbook. They are like personal diaries. If I want to remember a place that I have been I will pull a sketchbook off the shelf and flip through it. It all comes back. This was very different to what is expected of exhibitions in Nairobi. In a gallery called One Off contemporary art gallery in Nairobi, I had the sketchbooks and then printed out pages from the sketchbook so it was almost like a taster of what is inside. The actual sketchbook was behind Perspex. Somewhere in the middle. And then some smaller original artwork like watercolours that I ripped out of books. That is an easier way to have original work that can be sold. Some people really like something in a sketchbook and they want to buy it which doing them in a separate book solves that problem. So the exhibition was really a journey into what I look at and the two years previous and all of the travel that I had done. I wanted to make a statement about this part of my work that is not purely illustration it is a record for myself. I also had an exhibition in Bahrain in which musicians were rehearsing and I was drawing them right before the concert. When the concert was on, the big drawings I produced were exhibited in the foyer. I like drawing musicians very much. Here in Germany, I drew musicians in the philharmonic orchestra for their 150th anniversary. The drawings were all done on site with a famous violinist. I spent a few days squeezing myself in little corners drawing them as they performed and had the work in the foyer during the final performance. Since then if they every needed a gift for the orchestra or someone was leaving they asked to see if the work was available. It was very gestural. A lot of the time you could tell who was who but it was interesting to see the guys say 'is it this one or this one?' This exhibition I find interesting and I think they are more significant than having a big splashy grand exhibition which I love but I like the fact that the people I am drawing can come and see what I have done and engage with it and it is much more accessible for them. Those are different scenarios but they work well for me. I do also like quite informal settings. I have had work in cafes. And I do find that quite nice because people will have a coffee and look at your work and these are very different people and people who might not go to a gallery.

When you graduated from your BA did you position yourself as a reportage illustrator or were you doing different things?

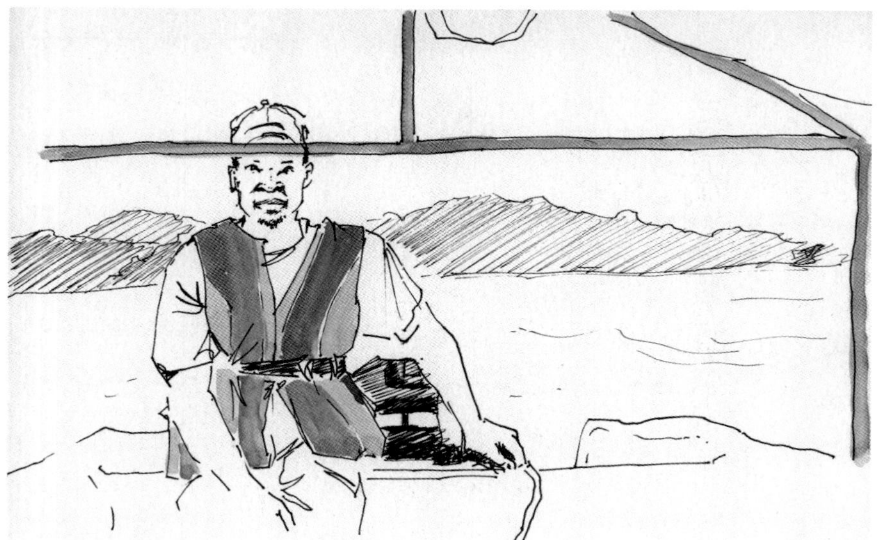

Figure 46 Boat driver, Lake Victoria, Uganda, 2019.
Source: Mercy Kagia

When I finished my BA the one distinct feeling I had was that I wasn't good enough to go out and start making work that I could sell. It goes back to the whole drawing people thing and with anatomy. I felt I needed to spend a little more time to develop my drawing so I went straight into an MA at Kingston University. It was an MA that doesn't exist anymore it was called Drawing as Process. It was brilliant. It was focused on not only drawing as an end result but looking at drawing as a thinking tool. And the different aspects of it so the idea was you don't focus on what you are producing at the end but focus on the mark making and thinking as your hand is moving you are processing whatever idea you have. That was very useful as well because as much I was then and am now figurative, there was this idea of mark making as a focus which was not about a tight line. I started teaching when I started my MA. And as a I went on, I finished my MA. I worked for a year at Kingston and then went back to Kenya. I taught for a year and developed the idea of a PhD. Mainly because I thought I really needed to reflect on what I was doing. Why am I doing what I am doing. Why do I keep getting asked if I will finish it because it is just a black and white line. Just! There were all of these questions going around in my mind and at this point I wasn't really … I would still make work that I would sell but not making work to sell. I was still making work, still drawing and filling sketchbooks but I wasn't making work with a view to sell it. When I started my PhD and when it ended, I was starting to make work with the intention to sell. I finished my PhD in 2012 and graduated in 2013.

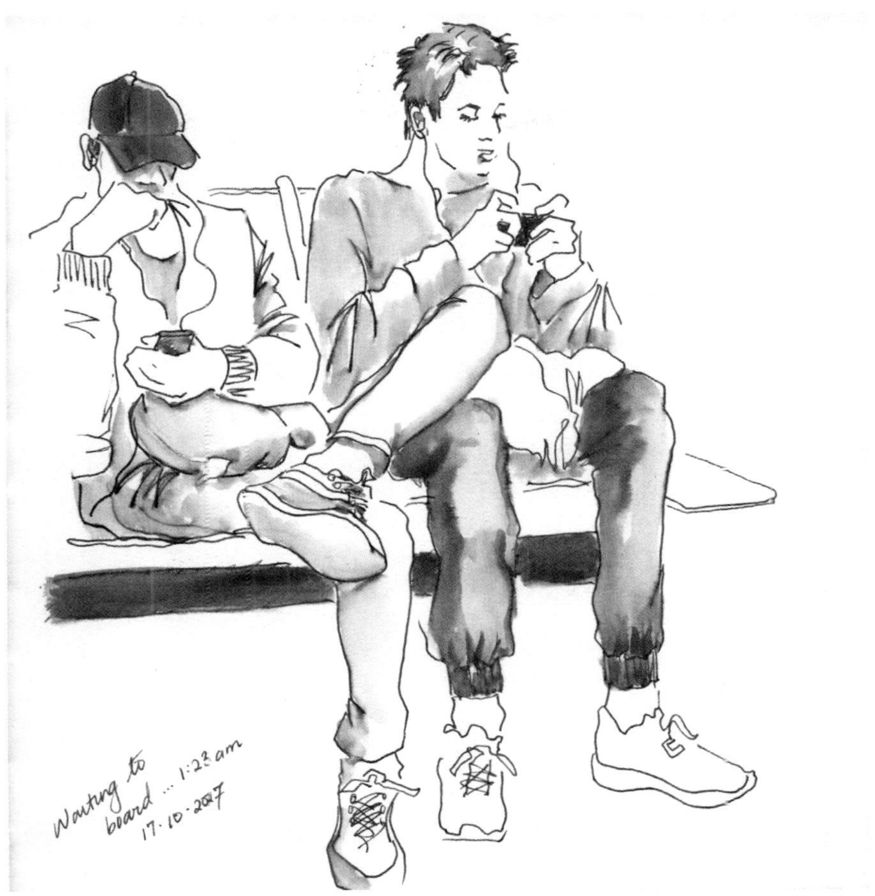

Figure 47 Waiting to board, Doha, Qatar, 2017.
Source: Mercy Kagia

I was still filling sketchbooks but I figured if I am going to pay my rent I need to figure out how to make this work commercial. This is when I started making the work on single sheets as people wanted sketches out of the sketchbook which I wouldn't do. So I would always take a sketchbook and a pad with me. Even if I don't have an exhibition coming up or work I will always be drawing. I am in my studio now. I have a studio at home and I look outside and I can see other flats and a view of the rathouse which is the city hall. And I will draw that. And I know over the next many years I will always have a drawing of that. I think this observation is key and it is always informing. It is also just reminding your brain how to look. Reminding your eyes to keep focused on this thing. And keeping your hand eye coordination going. I think it is as important as anatomy to keep stretching. It is the stretching and warm up and constant moving of muscles in drawing.

Conclusion

Mercy's work thoughtfully highlights the way in which reportage drawing identifies unique subjects among the plethora of options in fluid environments. Like many artists talked about in this book, it is the banality of life which can sometimes seem most compelling – the small moments that stand in contrast to a hectic reality or an established tourist destination. Travel makes us not only see and understand different cultures, it magnifies what connects us, and in the work of Mercy, we see a growing distractedness that she documents and a self-consciousness about the act of observing in a world that seems to be turning inwards. Like many reportage artists, the drawing holds a memory that for some is a more effective memory than photography. It is more effective because time and thought is invested in it. Mercy's detailed drawing demonstrates a deft observing hand and an evocative capture of the seen. Her sense of the historic record of the reportage drawing is a compelling idea but I wonder if there might be more to that notion. Perhaps her work can be better seen as a record less about times passage and more about her vision through it. Instead of a historical document, it is a trace of vision, attention and thought. It is a diary but not an inert record of the past; it lives a vivid new life with each viewing.

12
ARTIST SPOTLIGHT – DOMINIKA WROBLEWSKA

I first saw the work of Dominika in a graduate exhibition in London caled New Designers. I was genuinely blown away by the originality of her vision and the clear sophistication of her thinking. She had created a body of work around Norse fairy tales but had mixed them up with Scandi Noir elements. It had the sparkle of an original talent and I kept in touch, inviting her to speak to my students on a few occasions. Later, I was informed of new work that she was doing. Work that took her deep into caves near Manchester and creating highly evocative reportage work. Like her earlier work on Norse fairy tales, Dominika was submerged in her subject. Her tenacity and boundless energy to acquire knowledge and tell the story of cave explorers was well suited to reportage drawing. I interviewed her about this and her orientation to her work. Her art can be seen at www.domeeart.com.

Prior to your university education, was reportage drawing a term that you were familiar with?

I was not aware of something like this existing before I went to university. Actually, I think the very first time I heard of it was on my foundation year when they showed us some work by Olivier Kugler. When I saw it I was very impressed by it. It stayed somewhere at the back of my head. I don't think I put that consciously into my own practice until much later. Five years later in fact.

It is somewhat ironic that the most famous reportage artist is the Polish/ British artist Feliks Topolski.

Oh yes. I was completely unaware of that.

But then he probably wasn't very well known in Poland as he lived and worked in the UK.

We also have George Grosz. Was he German? He has a Polish surname so ....

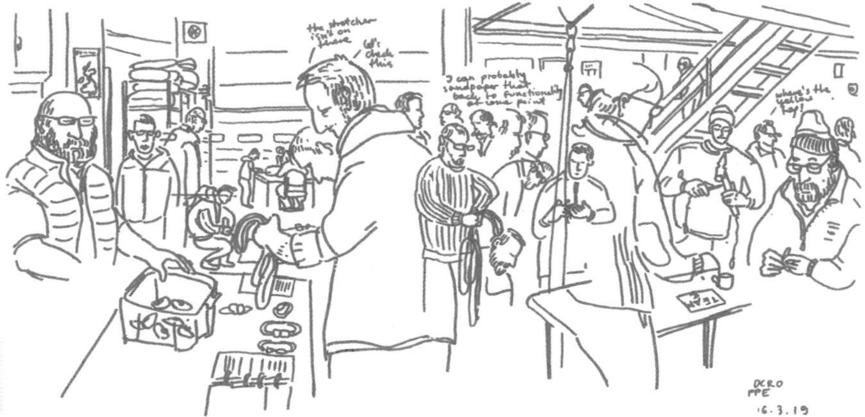

Figure 48 Dominika Wroblewska.

What was your art training prior to coming to the UK?

I went to high school before coming to the UK and I did go in an arts direction.
I had an art profile which enabled me to take extra classes but that was it. My
main education in the arts was in the UK.

That was in Manchester School of Art?

Yes, I did my foundation there, BA and then MA. It was an illustration with
animation degree.

So you did do a bit of animation?

I studied it and did a little bit. Not as much as I would have liked but in the
future I am thinking of re-visiting that area in my work.

The work that I saw at your graduate show was wildly experimental and based in fiction. How did you make this shift into documentary drawing?

It happened quite gradually and it started at the beginning of my master's
degree. I started to analyse my artistic practice and the methodologies behind
my projects. Then I realized that there were two things that all of my more
successful projects had in common. One was that the idea or concept behind
the project was always experiential. To do with observation of everyday life.
Putting myself in a location and gaining inspiration in that way.

Immersing yourself.

Yes.

So when you did Nordic folk tales you went there and soaked it up?

Yes. Exactly. Except it happened the other way around. I was obsessed with Norway. The landscape, the culture, the music … everything. That came first and then my illustrating Norwegian folk tales came after but I was using all of the experience gathered from these different trips to the country to seep into the illustrations. So there are quite a few hidden meanings that you wouldn't know if you haven't lived there for a while. So once I realized that this kind of immersion was part of my method I wanted to explore it further so the master's was the time I decided I should do it. At the time I was obsessed with two books: *In Patagonia* by Bruce Chatwin and *Island of the Colourblind* by Oliver Sacks. I loved the way that both authors depicted the reality around them. Intertwining historical or scientific events or facts with satire and also sensitive poetic observations. I found that this was my kind of language, my kind of thing. I was very excited by this and I have always been a kind of adventurous person so hiking, climbing, caving – all of those kinds of activities and that perhaps reportage illustration may enable me to explore them.

So back to the question. My shift from fiction was an understanding that real life had so much potential for incredible, bizarre stories that are as wild as anything in fiction. And if you are within that topic itself, you become part of the project, part of the story. Even though you are not portrayed within it, you are part of the illustration, you are there. It feels like an adventure that you are participating in.

Was your cave work entirely self-commissioned or was it part of a commission?

It was completely self-initiated. It happened during my master's degree. I did later on manage to get a grant from the British Cave Association which helped to develop the work further. So it started quite gradually. From a memory in fact. One of my earliest memories is from inside of a cave. It cropped up in my head from time to time and it just so happened to come to me again right at the beginning of my masters. And I started to question why it was such a strong memory and why have I been interested in exploring holes within rocks. If I see one I always must go in and see what is there. It was the perfect time to explore this obsession so I thought, let's see what I can do with it. It was a selfish reason for starting. It was all about me but then after starting and researching and going places, I realized there is a whole community of people who are also obsessed with caves. In fact so many people that it began to change the project and it really became reportage as my interest grew in who these other people were, why there were there and what they were doing.

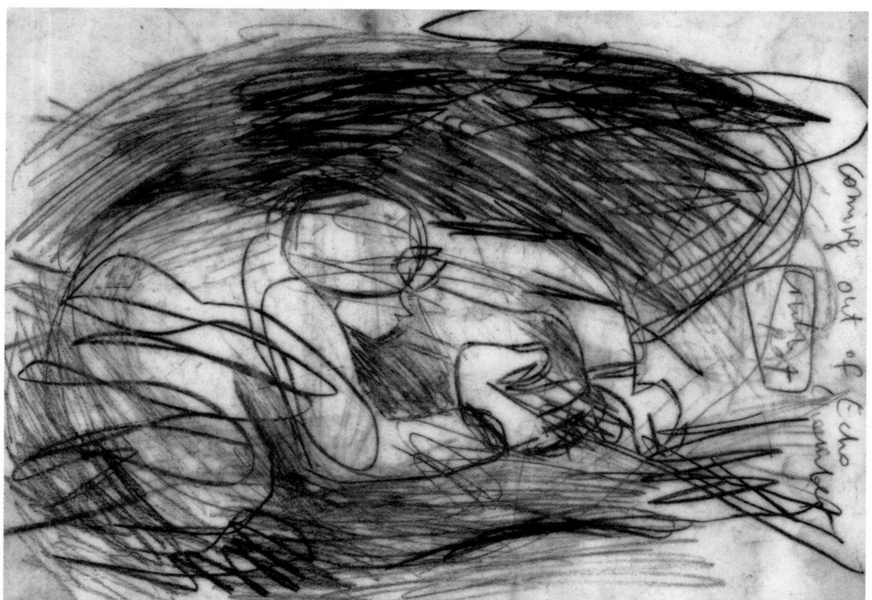

Figure 49 Dominika Wroblewska.

What are these activities underground that they are taking part in. I wanted to be a part of it but also share that story with others.

Is it because there was a community near you?

It was quite accidental. There are many strange things that happened in a very short space of time. One of the funniest moments was when we had a power outage at our house and I was walking around the house with my head torch, you know, like a cave. Our landlord came to fix the lights and he noticed something. I was reading on my computer which happened to be about caves. He then said, 'wow, back in the 60's when I was a kid I used to be a potholer'. I asked him what his favourite cave was and he told me and I went there. Then I bumped into a massive group of people underground. I wasn't expecting anyone to be there. This led to other discoveries and finally to one other caving club that is based in the Peak district in a little village called Castleton. The club has its own base in an old chapel connected to a dodgy looking garage. Such a great hidden world.

Do you see this project as connected to the tradition of reportage or journalism?

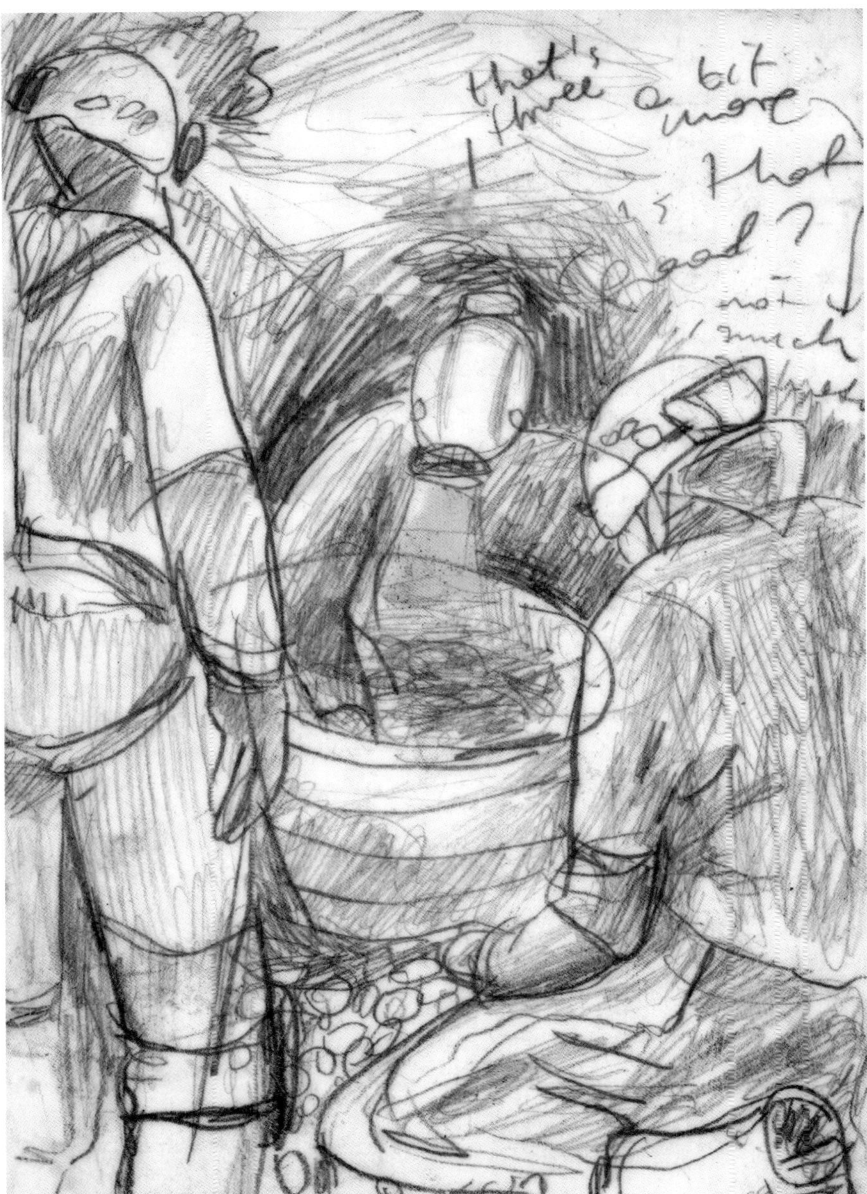

Figure 50 Dominika Wroblewska.

At the beginning I didn't really but later on … I guess the aim of the project became to reveal this hidden world of caves and these communities. For people on the outside but to offer a more insider perspective. So by joining the community and spending time making friends, having conversations and

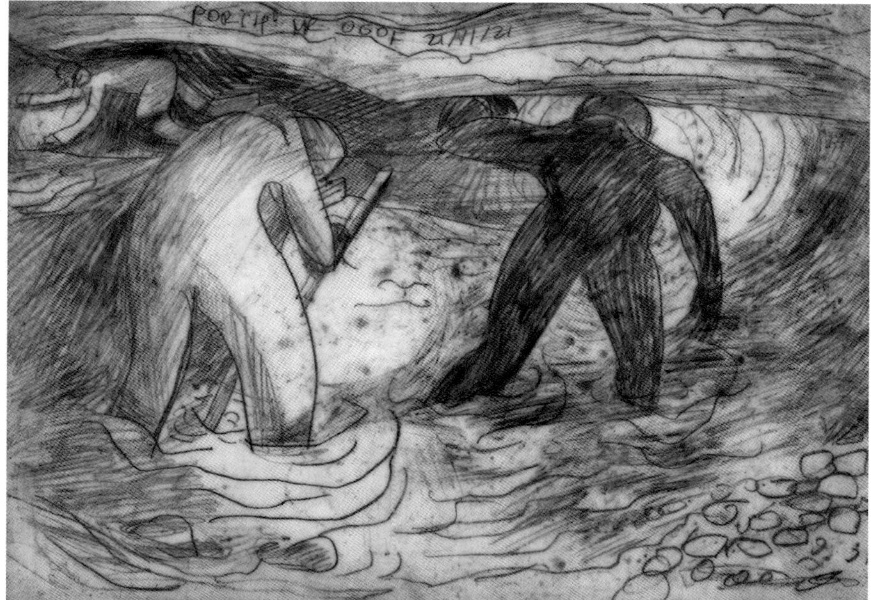

Figure 51 Dominika Wroblewska.

drawing a lot, you gain that insider knowledge. In terms of the tradition of reportage with illustrators travelling to different parts of the world to relay what it is like over there and show something new to a viewer. I think there is something similar there. It connects to that tradition.

Do you see yourself functioning as a visual journalist, artist or both?

Recently I feel I could class myself more around that term 'visual journalist'.

And maybe a diarist.

Diarist is a good word. I like that. I think probably both artist and visual journalist. I do a lot of different stuff but today the thing that excites me most is the diary, observation, journalistic sort of stuff.

Do you maintain other ways of working at the moment or are you just focusing on reportage?

I work full-time at the moment as a technician at Manchester Met. This takes up a lot of time. I don't have as much time for my other personal artistic work. I am always drawing however. Everywhere I go. I have a sketchbook with me. You never know when the perfect opportunity presents itself. You always have to be vigilant. I am hoping to create more time for my artistic practice. But reportage is the main thing for me at the moment. I am really using Instagram to post work and keep up to date with people and things. No commissions at the moment. I am working on some projects on the side but they are self-initiated. One is a digital platform called the northern dream archive. It is a kind of reportage type subject as you are reporting on your dreams and illustrating them. I have recorded dreams for two years and now I am beginning to create some content for them. I am hoping in the future this could be a platform for people to contribute and collaborate.

How do you see your drawing practice? Do you see drawing as your primary expressive medium or do you see drawing as part of your wider artistic practice?

At the moment it is certainly drawing. Mostly because of this obsession with recording what is happening around me. The reason I say obsession is because when you complete a drawing on location, it feels like you have just acquired a trophy. And now that trophy can be entered into the bank or archive of those other trophies of the different moments in time that you've recorded. Drawing is a way of collecting those moments in time. It lets you become connected to the world around you. Especially drawing on location. It trains your eye. You get to capture seemingly insignificant moments that normally we would forget about but there they are. I see it as a communication tool. Something to relay information with.

Do you feel a responsibility to your subject in terms of representation and narrative and do you think reportage creates a democratic space of understanding even though it is ultimately subjective?

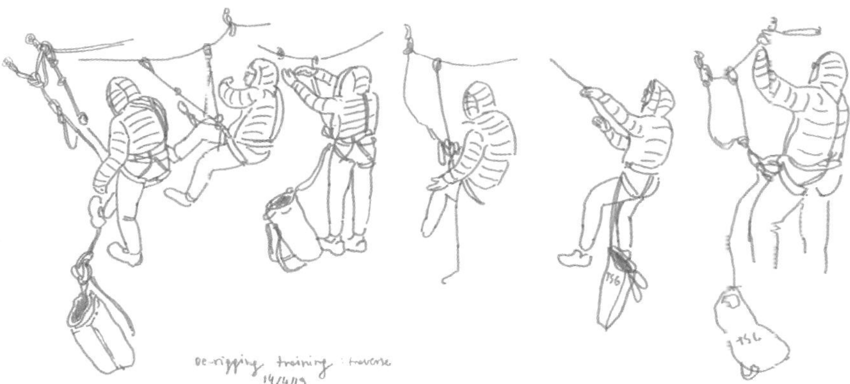

Figure 52 Dominika Wroblewska.

I think the written representation of what is seen should always be accurate in terms of facts. But the way you choose to present those facts can vary. The narrative can vary. For me, most of the time I try to go somewhere in between. Somewhere satirical or absurd or maybe something inquisitive or slightly more poetic. I think you usually just assess the situation and see what fits best with that situation. You have to also be quite careful about how you do it. There is always a lot of thought that goes behind the writing. For me, I find it excruciatingly painful but once it is done I am happy and it's amazing. But the process itself is extremely hard. In terms of the visual representation, there is always a lot of pressure for the drawing to be completed in time with the relevant amount of detail to get the point across. I am not too precious about the accuracy of the drawing. I am more concerned about capturing the whole scene of the overall atmosphere. I am not trying to completely reproduce everything. The drawings can be very expressive and very detailed, again, depending on how much time you have and the situation at that moment. There are so many other external factors that can affect the drawing as well.

In a way the quantity or lack thereof of information, or acquired details, in the moment is also part of that moment. It is all about the limitations that you are encountering. If a drawing is not very detailed there is likely a reason for that, a layer underneath it which has informed the drawing, such as it is too dark, too cold or limited vision ... that adds to the atmospheric qualities of the drawing. The absence of things.

Yes. And I think all of these qualities within the drawing allow the viewer to understand and interpret it.

That is a fascinating aspect of reportage drawing. It is as defined but what is not there as much as what is there. Piecing it together. Often that really connects you further to the experience of the artist and the vision.

Quite often I find that the more difficult the situation the more excited I am to have a go at it. To see what happens because you have even less control. Only then do you get a result that you were not expecting to get. Drawing in these situations like drawing on the go or drawing in the darkness is really hard to do. The moment before you start you think 'I am going to do this right here right now' you don't want to do it but you force yourself. Almost always you have a result that is extremely satisfying.

Do you learn things through drawing as a result of looking more intensely and how does drawing itself contribute to knowledge and understanding of people and contexts with reportage drawing?

I think when you are drawing on location with various things going on, there are different kinds of learning that occur. There is visual learning, experimenting with new ways of looking and documenting … I think you also end up learning about your own confidence. At first it is so difficult with people surrounding you and you look very out of place because you keep looking up and down and so forth. It looks unnatural. People want to find out what you are doing. You start conversations with people. Sometimes great conversations and sometimes it's questionable what you want to get out of it. You learn about your own confidence and it trains you to open up to people. You get into the flow of it and you become more laid back with the process. And the stuff outside of the drawing, all of the things that happens around it. That is also another story that the drawing holds that doesn't necessarily show but that is something can be maybe added in the writing.

Yes. Well, you see that and you remember that in the drawing. You remember the context.

Yes. And that is exactly the thing. The remembering. Drawing does help you memorize the place, the situation of the drawing but also the situation surrounding the drawing. What was happening that day? What was the weather like? What did this guy over there say to you?

All of the layers of observation and experience. Quite intimate. Like a conversation with yourself.

I quite often look at drawings later on and use it as a prompt to do the writing. The writing doesn't have to happen on the spot because that information is already recorded in the drawing. Connected to your brain through the subconscious and all it takes is to look at it again to access that information.

Do you think the image dominates text in this world? Do you think that is a good thing?

I think the image does dominate text. I think the image is more accessible when it comes to being able to quickly absorb information. And today we know that that is what everyone wants, for people to quickly absorb information. I don't think it is either good or bad. I would say it is natural because image precedes text historically. We painted images on the cave walls way before we could write. So images are a universal language. This is why I think something like reportage illustration can be very powerful because it can speak to people in a much more straightforward, clear way.

In your work, do you feel there is a link between art and activism?

The more I thought about this question the more I started to agree with it. The activism in my work is probably not very obvious. But I am trying to do something in my work, through my work. To encourage people to look at the world around them. To look with curiosity and some level of wonder even if those things they are looking at are not extremely exciting. I always like to present the side of things which is not obvious. I think there is activism in the work but not a strictly political form but some other kind.

I suppose it could be about getting people or encouraging them to have a greater awareness of their world and their experience. That is a form of activism. It is promoting a change of behaviour.

Do you have any future reportage adventures planned?

Well, I continue to gather images into my reportage collection. My bank or archive of images which one cay will become something. I will put these images on Instagram as it is a good way to prompt the writing about the images. I am waiting to see if some pattern emerges in the work that can make it a project. Now I am just happy to continue filling the bank but also looking at any possible topics that I can attach myself to and do another project. I am on the lookout or, maybe better to say, I am waiting for it to happen as quite often these thirgs just end up presenting themselves, rather than you choosing something. I think this can happen because you keep drawing and keeping your eyes open. I also want to find a publisher for my corona journal.

Lastly, I wanted to just touch upon something you mentioned to my students. You mentioned drawing on scuba slate in the caves because it was so damp. Can you tell me a bit more about that?

When you go down into a cave you have to consider all of those things such as mud, water, humidity, etc. You crawl through water, sometimes you have to swim through water and everything gets completely drenched. So sketchbook and paper will not do. I tried several different surfaces and materials throughout but then found the perfect one which is diving slate. It is made from a very thick PVC material around 3 or 5 mm thick. You sand it down to create a surface to draw on. They are designed for divers to draw or write underwater. The surface reveals the texture of the sanded plastic and pencil which is really beautiful.

Conclusion

Dominika's work has the closest connection to Mario Minichiello's In her work we see uncompromising vision and maturity. We see an almost overwhelming devotion to the subject of her art. In terms of reportage drawing, this energy, enthusiasm and breadth of investigation give us a gift of imbedded, infiltrated insight. As she notes, she becomes part of the story just as we have seen (quite literally) Mario in that car racing through bush fires. There is something both effortless and dense in Dominika's work. It is light but serious. This balance speaks to a tenacious mind and hand and contributes to contemporary reportage of a vision that aesthetically and conceptually doesn't play it safe. An adventure filled with the curiosity of its maker is the great promise of Dominika's work and it is a refutation of modern passivity.

13
THE CURRENCY OF REPORTAGE DRAWING

As demonstrated by this book, it is difficult to understand the contemporary practice of reportage drawing without an understanding of its historical origins and the ways in which illustration is practised and accessed today. The currency of contemporary reportage drawing is best understood through seeing it as a distinct part of illustrative practice and the diffusion of approaches that constitute the act. The future practice and relevance of reportage drawing is in three important areas. For one, reportage drawing is an activity which is practised by professional illustrators/artists and disseminated online, in mass media and in specialist publications. Here the illustrator is acting as a visual journalist. Secondly, commissioned and non-commissioned reportage artists and researchers are engaging in how reportage drawing can contribute to other fields and disciplines, for example, the sciences, historical subjects and contemporary social issues. Lastly, the impact of technology on the future of reportage drawing can be seen with virtual journalism, VR and digital drawing.

The currency of reportage drawing

Towards the end of the nineteenth century, through technical innovations and improvements to printing methods, the ability to replicate the effects of drawings and a range of tonalities was possible. Beyond the nineteenth century and into the early twentieth century, illustrators gained greater autonomy through establishing their own visual languages and, in some cases, choosing their own subjects as in reportage. The Ashcan School debuted in 1913 and were defined by their unflinching portrayal of the working class and poor in urban centres like New York (Doyle et al., 2019, p. 231). John Sloan, Robert Henri and Rodrigo Gruger were notable members and had a great impact on fellow illustrators and artists of their day through their deft and expressive draftsmanship and a vivacious approach to painting, which reflected the immediacy of their drawing. Sloan was to become the editor and chief artist of *The Masses* a socialist magazine in which his expressive, gestural and highly reductive drawing took on powerful issues of the day (Doyle et al., 2019, p. 325). This was dubbed social realism and marks a moment when the aesthetic of reportage drawing is being employed to engage viewers/readers as a witness through the impression of 'being there' in the quick, summative marks of the sketch. The liberation of the artist through technical improvements in printing led reportage towards greater editorial freedom which was enabled by a greater capacity for expression. Paul Nash's artwork, created as a witness during the First World War, was moving towards greater expressiveness and his own rationale for the work was to be 'a messenger who will bring back word from the men who are fighting to those who want the war to go on forever. Feeble, inarticulate, will be my message, but it will have a bitter truth, and may it burn their lousy souls' (Doyle et al., 2019, p. 340). The emotional currency of pictorial witnessing was a notable and exploited aspect of reportage practice in the early twentieth century and shaped the act in its development.

The development of reportage practice has inevitably been intertwined with technical advancements in both print and artistic visual language, and more philosophical developments such as existentialism (see the links between existentialism and expressionism). When the commissioning structures and conventions of the nineteenth century fade and the artist is not limited by technology, artistic progress and conceptual progress go hand in hand and developments in illustration mimic those in the other arts. As academic John Roberts notes, 'late nineteenth-century European capitalism does not just provide "new modern subjects" for the artist, but crucially transforms the *affective* space in which artists produce their work – how artists materially constitute the problem of representation – and as such how their works are received, transforming the questions of artistic value itself' (Roberts, 2010, p. 78). Technology enables the artist to identify and design an aesthetic approach and engage with the consequences and potentialities of new representational means. Professor of Illustration Alan Male notes 'the practice of expressing ideas rather than verbatim "scenes" or "pictures" has meant that *conceptual* illustration is now the dominant visual language' (Male, 2019, p. 88). He continues, 'whatever its genre of stylization … will be interpretive and present the "texture" of a topic and delve deep into its explication' (Male, 2019, p. 88). Although Male is largely referring to work that utilizes metaphor and allegory, the orientation to the subject in contemporary reportage as discussed in this book reveals a conceptual approach to both stylistic and subject choices and a wider awareness of the consequences of such choices on the reception and understanding of the work. Male has previously coined this 'visual intelligence' and defined this as 'identifiable maturity, experience, visual sophistication and contextual understanding' (Male, 2007, p. 52). In contrast, on objective drawing, Male notes three key elements to attain a 'knowledge-based discourse held within drawing'. Firstly, '*what* it is' its 'morphology'. Second, '*why* it exists' its 'ecology'. Lastly, '*how* it works' its 'biology' (Male, 2019, p. 122). This is a conception of drawing that for Male can be 'a significant strategy for an empirical approach to research' (Male, 2019, p. 122). Reportage drawing is then referred to as 'journalistic-style commentary' and 'less formal' (Male, 2019, p. 122). Male is reinforcing a perception that objectivity reflects a heightened engagement with a subject and that drawing that indulges in superficial attentions is lesser. While I disagree with the former, myself and other practitioners would largely agree that indulgence results in departures from the observed and that observation is an intelligence of seeing and is evidenced by specificities in the drawing. Paul Hogarth embraced changes to how reportage drawing was being pursued in the 1980s, noting 'the synthesis of the observed and the imagined … establishes their work as a viable and an exciting new approach in artist-reporting' (Hogarth, 1986, p. 174). Here Hogarth is referencing the work of Anita Kunz, Anne Howeson and Ian Pollock (to name a few) and acknowledges that 'some artists continue to work wholly or partly on location, whilst others who work from slides or remembered experiences, make a more oblique comment' (Hogarth, 1986, p. 175). The diffuse practice of reportage illustration has always reinforced both the differing conceptions and values around objectivity and subjectivity and the individual justifications that are the result of new approaches.

Contemporary approaches to reportage drawing are diverse in orientation to the subject and practice and yet reflect the same central desire of all reportage practice to transmit the experience in situ and engender intimate connections. Additionally, some contemporary practitioners are incorporating other media along with reportage drawing to connect to other realms of experience. This can be seen as a desire to provide more context to the work and this was noted by Gary Embury (see Chapter 8) as a desire for his work in the future. Olivier Kugler's work utilizes photography to capture rich details on location and he uses an audio recorder to get testimony from drawn subjects. Stacey Clarkson, the editor of *Harper's* magazine, noted of Kugler's work: 'Olivier has a very strong instinct for stories that will resonate over time and deep compassion. He foregrounds the voices of the refugees as they elucidate their experiences of escape and survival in an empathetic and moving way' (Walters, 2017, p. 46). With written notes on his drawing and the clear help of photographic reference, Kugler is delivering a hybrid form which has made him one of the most recognizable voices in contemporary reportage. The term 'empathetic' used by Clarkson confirms the value of drawing among commissioners for engaging with stories in an intimate way. John Walters notes the 'personal odysseys' of artists like Joe Sacco which heighten our personal connection to journalism, and in Sacco's case, including depictions of the author/illustrator on location (Walters, 2017, p. 48). Speaking of Sacco's journalism in comparison with Spiegelman's Maus, academic Hillary Chute notes 'both projects hinge on the plenitude of the visual, the ability to present an uncategorizable excess that is outside of the logic of the denotative' (Chute, 2016, p. 222). Seen in terms of the currency of reportage drawing and drawn imagery as a lens on our world, this statement reflects the way in which the inherent abstraction that drawing represents can vividly take us closer to a reality which is both atomized through depiction and exploded, opening the depicted moment to scrutiny and reception of all its effects and meanings. Contemporary reportage drawing has changed with access to technologies and a changing media environment; however, the connection to the personal, emotive and idiosyncratic vocabulary of drawing is central to its potency.

Other examples of extended reportage practice can be seen in the project *Reflections* organized by UK reportage artist Harry Morgan as a multimedia approach to capture the aftermath of the Nepal earthquake in 2015. The project brought together photojournalists, local artists, residents and reportage artists and resulted in a multimedia installation which was a true collaborative effort (Brazell, 2016, p. 50). Aligned with the commentary on Kugler's work, *Reflections* had the aim of 'foregrounding the impact on the lives of Nepali people' (Brazell, 2016, p. 50). Here, reportage drawing is nested within other media to deliver a wider context to the viewer of the stories of victims and flattened professional hierarchies, with professional and enthusiastic amateur artists and reporters sharing the same space. The work has been featured on the *Reportager* blog and there is a call on the project website to 'submit a story' (Brazell, 2016, p. 52). The emphasis on story with Kugler and Morgan's work indicates the contemporary desire to package reportage drawing into a narrative and extend pure drawing into multimedia platforms that align with trends in media consumption.

French animation artist Loup Blaster (see Chapter 10) used reportage methodologies in the creation of her film about the refugee crisis in Calais. The emphasis on story is clear in her own thoughts about the project but equally she notes 'storytelling can take any form … we are beyond questions of gender, style, techniques. Our eyes get to understand things really fast' (Blaster, 2017, p. 23). She adds, 'we need to ask what keeps the viewer curious, active and enriched from the experience of watching?' (Blaster, 2017, p. 23). She refers to her own approach to documenting Calais as a 'collage' of things she saw and she didn't storyboard her animation. She notes that a viewer described it as 'impressionism' and that relates to the way reportage drawings function in delivering textures of experience often without a deliberate narrative (Blaster, 2017, p. 23). She notes her final work 'gives an impression of reality, but using a sensitive approach that gives room for emotions' (Blaster, 2017, p. 23). It is perhaps this point which connects this work to wider reportage practice and the currency of the act in contemporary terms. In a media environment that is saturated with photo and video, the drawing or the animated drawing connects to new textures of experience and a new portal to understanding, enabled, in part, by the relative novelty of the form and the expansive vernacular of its application. Seeing reportage drawing as visual journalism, it is relevant to consider the context and means of dissemination in the current multimedia environment. Linus Abraham notes:

> Visual communication skills that were once defined separately, for example graphic illustration and photography are becoming increasingly integrated because of new media technology. The pace towards integration is also accelerated by the demands of the new medium of communicator, the Internet, by its very nature characterised by multimedia and integrated modes of communication. (Abraham, 2002, p. 178)

While the above quote is referring to visual journalism which is not necessarily reportage drawing, the contemporary reportage artist must acknowledge and respond to new and emerging platforms to stay current, relevant and impactful. Because of the popularity of comics, many artists are taking reportage assignments into the comic form and bringing in new audiences but also challenging established forms of the comic medium and thereby moving both practices to new places and forms. Phoebe Gloeckner is best known as the artist and author behind *The Diary of a Teenage Girl* graphic novel and is working on a large-scale and ongoing project exploring the death of young women in the violent Mexican city of Ciudad Juárez. The project is called *The Return of Maldoror* and is envisioned as an eBook which incorporates 'drawing, photography, text, sculpture, and animation, mixing narrative forms and genres, such as traditional reporting with the photo novella' (Chute, 2016, p. 263). This also includes creating a large three-dimensional set of Juárez with anatomically correct figures to re-enact sex crimes (Chute, 2016, p. 263). Gloeckner notes on her blog about the project that 'my purpose was not to report news, and my work wasn't intimately bound to factual details as a reporter's would be. My second impulse was to find the beauty in death, which is, naturally, usually obscured by horror or grief' (Charmy). Gloeckner's hybrid approach to visual reporting and narrative opens up new ways to engage with real places and events through novel aesthetic approaches and a conscious break from expected norms of depictive reality (see Kirshner, 2008).

Part of the currency of contemporary reportage practice is in its flexibility and its openness to new terrain and new avenues for practice and dissemination. However practised, reportage drawing, in all of its forms, mutations and adaptations, must go back to the central record of the witness and rely on first-hand observation. Writer John Carey notes that for reportage reporting 'eye-witness accounts have the feel of truth because they are quick, subjective and incomplete, unlike "objective" or reconstituted history, which is laborious but dead' (Carey, 1987, p. xxix). Carey is referring to written reportage but this is also central to drawn reportage, even hybrid forms, which engage the viewer through our understanding of the image as witnessed in some form by the artist.

Reportage and observational drawing as a contributing element to research in the sciences is an established practice both formally and informally, both public and private. Julia Midgley is a reader in documentary drawing at the Liverpool School of Art and Design and has had several residencies in which she was tasked with drawing on location for long periods of time to document how medicine and science were being practised, specifically the human story. She has worked on archaeological sites, in hospitals, at Blackpool's pleasure beach and on construction sites. She notes that drawing 'efficiently conveys the tensions and passions witnessed on location. The drama of surgery, for example, powerfully affects the artist, whose artworks will inevitably reflect emotive responses' (Midgley, 2010, p. 2). Midgley sees her work in these locations as collaborations and notes 'ideas are conceived which would not have been born without the access afforded by such collaborations ... To them, the artist is part lay-person, part professional observer, who presents objective, possibly novel, interpretations of their work' (Midgley, 2010, p. 6). Midgley found in all her residencies that the feedback to her drawings, both emotional and quizzical, revealed a surprising understanding of the function of reportage drawings to generate discussion, contemplation and an amplified understanding of an event. Archaeologists she observed working at the Chester Roman Amphitheatre site noted (about her drawings) 'they were emphatic that the drawings "were so familiar" that they recognisably portrayed not the research and academic rigour of excavation but the reality of archaeology' (Midgley, 2010, p. 11). As noted previously, reportage drawing has the ability to connect human stories to human experience through the imperfect yet indicative forms of drawing and through the re-creative act of looking. Midgley notes of works she produced in her residencies which are of emotional scenes, such as the death of a patient in a hospital or the uncovering of an infant's skull in an archaeological dig, and how the drawing becomes a record of the emotions felt by the artist and then the viewer, creating a 'cross fertilisation of sensitivities' (Midgley, 2010, p. 14). For Midgely, the currency of reportage practice is in its ability to present and exchange ideas and ultimately reveals our fascination with the human condition, providing a new lens from which we can share 'knowledge, perspectives and skills' (Midgley, 2010, p. 18).

Technology plays a significant role in the development and currency of reportage drawing, particularly when considering dissemination and aesthetics. Inherent in this is a question about the relevance of drawing itself and how, in what some call the de-skilling of art education, reportage drawing can maintain quality with arguably less skilled practitioners. Although another, possibly more convincing argument is that great art, even great drawing is about a conceptual orientation to the act and that rendering great art need not be about technical mastery. John Roberts notes about the shifting nature of skills and art 'reflections *on* skill (as a withdrawal from received skills), as much as the development of new skills become part of the restless, ever-vigilant positioning of art's critical relationship to its own traditions of intellectual and cultural formation and administration' (Roberts, 2010, p. 94). Technology may provide new skills which when learned may be capable of reflecting what is achieved in reportage drawing, but in a very different way. Roberts additionally notes 'conceptualisation serves to split the judgment of a work's skilfulness from the fetishistic evaluation of technical skills. The artist may choose to be a master of a given technical process … but this does not determine our judgment of the artist's skill overall' (Roberts, 2010, p. 92).

Mario Minichiello (see Chapter 9), an established reportage artist who has worked for the BBC and *Guardian* newspaper, conducted a study exploring the reaction to and reception of reportage drawing in comparison with newspapers, radio television and internet reporting. This was conducted through questionnaires that were distributed to visitors of his exhibition of drawings done from correspondent reports during the Afghan war in the early 2000s. He noted that '42% of respondents felt that "reportage" artwork had the greatest credibility' and '84% trusted the artist to be "fully in control' of their work whereas film and print were seen as the most compromised with only 13% trusting that film had not been subjected to bias or interference' (Minichiello, 2006, p. 145). Minichiello's emotive drawings have the impromptu effects of drawing in situ from a directly observed subject but push the viewer towards greater abstraction as seen in his images which create impossible compositions, focusing on texture, atmosphere and the macabre aspects of war. The currency of reportage, as evidenced here, is linked to the perceived authority of the artist and the perception that drawn works are a construct of the artist alone and therefore are authentic. This perception is key for reportage drawing to consider as it moves into new forms and opens itself up to the scrutiny and distrust of other forms of digital media.

Virtual reality is a developing field which encompasses a wide range of applications yet is limited by access to specialized hardware Immersive journalism is a term which describes attempts to deliver news stories in VR and engage viewers/experiencers in the on-the-ground confrontations of journalists. Donghee Shin and Frank Biocca conducted an experiment exploring the immersiveness of immersive journalism with fifty people and with two different ways to engage with the content (VR headset and flat-screen TV) (Shin & Biocca, 2017). It was notable that immersiveness was not a given for participants and through further questioning it was revealed that 'immersion depends on the users' traits and contexts; the function of immersion is strongly dependent upon user sense-making and intention' (Shin & Biocca, 2017, p. 3). Shin and Biocca further this, noting 'the immersive experience in IJ, where the viewer feels as though they are part of the action. is not directly given by HMD, VR goggles, stereoscopic video, or 360-degree camera … rather, it is reconstructed via user cognition and the stories of VR are reprocessed using user sense-making processes' (Shin & Biocca, 2017, p. 12). With immersive journalism, as opposed to reportage drawing, the medium or delivery mechanism itself is the barrier for total immersion as is the nature and content of the story which motivates the user to engage. To be clear, the immersive journalism discussed in this study refers to computer-generated environments and avatars, and there is little indication of the aesthetic look and feel of these environments. The BBC has had a few forays into VR and even offers a free app on their website for content created for the Oculus VR system. One such VR experience which can be considered immersive journalism is the story *We Wait* which takes the viewer/experiencer on a boat ride with a terrified migrant family escaping war in Syria and travelling on the sea (*We Wait* VR, 2016). The aesthetic of the animation reflects a generic avatar common to VR applications and does not have the aesthetic or urgency of reportage drawing. A project that more closely replicates the qualities of drawing within the immersive environment of VR is the project *Drawing Room. Drawing Room* uses the drawings done by Dutch artist Jan Rothuizen of Amsterdam from the high tower of a department store. Working with interactive designer Sara Kolster, they created an immersive, interactive environment that Jan described as 'drawn reality' (Drawing Room). The project won the IDFA (International Documentary Film Festival Amsterdam (2015)) award for digital storytelling and was praised for the inherent contrasts between the poetic drawn environment and the more photo-real environments that are typical of VR. These forays into VR and challenges to its nascent aesthetic are important for the future of drawn reportage as it inevitably evolves with technology.

Jenny Soep is a reportage artist who specializes in drawing alternative music performances and has developed a successful career, drawing Bjork, Patti Smith, Paul Simon and Yo-Yo Ma among many others (Embury & Minichiello, 2018, p. 88). She draws with an iPad Pro and this choice enables her trademark trace of movement and ability to add colour which enables great flexibility, atmosphere and digital effects. In addition to musical performances, Soep has drawn weddings, interviews, music prizes and dance performances. Soep's choice of reportage subject matter is unique and the recognition and interest in her work from musicians and other artists confirm her contribution to capturing those events. Using an iPad is less of a dramatic departure from reportage practice for Soep but does reflect a desire for immediate dissemination and some of the seductive tools that digital drawing provides.

Conclusion

The currency of reportage drawing has always been its connection to human stories, rendered by hand and therefore imperfect and connected to individual vision and attentions. Ronald Searle said of his drawings of Paris that they were more 'family snaps' than 'grandiose panoramas' and that he was 'haunted' by the many representations of Paris created previously and preferred to present a vision of what it '*feels* like to live in Paris, rather than what one might imagine it is like' (Searle, 1988, pp. 8–9). At the centre of the question around the currency and future of reportage drawing is its perception as an article of truth and this relates as much to the changing perception of the artist and media in general as it does to an evolution in the way we see drawing. Alfredo Cramerotti in his book *Aesthetic Journalism* notes 'we no longer consider artists as specialised craftspeople: to produce sense socially and politically one has to abandon the notion of artisanship in favour of innumerable forms of expression, which include film festivals, newspapers, television, internet, radio and magazines' (Cramerotti, 2009, p. 22). This reflects the diversity of projects mentioned above and supports a vision of reportage drawing which does not hide its subjectivities and, as Cramerotti notes, 'employ(s) fiction as a subversive but meaningful and effective agent of reality' (Cramerotti, 2009, p. 22). As Jil Gibbon (see Chapter 6) notes, 'drawing requires a different kind of looking' and for her this enables an alternative vision to the 'regime' of surveillance she witnesses at arms fairs (Gibbon, 2018). Drawing also benefits from the perception of it as an act of one hand and vision, and although able to be manipulated, there is an assumption that such alterations would be done by the artist. W. J. T. Mitchell notes that the artist and his or her images are seen differently from the digital or photographic image. He notes 'a painter, firstly, is traditionally seen as an artificer, a patient maker, an urbanized craftsperson who transmutes formless raw materials into images. We naturally use the language of personal intention – reference, comment, expression, irony, conviction, truthfulness, and deception – to describe this process' (Mitchell, 2001, p. 56). Mitchell contrasts this with the digital image economy and notes 'the currency of the great bank of nature has left the gold standard: images are no longer guaranteed as visual truth – or even as signifiers with stable meaning and value' (Mitchell, 2001, p. 57). Andrew Hoskins notes a similar crisis of meaning and trust occurring in journalism, noting 'the massively increased pervasiveness and accessibility of digital technologies, devices and media – has ushered in a "post-scarcity culture" and charged a wholesale reappraisal of the nature and the value of journalism' (Zelizer & Tenenboim, 2014, p. 179). In a media environment inundated with photographic and video content, drawing asserts itself as a medium that despite inherent subjectivities, through its connection to its maker, moves us towards mutual experiences with the world around us and gives us new ways to construct meaning and understanding.

14
CONCLUDING COMMENTS

Reportage drawing can be individually seen as both a recorded experience and, as Berger has noted, the 'simultaneity of a multitude of moments' (Here he is referencing the process of drawing as well as the experience of the subject.) (Berger, 2008, p. 71). It can also be said that drawings are never singular in their meaning. They are containers of a range of experiences in the making of the drawing and the engagement with the subject. As such, the reading of the images is always more expansive and unfixed. Political satirist and avid street sketcher George Grosz noted about drawing that 'maybe my pictures outwardly seem like baskets; that there is, naturally, something inside those baskets is something else again. I believe drawing may have originated in man's inborn sense of braiding and weaving' (Grosz, 1998, p. 34).

While the contemporary practice of reportage drawing is expansive and popular (see urban sketchers movement), its visibility in mainstream media does not reflect this and besides courtroom sketch artists, we rarely see and engage with drawing as mediated vision.

A notable contemporary example of reportage in book form is Victoria Lomasko's *Other Russias*. She called her own work 'graphic reportage' noting an affinity to graphic novels but preferring a singular approach to subjects which is more in the tradition of reportage drawing. She eloquently states her interest in reportage saying, 'I felt the need to complete my drawings on the spot, to serve as a conductor for the energy generated by events as they happened. I refused to make drawings from photos and videos.' She further says, 'what I was trying to do, above all, was to break through to a more direct grasp and reflection of the reality around me' (Lomasko & Campbell, 2017, p. 8). This last point is particularly relevant to the wider question 'why reportage drawing'. It s this direct engagement with experience and witnessing that is so critical. The drawings accumulate interest and complexity when we know they are real people and equally, in the construction of the drawing, where we see vision being wrestled into coherence. The vision and the struggle is a defiantly human one and a critical understanding for the potential of reportage drawing as a media form.

In reportage drawing, as artist Ben Shahn noted, 'form is formulation .. form is as varied as the accidental meetings of nature. Form in art is as varied as idea itself' (Shahn, 1957, p. 53). For Shahn, form is content and content is form, and reportage drawing provides another way to see and understand the realities on the ground through the topographies of drawn lines. People and places inhabit each other. The mystery lies in what the artist is ultimately capturing and how closely it approximates reality. As shown in this book, the success of a reportage drawing is largely self-regulated by the artist, but the viewer will have different ideas, formed by their ability to align with the artist's vision, experience and visual language.

Reportage drawing happens in mere moments, but it reflects the merger of thought, action and feeling. Ernst Kris notes about inspiration that 'inspiration designates, as we said, the sudden arising of visions or thoughts, and in this sense, inspiration may be called almost the everyday version of the creative process … a flash of thought' (Kris, 1964, p. 296). The flash of thought is often the impetus for getting out the drawing implement and doing a drawing. It reflects something in the person, place or thing that is compelling and possibly symbolic. A passing thought or 'flash' becomes an immediate scrawl with purpose. This is highly subjective and may pollute drawings with overt subjectivity. However, the drawings are responsive to something seen. They would not exist if they were not 'inspired' by the real. They are designed to counter 'over-thinking' and relish the battle to wrestle vision into form. Through this immediacy, reportage artists attempt to purge their drawings of artifice. The sketch does not hide its formation, it embraces the trace of creation.

Baudrillard is a writer who, for me, manages to capture in writing what the image often does when seen as a text. His exploration of America (a place I know well) is evocative like a Basquiat painting, letting ideas merge with effortless ease, seemingly chaotic but urgent and dead eyed. In his wide-ranging meditation on America called *America*, he notes of California that 'even nature in California is a Hollywood parody of ancient Mediterranean landscapes: a sea that is too blue, mountains that are too rugged, a climate that is too gentle or too arid, an uninhabited disenchanted nature, deserted by the gods: a sinister land beneath a sun that is too bright' (Baudrillard, 1988, p. 103). Like these words from Baudrillard, all drawings function as provocations and fire our imaginations to see connections, parallels and, ultimately, confront our own ideologies. Drawings proclaim to be something of 'reality', but they are just dirt marks and scrawls. When assembled in the mind, they, like a piece of poetry, cobble the realms of the real and imagined, making something new. Something that approximates not life but the experience of life. Something the psychogeographers perhaps desired.

The artists featured in this book and the way they encapsulate the contemporary act of reportage drawing reveal a return to fundamentals. Vision mediated through the limitations of hand, mind and circumstance delivers imperfection and incompleteness. In most other media forms this would be an obvious disadvantage. In the realm of reportage drawing, it enables us to connect to the artists' vision, like putting on a VR headset and retracing the drawing act. The fallibility of drawing reflects our own fallibility, and we move towards completing the act, filling the gaps and finding closure. We do it because we believe in the record and more than just our visual senses are engaged. The feedback for the artist and the viewer is rewarding. Drawing maintains two powerfully opposing features: that of the primitive and the sophisticated. Like the marks on a wall made thousands of years ago, there is a magician's turn in rendering pictures on a surface.

Drawing allows us a human lens from which to see. Drawings capture the experience of seeing and witnessing. A drawing is an empathetic dialogue with the viewer. It invites participation and re-creation. They are rooted in observation, but they are deliberate constructions, made at the point when seeing becomes looking and looking becomes feeling.

Reportage drawing has a long and rich history and the contemporary act persists in defiance of more comprehensive, more accurate and ever more spectacular technologies. Its formal, creative challenges become, after much practice, a synthesis of thought, feeling and artistic intent. As filled with intent as the drawing is, it rarely just reflects back those intentions. Its meaning is never fully controlled and it is pulled further from control by the viewer who will inevitably bring a new lens, a new understanding. In this sense, drawing is not just a summation, it

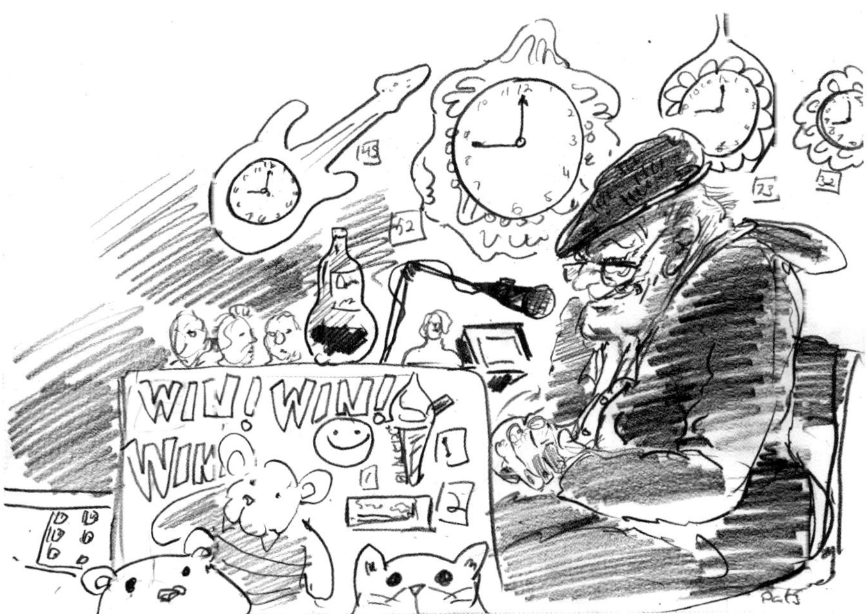

Figure 53 Blackpool, Lancashire.
Source: Louis Netter

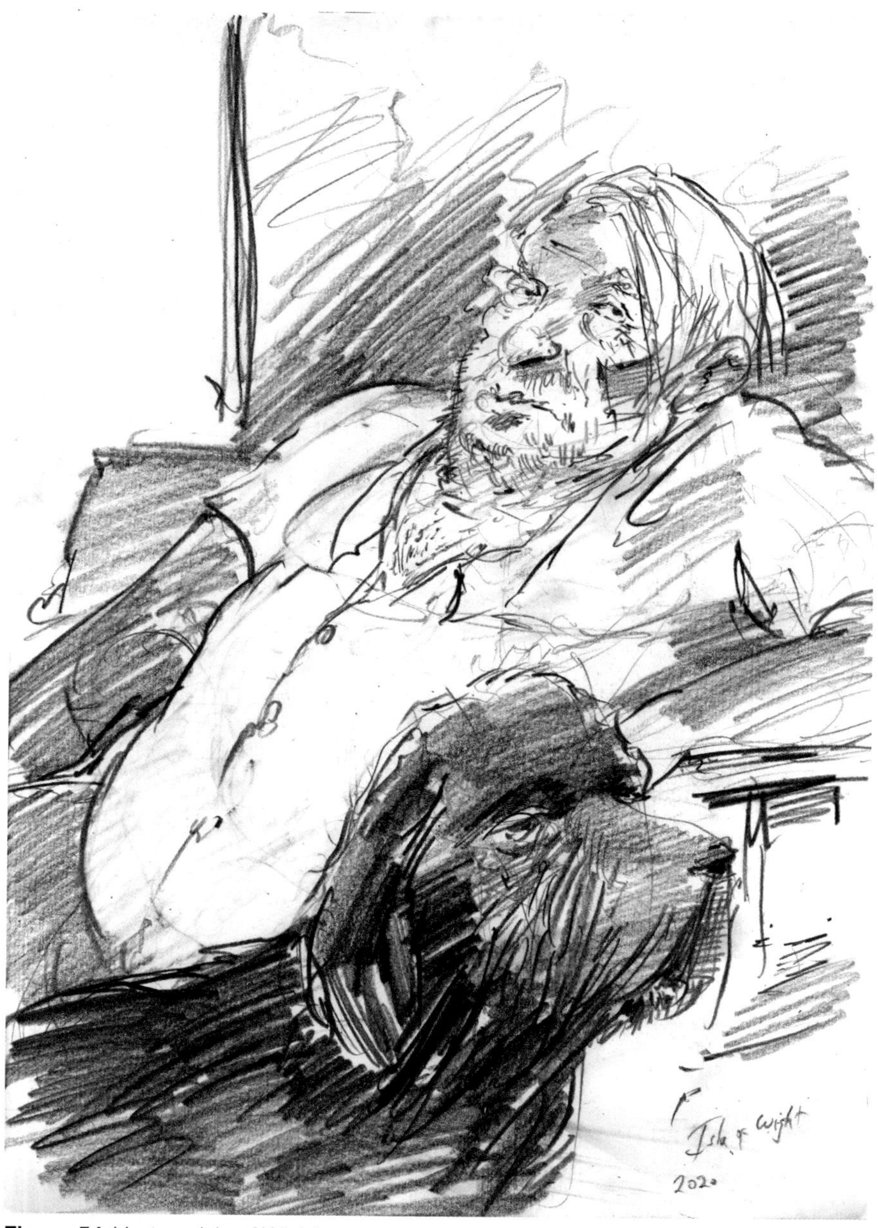

Figure 54 Ventnor, Isle of Wight.
Source: Louis Netter

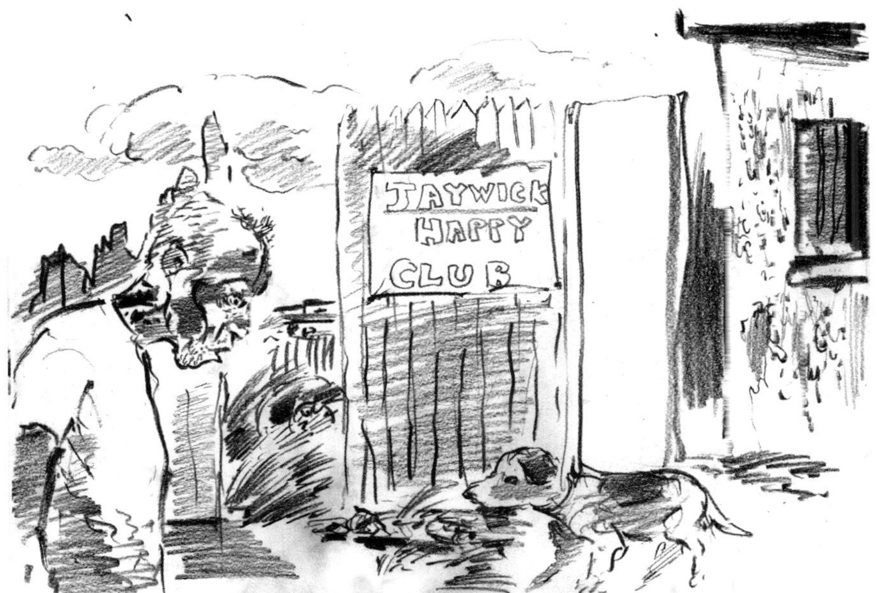

Figure 55 Jaywick, Essex.
Source: Louis Netter

is a new vision, a vision which is ultimately reflexive, an epistemological challenge. Reportage drawings teach us new things about the limits of vision and the playful dance between what we know, see, feel and think in the work.

When I take a photograph it is rushed, and like so many other people, I rarely ever look at it again. When I draw, the drawing holds a kind of power, like Dominika Wroblewska's trophies of captured reality (see Chapter 12). No matter if the drawing is stacked with many other drawings from a similar trip, it is there, like a piece of my own psyche, waiting to be revisited. And I do, often. It transports me back to the circumstances of its production and all the feelings I had, both connected to the subject and tangential insights and circumstantial memories. Drawings quickly obtain their own autonomy once drawn. They are masters of their own domain. You have made them, but if successful, they are a complete statement, they are whole. They also look back. They question you. I hope this book has enabled you to see the richness in reportage drawing and how the act is formulated, its historical shifts and the valuable contribution it makes to rendering meaning about the world. Further research into the ethics of reportage drawing, its potential in emerging technology and its continued relevance in a rapidly digitizing world are all possible extensions of this work.

If you see me with a sketch pad under my arm, please come up and say hello. If I appear to be drawing you, please don't move so much. Oh, and sorry in advance (Figures 53 to 55).

REFERENCES

Abraham, L. (2002). Visual journalism: An integrated conception of visual communication in journalism education. *Journal of Visual Literacy, 22*(2), 175–90. doi: 10.1080/23796529.2002.11674588.

Adams, T. E., S. Holman Jones, & C. Ellis (2015). *Autoethnography*. New York: Oxford University Press.

Arnheim, R. (1954). *Art and visual perception – A psychology of the creative eye*. London: Faber and Faber.

Arnheim, R. (1969). *Visual thinking*. London: Faber and Faber.

Atweh, B., S. Kemmis, P. Weeks, & M. Wilkinson (1998). *Action research in practice: Partnerships for social justice in education*. London: Routledge.

Barrett, E., & B. Bolt (2007). *Practice as research: Approaches to creative arts enquiry*. London: I.B. Tauris.

Barthes, R., & S. Heath (1977). *Image, music, text*. London: Fontana.

Baudelaire, C., & J. Mayne (2006). *Painter of modern life and other essays*. London: Phaidon.

Baudrillard, J., & C. Turner (1988). *America*. London: Verso.

Beatty, C., S. Fothergill, & I. Wilson (2008, November). *England's seaside towns a 'benchmarking' study*. Assets Publishing Service. Retrieved 25 February 2022, from https://assets.publishing.service.gov.uk/government/uploads/system/uploads/atta chment_data/file/7624/englishseasidetowns.pdf.

Benjamin, W. (1998). *Understanding Brecht*. London: Verso.

Berger, J. (1991). *About looking*. New York: Vintage.

Berger, J., & J. Savage (2008). *Berger on drawing*. Aghabullogue: Occasional Press.

Blaster, L. (2017). Tell me a story. *Varoom*, (35), 22–3.

Bolter, J. D., & R. Grusin (2000). *Remediation: Understanding new media*. Cambridge, MA: MIT Press.

Brazell, D. (2015, Winter). Street stylings. *Varoom*, (28), 16–18.

Brazell, D. (2016, Spring). After the earthquake. *Varoom*, (33), 50–4.

Brazell, D. (2017, 1 January). Derek Brazell selects Melanie Reim's drawings from the USA election. *Varoom*, (35), 42–5.

Brown, J. (2006). *Beyond the lines: Pictorial reporting, everyday life, and the crisis of gilded age America*. Berkeley: University of California Press.

Burgin, V. (1994). *Thinking photography*. Houndmills: Macmillan.

Carey, J. (1987). *The Faber book of reportage*. London: Faber and Faber.

Carter, P. (2004). *Material thinking: The theory and practice of creative research*. Carlton: Melbourne University Press.

Causey, A. (2017). *Drawn to see: Drawing as an ethnographic method*. Toronto: University of Toronto Press.

Certeau, M. D., & S. F. Rendall (2011). *The practice of everyday life*. Berkeley: University of California Press.

C h a r m y. (n.d.). Retrieved from https://ravenblond.wordpress.com/

Chute, H. L. (2016). *Disaster drawn*. Cambridge, MA: Harvard University Press.

Collins, H. (2019). *Creative research: The theory and practice of research for the creative industries*. London: Bloomsbury Visual Arts.

Connelly, F. S. (2014). *The grotesque in Western art and culture: The image at play*. New York: Cambridge University Press.

Coughlan, S. (2021, 21 July). *Seaside poor health overlooked, warns Whitty*. BBC News.

Coverley, M. (2010). *Psychogeography*. Harpenden: Pocket Essentials.

Crabapple, M. (2013, September). It dcn't Gitmo better than this: Inside the dark heart of Guantanamo Bay. *VICE, 11*(8), 100–9.

Cramerotti, A. (2009). *Aesthetic journalism: How to inform without informing*. Bristol: Intellect.

Crary, J. (1990). *Techniques of the observer: On vision and modernity in the nineteenth century*. Cambridge, MA: MIT Press.

Crary, J. (2001). *Suspensions of perception attention, spectacle and modern culture*. Cambridge, MA: MIT Press.

Creswell, J. W., & J. D. Creswell (2017). *Research design: Qualitative, quantitative, and mixed methods approaches* (4th edn). Newbury Park: Sage.

Denbeaux, M., S. M. Haire, T. Laing, K. Guldner, D. Pope-Ragoonanan, A. Casner, B. Lewbel, T. Paulson, T. Profeta, J. Sobh, N. Waters, & B. Zahriyeh (2019). How America tortures. *SSRN Electronic Journal*. https://doi.org/10.2139/ssrn.3494533.

Dewey, J. (1929). *Experience and nature. Lectures upon the Paul Carus Foundation* (2nd edn). Chicago: Open Court Publishing Comp.

Dewey, J. (2005). *Art as experience*. New York: Berkeley.

Doyle, S., J. Grove, & W. Sherman (2019). *History of illustration*. New York: Fairchild Books.

Drawing Room. (n.d.). Retrieved from https://www.doclab.org/2015/drawing-room/.

Edwards, J. D., & R. Graulund (2013). *Grotesque*. Abingdon: Routledge.

Eisner, E. W. (2002). *The arts and the creation of mind*. Yale: Yale University Press.

Embury, G. (2014). *Witness: Reportage and documentary*. Penryn: Atlantic Press.

Embury, G., & M. Minichiello (2018). *Reportage illustration: Visual journalism*. London: Bloomsbury Visual Arts.

Evans, K. (2017). *Threads: From the refugee crisis*. London: Verso.

Field, A. (2015, Spring). American histories: Official & unofficial. *Varoom*, (29), 34–5.

Garner, S. W. (2008). *Writing on drawing: Essays on drawing practice and research*. Bristol: Intellect.

Gibbon, J. (2018). *The etiquette of the arms trade* (1st edn). Nottingham: Beam Editions.

Gombrich, E., & E. Kris (1938). The principles of caricature. *British Journal of Medical Psychology, 17*, 319–42. doi: 10.4000/books.pupo.2233.

Gombrich, E. H. (1963). *Meditations on a hobby horse*. Oxford: Phaidon.

Gombrich, E. H. (1972). *Art and illusion: A study in the psychology of pictorial representation; … lectures …*, Nat. Gallery of Art, Washington, 1956. Princeton, NJ: Princeton University Press.

Gombrich, E. H. (1994). *Meditations on a hobby horse: And other essays on the theory of art*. London: Phaidon.

Gough, M. (2013). Drawing between reportage and memory: Diego Rivera's Moscow sketchbook. *October, 145*, 67–84. doi: 10.1162/octo_a_00148.

Gray, C., & J. Malins (2004). *Visualizing research: A guide to the research process in art and design*. Aldershot: Ashgate.

Gross, J. (2019, 16 November). *The 50 best non-superhero graphic novels*. Rolling Stone. 31 May 2022, Retrieved from https://www.rollingstone.com/movies/movie-lists/drawn-out-the-50-best-non-superhero-graphic-novels-29579/m s ter-x-dean-motter-and-various-157831/.

Grosz, G. (1998). *George Grosz: An autobiography*. Berkeley: University of California Press.

Groth, G. (2004). *Drawing the line: Interviews with Jules Feiffer, David Levine, Edward Sorel, Ralph Steadman*. Seattle: Fantagraphics Books.

Halliday, M. A., & J. Webster (2009). *The essential Halliday*. London: Continuum.

Heath, C., J. Hindmarsh, & P. Luff (2010). *Video in qualitative research: Analysing social interaction in everyday life*. London: SAGE.

Hibbert, C. (1975). *The Illustrated London News' social history of victorian britain*. London: Angus & Robertson.

Hofmann, W. (1957). *Caricature: From Leonardo to Picasso*. London: John Calder

Hogarth, P. (1986). *The artist as reporter*. London: Gordon Fraser.

Hogarth, P., & G. Greene (1986). *Graham Greene country*. London: Pavilion Books.

Hogarth, W., & R. Paulson (1997). *The analysis of beauty*. New Haven, CT: Published for the Paul Mellon Centre for British Art by Yale University Press.

Hulton, P. (1984). *America 1585: The complete drawings of John White*. Chapel Hill: University of North Carolina Press.

Hustvedt, S. (2013). *Living, thinking, looking*. London: Sceptre.

Illustrationclass. (2017, 30 October). The Weave. American Illustrator Robert Weaver. Retrieved from https://illustrationconcentration.com/2017/10/29/the-weave-ameri can-illustrator-robert-weaver/.

Ingold, T. (2016). *Lines*. Abingdon: Routledge Classics.

Ivins, W. M. (1969). *Prints and visual communication*. New York: Da Capo Press.

Jewitt, C. (2017). *The Routledge handbook of multimodal analysis*. Abingdon: Routledge.

Jussim, E. (1974). *Visual communication and the graphic arts; photographic technologies in the nineteenth century*. New York: R.R. Bowker.

Kentridge, W. (2014). *Six drawing lessons*. Cambridge, MA: Harvard University Press.

Kirshner, M. (2008). *I live here*. New York: Pantheon Books.

Kitson, L. (1982). *The Falklands War: A visual diary*. London: M. Beazley in association with the Imperial War Museum.

Kovats, T. (2005). *The drawing book*. London: Black Dog.

Kris, E. (1964). *Psychoanalytic explorations in art*. New York: Schocken Books.

Lambourne, L. (1983). *An introduction to caricature*. London: H.M.S.O.

Lavin, I. (1981). *Bernini and the art of social satire*. The Art Museum: Princeton University.

Leddy, T. (2006, 29 September). Dewey's Aesthetics. 9 May 2017. Retrieved, from https://plato.stanford.edu/entries/dewey-aesthetics/#toc.

Leeuwen, T. V. (2005). *Introducing Social Semiotics*. Abingdon: Routledge.

Lomasko, V., & T. Campbell (2017). *Other Russias*. London: Penguin Books.

Lowenfeld, V., & W. L. Brittain (1987). *Creative and mental growth* (8th edn. Upper Saddle River, NJ: Prentice-Hall.

Lubbock, T., & M. Coutts (2012). *English graphic*. London: Frances Lincoln Limited.

Male, A. (2007). *Illustration: A theoretical & contextual perspective*. London: AVA.

Male, A. (2019). *The power and influence of illustration: Achieving impact and lasting significance through visual communication*. London: Bloomsbury Visual Arts.

Massey, D. (2005). *For space*. London: SAGE.

Maynard, P. (1997). *The engine of visualization thinking through photography*. Ithaca, NY: Cornell University Press.

Maynard, P. (2005). *Drawing distinctions: The varieties of graphic expression*. Ithaca, NY: Cornell University Press.

Midgley, J. (2010). Drawing lives – Reportage at work. *Studies in Material Thinking, 4*, 1–18.

Miles, M. B., & A. Huberman (1994). *Qualitative data analysis: 2nd ed*. Thousand Oaks, CA: SAGE.

Minichiello, M. (2006). The art of conflict: Making art about ourselves. *The International Journal of the Arts in Society: Annual Review, 1*(2), 141–62. doi: 10.18848/1833-1866/cgp/v01i02/35530.

Minichiello, M. (2012). On drawing in mass media contexts. In P. Israsena, J. Tangsantikul & D. Durling (eds), *Research: Uncertainty contradiction value – DRS international conference 2012*, 1–4 July, Bangkok, Thailand. https://dl.designresearch society.org/drs-conference-papers/drs2012/researchpapers/91.

Mitchell, W. J. (2001). *The reconfigured eye: Visual truth in the post-photographic era*. Cambridge, MA: MIT Press.

Mitchell, W. J. (2005). *What do pictures want? The lives and loves of images*. Chicago: University of Chicago Press.

Mitchell, W. J. T. (1980). *The language of images*. Chicago: University of Chicago Press.

Mumford, S. (2005). *Baghdad journal: An artist in occupied Iraq*. Montreal: Drawn & Quarterly.

Nisbet, P., & C. Lauer (1993). *The sketchbooks of George Grosz*. Cambridge, MA: Harvard University Art Museums.

O'Toole, L. M. (2011). *The language of displayed art*. New York: Routledge.

Owens, S. (2013). *The art of drawing*. London: V & A Publishing.

Patton, M. Q. (2015). *Qualitative research and evaluation methods: Integrating theory and practice*. Thousand Oaks, CA: Sage.

Perri 6, & C. Bellamy (2012). *Principles of methodology: Research design in social science*. London: Sage.

Petherbridge, D. (2010). *The primacy of drawing histories and theories of practice*. New Haven, CT: Yale University Press.

Rawson, P. S. (1969). *Drawing*. London: Oxford University Press.

Read, H. E. (1967). *Art and alienation: The role of the artist in society*. London: Thames and Hudson.

Ritchie, J., & J. Lewis (2003). *Qualitative research practice: A guide for social science students and researchers*. London: SAGE.

Roberts, J. (2010). Art after deskilling. *Historical Materialism, 18*(2), 77–96. doi: 10.1163/156920610x512444.

Robertshaw, U., & L. D. Vries (1995). *History as hot news, 1842–1865: The world of the early Victorians as seen through the eyes of the Illustrated London news*. London: John Murray.

Rosand, D. (2002). *Drawing acts: Studies in graphic expression and representation*. Cambridge: Cambridge University Press.

Rose, G. (2012). *Visual methodologies: An introduction to researching with visual materials*. London: SAGE.

Ruskin, J. (1971). *The elements of drawing*. New York: Dover.

Searle, R. (1988). *Ah yes, I remember it well: Paris 1961–1975*. Topsfield, MA: Salem House Pub.

Searle, R. (2010). *Ronald Searle: Graphic master*. London: Cartoon Museum.

A sense of permanence?: Essays on the art of the cartoon: Celebrating the 21st anniversary of the centre for the study of cartoons and caricature (1997). University of Kent.

Shahn, B. (1957). *The shape of content*. Cambridge, MA: Harvard University Press.

Shin, D., & F. Biocca (2017). Exploring immersive experience in journalism. *New Media & Society*, *20*(8), 1–24. doi: 10.1177/1461444817733133.

Sloan, K., J. E. Chaplin, C. F. Feest, & U. Kuhlemann (2007). *A new world: England's first view of America*. London: The British Museum Press.

Sontag, S. (1979). *On photography*. London: Penguin Books.

Tagg, J. (1995). *The burden of representation essays on photographies and histories*. Minneapolis: University of Minnesota Press.

Taussig, M. T. (2011). *I swear I saw this: Drawings in fieldwork notebooks, namely my own*. Chicago: University of Chicago Press.

Taussig, M. T. (2015). *The corn wolf*. Chicago: University of Chicago Press

Taylor, J. C. (1957). *Learning to look; a handbook for the visual arts*. Chicago: University of Chicago Press.

Topolski, F. (1968). *Holy China*. Boston, MA: Houghton Mifflin.

Topolski, F., & C. Riddell (1988). *Fourteen letters: Autobiography*. London: Faber and Faber.

Tuan, Y. (1977). *Space and place: The perspective of experience*. Minneapolis: University of Minnesota Press.

Vormittag, L. (2017). Luise Vormittag selects Anne Howeson's King's Cross St Pancras project. *Varoom*, (36), 58–9.

Walters, J. L. (2017, 1 January). Olivier Kugler: Bearing witness. *Eye*, (93), 42–55.

We Wait VR. (2016, 9 June). Retrieved from https://www.bbc.co.uk/taster/pilots/we-wait/trailer.

Weissová-Hošková, H. (2017). *Zeichne, was Du Siehst: Zeichnungen eines kindes aus Theresienstadt/Terezín = Maluj, Co vidíš = draw what you see*. Göttingen, Germany: Wallstein Verlag.

Whitehead, Dan, west of England correspondent. (2019, 11 August). *Decay and decline: Seaside towns desperate for investment*. Sky News. 25 February 2022. Retrieved from https://news.sky.com/story/decay-and-decline-seaside-towns-desperate-for-investment-11778384.

Yu, J. (2019, Spring). Distant memories. *Varoom*, (39), 4–17.

Zelizer, B., & K. Tenenboim-Weinblatt (2014). *Journalism and memory*. Houndmills: Palgrave Macmillan.

INDEX